# THE CODES OF ADVERTISING

## FETISHISM AND THE POLITICAL ECONOMY OF MEANING IN THE CONSUMER SOCIETY

# THE CODES OF ADVERTISING

## FETISHISM AND THE POLITICAL ECONOMY OF MEANING IN THE CONSUMER SOCIETY

## SUT JHALLY

**ROUTLEDGE**   New York   London

Published in 1990 by

Routledge, an imprint of
Routledge, Chapman and Hall, Inc.
29 West 35 Street
New York, NY 10001

Published in Great Britain by

Routledge
11 New Fetter Lane
London EC4P 4EE

**Published by arrangement with Pinter Publishing, Ltd.**
Published in 1987 by St. Martin's Press

Library of Congress Cataloging-in-Publication Data

Jhally, Sut.
    The codes of advertising.

    Bibliography: p.
    Includes index
    1. Advertising—Social aspects. 2. Symbolism in
advertising. 3. Mass media.      I. Title.
HF 5827. J49     1987      659.1'042      86-20349
ISBN 0-312-00211-4
ISBN 0-415-90353-X (pb)

British Library Cataloguing in Publication Data

Jhally, Sut
    The codes of advertising: fetishism and the political
    economy of meaning in the consumer society.
    1. Advertising—Sociological perspectives
    I. Title
    302.23
    ISBN 0-86187-584-2
    ISBN 0-415-90353-X

For my parents
Dalip Singh and Pritam Kaur Jhally

# Contents

# Acknowledgements

The initial stage of this work developed from 1980 to 1984 at Simon Fraser University in Vancouver, Canada. I consider myself extremely fortunate to have been able to participate in the fertile, stimulating and challenging intellectual and social environment that I found in Vancouver in these four years. I wish to thank Martin Laba, Paul Heyer, Heribert Adam, Russell Jacoby, Rick Gruneau, Dallas Smythe, Ian Angus, Liora Salter,Mike Lebowitz, Debbie McGee, Rohan Samarajiwa, Peter Cook, Lynda Drury, Diane Charbonneau, Robert Davidson, Cam Landell and Verla Fortier. Lynne Hissey deserves special mention for her copy-editing of the first draft manuscript.

The final version of the manuscript was completed at the University of Massachusetts in Amherst, USA, from 1985 to 1986. I wish to thank David Maxcy, Jarice Hanson, Dianne Cherry, Michael Morgan, Barnett Pearce, Vern Cronen, Mary Goodlett, Eileen Mahoney, Carolyn Anderson and Rhonda Blair.

Thanks are also due to my editors, Peter Moulson and Kermit Hummel, for their support of this project.

I would like to thank Methuen, Inc. (Toronto) for permission to use some material from *Social Communication in Advertising* (1986) by William Leiss, Stephen Kline and Sut Jhally.

This book could not have been written without the profound influence of three people on my life and my work. I acknowledge my debt and thank Bill Leiss (who taught me how to think critically), Steve Kline (who taught me how to study advertising), and Bill Livant (who allowed me to latch on to his unfettered genius). I look forward to many more years of learning, friendship and collaboration.

# Preface

This book has a strange ontogenesis. Like many other works it started as research for a doctoral dissertation that began in 1980 and was completed in the summer of 1984. Immediately after finishing this, I started work on a collaborative project with Bill Leiss and Steve Kline. This was published in 1986 as *Social Communication in Advertising: Persons, Products and Images of Well-Being* (hereinafter referred to as *SCA*). It included a comprehensive review of the field of advertising and culture and a thorough historical analysis of the development of the link between media, marketing and the advertising industry. Reported were the results of an extensive study of magazine advertising in which we identified four major epochs in the development of advertising form and content. This empirical material was woven into a highly theoretical analysis of the cultural role that goods play as satisfiers and communicators in modern society and the relationship of advertising to this cultural process. In seeking to understand the *system* of commercial messages, we took an *institutional* approach that examined the advertising industry as being located at the crucial conjuncture where media, industry and popular culture all converged and interacted. The evolution of the four stages was explained by an historical tracing through of the changing relationships between these three domains.

The present work was written after completion of *SCA* and has been substantially changed by the arguments we developed there. While much of the original thesis material was used in *SCA*, the central core of the argument was not developed and expanded in that work. Although the present book is concerned with many of the same issues and problems, it approaches them from a very different perspective. The central analytical dynamic in this work is the material social relations of advanced capitalism as an economic system. The understanding of advertising's social role is developed in relation to the accumulation dynamic of modern capitalism operating in the economy in general and also more specifically internal to the system of commercial television. I will argue that the symbolic dimensions of needing and culture and the economic dynamic of capital accumulation are symbiotically intertwined in the new 'communication age' of advanced capitalism. As such the arguments developed here and in *SCA* form part of a single explanatory framework on the role that advertising plays in the modern mediation of the person–object relationship.

# 1 Introduction: fundamentals and starting points

## People and things

It could be argued that advertising is the most influential institution of socialisation in modern society: it structures mass media content; it seems to play a key role in the construction of gender identity; it impacts upon the relation of children and parents in terms of the mediation and creation of needs; it dominates strategy in political campaigns; recently it has emerged as a powerful voice in the arena of public policy issues concerning energy and regulation; it controls some of our most important cultural institutions such as sports and popular music; and it has itself in recent years become a favourite topic of everyday conversation. However, we should not let its enormous presence in a wide variety of realms obscure what it is *really* about. At the material, concrete and historical level advertising is part of a specific concern with the marketing of goods. It rose to prominence in modern society as a *discourse through and about objects*. It is from this perspective that an analysis of advertising has to unfold. More particularly, this discourse concerns a specific, seemingly universal relationship: that between people and objects.

The relationship between people and their things should not be considered a superficial or optional feature of life. It is in fact a definitional component of human existence. All societies are based upon the use of nature by humans. Humans as a species are only able to survive by the 'appropriation' of the material elements that surround us. We eat the food of nature, we shelter under materials provided by it, and we clothe ourselves in fabrics woven from its raw materials. This relation between people and objects has been described as one of 'objectification'—we objectify ourselves and our lives in the materiality of the concrete world. We continually take what exists outside of us, and, by our activity, make it a part of our daily existence. Herbert Marcuse (1972b) believes this objectification is not merely a small part of what constitutes the human experience, but is its 'deeper foundation'. In fact, objectification lies at the basis of what we can call a distinctive human experience, the mediation of human need through objects.

Based on this understanding, Jean-Paul Sartre (1976, p. 79) writes that 'the crucial discovery of dialectical investigation is that man is "mediated" by things to the same extent as things are "mediated" by man'. While it seems obvious that things are mediated by humans—in that without us things might have existence but not meaning—and that in this sense *things need people*, it is equally true that *humans need things*. The evidence from history and anthropology on our necessary intimate interaction with objects is overwhelming. A widely accepted theory holds that the utilisation of objects as tools was a decisive step in the evolutionary process of humanity. Indeed, the authors of a book titled *The Meaning of Things* remark that, 'Man is not only *homo sapiens* or *homo ludens*, he is also *homo faber*, the maker and user of objects, his self to a large extent a reflection of things with which he interacts' (Csikszentmihalyi and Rochberg-Halton 1981, p. 1). Advertising then, as a discourse concerning objects, is dealing with one of the fundamental aspects of human behaviour. This should be the starting point for an analysis of advertising's social role.

## Use, symbol and power

The social debate concerning advertising has diverged considerably on the contemporary person–object relationship (for a full discussion see *SCA*, Chapters 2 and 3). The many critics of advertising claim that it is a tool whereby consumers are controlled and manipulated by the producers of goods (on whose behalf advertising is waged) to desire things for which they have no real need. The imperative for this creation of demand comes from the huge number of goods that capitalism as a system is able to deliver. To avoid stagnation and the ultimate demise of capitalism through a depressed economy, manufacturers have to ensure that what is produced is also consumed. Advertising is the main weapon that manufacturers use in their attempt to 'produce' an adequate consuming market for their products. To this end advertising works to create false needs in people (false because they are the needs of manufacturers rather than consumers). Writers from a variety of viewpoints (John K. Galbraith, Stuart Ewen, Herbert Marcuse, Raymond Williams, Paul Baran, Paul Sweezy, Ernest Mandel, Guy DeBord, Vance Packard, Jerry Mander) seem to be agreed on this point. Particularly, it is the manner in which this is achieved that is held to be socially harmful. In his important book *Captains of Consciousness* (1976), Stuart Ewen argues that in the early years of this century the need to create desires in the newly enfranchised consuming public necessitated a shift away from a stress solely on products, to a context where it was the relationship *between* people and products that was important. If demand for products had to be created by the marketplace itself (rather than reflecting the true needs of consumers) advertising would have to incorporate more direct references to the audience. Increasingly, advertising integrated the consumer within a rich and complex web of social status and symbolic meaning.

The cultural theorist and historian, Raymond Williams, believes that this social and symbolic significance conferred on goods by advertising shows us that it is wrong to regard modern society as being too materialistic, as putting too much emphasis on the possession of goods. Rather, we are in fact *not materialistic enough* (Williams 1980, p. 185):

If we were sensibly materialist, in that part of our living in which we use things, we should find most advertising to be of insane irrelevance. Beer would be enough for us, without the additional promise that in drinking it we show ourselves to be manly, young at heart or neighborly. A washing machine would be a useful machine to wash clothes, rather than an indication that we are forward looking or an object of envy to our neighbors. But if these associations sell beer and washing machines, as some of the evidence suggests, it is clear that we have a cultural pattern in which the objects are not enough but must be validated, if only in fantasy, by association with social and personal meanings which in a different cultural pattern might be more directly available.

There are two important points to be distinguished here, one of which is valid and one which is problematic. Williams is correct in noting that modern capitalism provides social and personal meanings through the consumption of goods that were previously (and could be again) more directly available. The conclusion that Williams draws from this is, however, questionable: that is, without advertising and in a 'sensibly materialist' society, goods would only be seen as things which are practically useful but socially meaningless. It is the general acceptance of this proposition which, I believe, has stalled a truly adequate critical perspective on the role that advertising plays within modern consumer societies. The contention that goods should be important to people for what they are *used* for rather than their *symbolic* meaning is very difficult to uphold in light of the historical, anthropological and cross-cultural evidence. In all cultures at all times, it is the relation between use and symbol that provides the concrete context for the playing out of the universal person–object relation. The present radical critique of advertising is unbalanced in its perception of the 'proper' or 'rational' relation between use and symbol. It suffers from what could be called 'commodity vision'—the problem of capitalist commodities has not been sufficiently distinguished from the problem of objects in general. While the person–object relation has been set within the context of *power*, the critique as presently conceptualised has lost the link with culture and history. That Raymond Williams should fall into this misperception is extremely surprising, for in the rest of his magnificent corpus of writings he strongly focuses on the central role that culture has played in the development of human societies.

The recognition of the fundamentally symbolic aspect of people's use of things must be the minimum starting point for a discourse that concerns objects. Specifically, the old distinction between basic (physical) and secondary (psychological) needs must be superseded. The anthropologist Marshal Sahlins (1976) points out that all utility is framed by a cultural context—that even our interaction with the most mundane and 'ordinary' of objects in daily life is mediated within a symbolic field. Csikszentmihalyi and Rochberg-Halton (1981, p. 21) note that:

Even the use of things for utilitarian purposes operates within the symbolic province of culture. The most 'utilitarian' objects in the home, such as running water, toilets, electric appliances, and the like, were all introduced into general use no more than 150 years ago by advances in Western technology—all considered luxuries when introduced. Thus it is extremely difficult to disentangle the use-related function from the symbolic meanings in even the most practical objects.

William Leiss (1976), too, refers to the dualistic nature of human behaviour and argues that every facet of human needing has both symbolic and material correlates, and that even our basic physiological requirements (food, shelter, clothing) have always been 'firmly embedded in a rich tapestry of symbolic mediation' (Leiss 1976, p. 65). (See *SCA* for fuller discussion of these points.)

The importance of the symbolic constitution of utility has not been lost on writers from within marketing and business circles who have been called upon to answer the attacks directed against advertising. Indeed, they have made it the cornerstone of their legitimation of advertising's symbolic aspect. Theodore Levitt goes so far as to equate advertising with art. Art presents by definition a 'distortion' or inter-pretation of reality with the aim of influencing an audience to think in a particular way—beyond functionality and practicality to abstraction. Advertising has the same goals, uses similar means and so should be evaluated by the same noble criteria as art.

One does not need a doctorate in social anthropology to see that the purposeful transmutation of nature's primeval state occupies all people in all cultures, and all societies at all stages of develop-ment. Everybody everywhere wants to modify, transform, embellish, enrich and reconstruct the world around him, to introduce into an otherwise harsh or bland existence some sort of purposeful and distorting alleviation. Civilisation is man's attempt to transcend his ancient animality: and this includes both art and advertising... Both represent a pervasive and I believe *universal* characteristic of human nature—the human audience *demands* symbolic interpretation in everything it sees and knows. If it doesn't get it, it will return a verdict of 'no interest' (Levitt 1970, pp. 87, 89).

Because humans are not confined to pure utility in their use of objects, the messages of the marketplace (advertising) must reflect the symbolic breadth of the person–object relation. The symbolism of advertising reflects a deeply felt human need. Only deception and outright lies are considered inappropriate for this discourse. Michael Schudson (1984) also uses what may be called an anthropological perspective to build his case against the 'puritanical' critics of advertising. Noting that needs are socially relative in any society and that the true–false distinction is an exceedingly difficult one to sustain, he argues that the real issue is not 'false' symbolism, but the direction that symbolism takes in any society.

However, the defenders of advertising are just as one-sided as the critics in their analysis. While they recognise the symbolic element in all human needing, they ignore almost totally any discussion of the dimension of *power* or of the *social effects* of advertising. The appropriation thus from anthropology is incomplete, for just as it is true that the symbolic mediation of human needing is a vital feature of human existence, so it is just as true that power also clouds and influences all social relations. Goods always mean something within a social context where different interests are being played out. On this the defence is virtually silent, falling back on a vague belief in the market as an institution where conflicting interests are given an impartial mediation. If the evidence from anthropology is to be introduced into the debate, then it is important that all the evidence is used, and not just selected fragments of it. All utility may be symbolic—but for whom and with what ends?

## Goods and social communication

The most important attempt so far to initiate what could be called an 'anthropology of consumption' has been *The World of Goods* by Mary Douglas and Baron Isherwood (1978). Noting that in traditional economic thought two main assumptions are made about human needs (materialism and envy) that do not stand up to sustained analysis, they suggest instead that an anthropological approach would regard consumption as part of the *cultural pattern* in any society (Douglas and Isherwood 1978, p. 59).

Instead of supposing that goods are primarily needed for subsistence (materialism) plus competitive display (envy), let us assume that they are needed for making visible and stable the categories of culture. It is standard ethnographic practice to assume that all material possessions carry social meanings and to concentrate a main part of cultural analysis upon their use as communicators.

A communication theory of consumption tied to the concept of ritual is invoked to analyse the 'world of goods'. Ritual, in the anthropological sense, seeks to give shape and substance to dominant social meanings, to anchor social relationships. 'Rituals serve to contain the drift of meaning.' For any society to operate without some form of ritual is for a society to live without a shared collective memory. While ritual can take a verbal form, it is more effective when tied to material things. 'Goods, in this perspective are ritual adjuncts: consumption is a ritual process whose primary function is to make sense of the inchoate flux of events' (Douglas and Isherwood 1978, p. 65). Goods are used in the negotiation of social life, and act as meaningful 'markers' of social categories. The precise form that this takes is framed by both cultural and economic relations—that is, by *social power*.

   The use of goods as social markers has been extensively documented in the anthropological study of 'primitive' societies. In many such societies, the economy is divided between the prestige and subsistence sphere, with very little exchange between them. The 'subsistence' economy includes those materials related to food, clothing and shelter and fairly easy to obtain. The 'prestige' economy consists of less readily available, socially scarce goods, possession of which in ritual settings translates material values into abstract values of prestige, reputation and status. The native society of Ponapea had such a dual economy, with specially grown and cared for yams acting as the prestige goods of the upper sphere. Similarly, the potlatch ceremonies of the Kwakiutl of British

Columbia demonstrate the value of certain goods acting as social markers between social groups. (Leiss, 1978)

The Tiv people of Nigeria had a more elaborately ranked three-tiered system which included two spheres of the prestige economy. The higher of these consisted of holding rights over women, while the lower was made up of goods such as metal rods, cloth, guns and slaves. The subsistence economy was concerned with domestic goods. The goods of the lower part of the prestige economy could be obtained either through outside trade or through conquest in war, and it was the metal rods of this sphere that acted as a kind of 'currency' for the whole economy. Social action was based upon the conversion of lower-level to higher-level goods. However, because it was solely men who had access to prestige goods, it was impossible for women to move into the prestige economy except as objects of prestige themselves. By making only some goods for prestige (and hence access to power) and then by limiting access to these goods to certain privileged groups, the contextualisation of goods within a symbolic/material field sought to stabilise the existing organisation of social power.

The critical anthropologists Rey and Dupre (1973) also focus on how goods are used for social control and domination and show how power was exercised in West African lineage societies both materially and symbolically. They start their analysis by focusing on a key problem—how goods produced by one group (cadets—unmarried, young, male) can be entirely controlled by another group (the elders). After rejecting a number of conventional explanations based on physical coercion, they argue that the vital element is that the elders

reserve for themselves control of social knowledge (knowledge of genealogies, of history, or marriage regulations) and their control is prolonged in the spheres of artifice (magic, divination, cultural rites). Above all, they reserve for themselves control of the cadets' and their own access to women, and they guarantee this control by holding the 'elite' goods which are indispensable for marriage (Rey and Dupre 1973, p. 145).

They control the objects and symbolic knowledge then that a cadet needs to become an 'objectively individuated man'. If symbolic processes are always played out in contexts of power, there is no reason to think that the symbolism of advertising should be exempt from this, especially when it is so clearly controlled by a small clearly identifiable group using it for particular ends.

## The capitalist market and goods

The anthropological evidence shows that goods are simultaneously *communicators* (about social ideas and power) and *satisfiers* (of human needs). This added to the person–object, use–symbolism and symbolism–power relations is the minimum starting point for any analysis of the modern institution of advertising. However, while the literature I have examined thus far has stressed the *similarity* between modern and traditional types of society, we must not lapse into these generalisable relations as explanations *in themselves* of modern social relations. They merely provide a framework with which to approach the problem. What we have to examine rather are the different social forms in which these dimensions have been cloaked, or 'the various modes of representation for it that correspond to qualitative differences in forms of social organisation' (Leiss 1983b, p. 2).

In order properly to contextualise these seemingly universal relations within the contemporary situation of Western industrial societies we need to understand the arena where these relations are 'represented' in the capitalist economy—the market. Modern society has 'collapsed' the separate spheres of traditional economies into the one sphere of general consumption. However, Douglas and Isherwood (1978, p. 150) argue that there is little difference between the two contexts and that the modern market works pragmatically in fact to produce separable spheres of activity.

That which disguises itself as a disinterested, friendly, hospitable consumption sphere in practice draws up dividing lines between those in control and those they are excluding. The ethnography suggests that we will find these consumption spheres, distinct and ranked, here as well as among the Tiv and the Yurok, and that these should yield a basis for discerning groupings among goods.

Sahlins (1976) agrees that social differentiation in modern society has similarities with distinctions in older societies, but he invokes instead the anthropological concept of *totemism* in his analysis of 'Western society as culture'. Totemism is the symbolic association of plants, animals or objects with individuals or groups of people. In the most sophisticated exposition of totemism, Levi-Strauss argues that the essence of the concept consists of the almost universal tendency of cultures to divide nature into different groups of species and things and to correlate these with differentiations in the social world of people. For Sahlins modern society has simply substituted manufactured objects for species, with exchange and consumption acting as the means of communication of the totemic order.

The object stands as a human concept outside itself, as man speaking to man through the medium of things. And the systematic variation in objective features is capable of serving, even better than the differences between natural species, as the medium of a vast and dynamic scheme of thought: because in manufactured objects many differences can be varied at once, and by a godlike manipulation . . . The bourgeois totemism, in other words, is potentially more elaborate than any wild (*sauvage*) variety, not that it has been liberated from a natural-material basis, but precisely because nature has been domesticated (Sahlins 1976, p. 178).

Sahlins looks at the American clothing system for what it indicates about the symbolic scheme of social classification and differentiation in modern capitalism. Clothes reflect many things (time and place of activity, social status, age, ethnicity, subcultures) but what is produced through the clothing system is not simply the boundaries but the 'meaningful differences' between categories. Moreover, the meaningful differences are not simply the results of the imposition of an ideology of fashion through 'the deceits of advertising', nor do they reflect the wishes of the consumer. Sahlins notes that: 'It should be possible to transcend all such subjective representation for an institutional description of capitalist production as a cultural process' (Sahlins 1976,

p. 185). Neither Sahlins nor Douglas and Isherwood locate advertising as a powerful actor in the cultural process of modern society. However, as McCracken and Pollay (1981, p. 2) point out:

If goods have a symbolic aspect it is largely because advertising gives them one. They plainly do not spring from the factory fully possessed of their ability to communicate. It is advertising that enables them to assume this ability . . . It is part of the process with which we endow objects with certain meaningful properties. It is advertising that makes goods 'communicators'.

Such an integration of advertising would also help to give the motivational impulse to Sahlins' claim (1976, p. 184) that the symbolic code (mediated through the market) 'works as an open set, responsive to events which it both orchestrates and assimilates to produce expanded versions of itself'.

The modern French social theorist Jean Baudrillard (1975; 1981) also places the concept of symbolic code at the centre of his analysis of advanced capitalism. He argues that it is time to transcend the work of Marx as an adequate description of advanced capitalism because society has gone through a radical transformation since the nineteenth century. Marx analysed a capitalism where only 'material production' was alienated in the exchange of political economy. Today, however, almost everything (virtue, love, knowledge, consciousness) falls into the sphere of exchange value (that is in the realm of the market). This latter stage constitutes not merely an extension of the first but a radical rupture with it. Thus traditional Marxist concepts such as reification are not sufficient analytical tools, because we have moved from a phase where the commodity-form was dominant to one where the *sign-form* prevails. Consumption today is concerned with the 'systematic manipulation of signs' within the workings of a broader behavioral code. As for Sahlins, so too for Baudrillard, the manipulation of a symbolic code is the most important feature of advanced capitalism. Objects lose any real connection with the basis of their practical utility and instead come to be the material correlate (the signifier) of an increasing number of constantly changing, abstract qualities.

It is this logic of signification that is the true essence of advanced capitalism.

In an important social change, Baudrillard argues (1975, pp. 127–8), monopoly capitalism has shifted the locus of control away from production into consumption, with control over demand and socialisation by the code (in which advertising plays a leading role).

The monopolistic stage signifies less the monopoly of the means of production than *monopoly of the code* . . . The form-sign describes an entirely different organisation: the signified and the referent are now abolished to the sole profit of the play of signifiers, of a generalised formalisation in which the code no longer refers back to its own logic . . . The sign no longer designates anything at all. It approaches its true structural limit which is to refer back only to other signs. All reality then becomes the place of a semiurgical manipulation, of a structured simulation.

Control over demand and symbolism, rather than contradictions in production, becomes the vital focus of advanced capitalism. This is achieved through control of the symbolic code such that commodities can be given any meaning (totally divorced from what they are used for) by the manipulation of their relationship to other signs. Further, as more and more 'needs' are brought into the realm of sign consumption, individuals lose autonomous control and surrender to the code: 'the system no longer needs universal production: it requires only that everyone play the game' (Baudrillard 1975, p. 132). Again the market is the central institution in this new monopoly of the code.

## The paradox of affluence—commodities and satisfaction

The notion that goods are communicators and satisfiers is based upon a *relational* view of consumption, not as a private affair but a social activity. One of the first thinkers to apply this to modern society was Thorstein Veblen (1953) who coined the famous phrase 'conspicuous consumption' as a description of the 'ceremonial' nature of the phenomena. It was his analysis of the implications of this for the 'satisfaction of needs' however that is especially pertinent here. Because consumption is socially based (and judged) it describes a *relative* rather than an absolute activity. The satisfaction that people derive from this is then also relative. Satisfaction is measured against a social scale, or an average standard. As a society gets richer and more goods are available to a wider group of people, so the average standard also rises and the 'level' of satisfaction remains stable. The numbers above and below the average standard remain constant.

Veblen's formulation of the problem proved remarkably prophetic. In an extremely important article, in which the major research studies regarding 'happiness' are brought together to form an historical and cross-cultural comparison, Richard Easterlin (1974) questions the traditional stress in economic theory on the correlation between economic *growth* and welfare—between mass affluence and happiness. He addresses three key questions: Is there a positive correlation between income and happiness (1) within a country, (2) between countries, (3) over time in a single country? Although the data are ambiguous at times, Easterlin is able to give a positive evaluation of the posited relation between economic growth and social welfare (measured subjectively) only for (1), and a fairly substantial negative evaluation for (2) and (3). In looking at the data on within-country comparisons, there is a clear indication here that income and happiness are positively associated, that is to say, that those at the higher end of the income scale report themselves happier than those at the lower end. However, when the international comparisons are made it seems that there is little difference in the overall level of reported happiness between rich and poor *countries* in that the proportions of people who reported themselves to be 'happy' were about the same in both rich and poor countries. The expected correlation between economic growth and happiness is not borne out. Finally, in examining a series of surveys, taken at different times since 1945, that addressed the question of happiness in the United States, Easterlin shows that although there was a substantial rise in incomes for all groups, the proportion of the total population who considered themselves happy remained relatively stable. He explains these results by reference to a 'relative income' model by which people judge their subjective level of happiness in comparison with what others *within society at that time* have (Easterlin 1974, p. 112).

There is a 'consumption' norm which exists in a given society at a given time, and which enters into the reference standard of virtually everyone. This provides a common point of reference in self-appraisal of well-being, leading those below the norm to feel less happy and those above the norm, more happy. Over time, this norm tends to rise with the general level of consumption, though the two are not necessarily on a one-to-one basis.

Easterlin does not pose the question of what role advertising plays in the constitution of this 'consumption norm'.

Tibor Scitovsky in *The Joyless Economy* (1976) seeks to explain this intuitive paradox between affluence and happiness. His focus of critique is traditional economic theory's stress on the rational consumer and consumer sovereignty. He argues that the theory is *unscientific* in its portrayal of human psychology (because it cannot account for variations over time in individual taste) and is incapable of explaining the results of the 'happiness' surveys. He offers four possible explanations for the stable pattern of satisfaction which are bought together in the concept of 'rankhappiness': (1) satisfaction is derived from relative social ranking and status as measured against a consumption norm; (2) work provides satisfaction and this is likely to be more rewarding and stimulating the higher one's position on the income scale; (3) satisfaction is derived from novelty and stimulation in consumption, but capitalist production tends to homogenise experience and stress standardisation instead; (4) comfort, resulting from consumption, is addictive, and since we take it for granted it ceases to be a source of stimulation (and thus satisfaction) for us.

The third and fourth factors are important points of reference in Scitovsky's critique of the theory of consumer sovereignty. The theory, the basis of marketing theory, holds that the market is the place where consumers 'vote' with their money, so that what is available is the result of the free choice of consumers. Scitovsky (1976, pp. 7–8) writes that:

The doctrine of consumer sovereignty is a gross oversimplification, especially in an age of mass production, when almost nothing gets produced that cannot be produced in the thousands . . . Even if we accept this proud claim, it leaves some of the most important questions unanswered. There are millions of consumers. Are all of them sovereign? Are they equally sovereign? And, if not, what determines their relative influence on the nature and quality of goods and services produced?

If the market is like a voting machine then it will most reflect the 'choices' of those who have most to spend. Thus consumer sovereignty at one level is a rule of the rich. However, there are counterbalancing forces, the most important of which are the economies of scale which ensure that the things bought by many can be produced more cheaply than those bought by only a few. Plutocracy and mob rule thus are the twin features of the capitalist marketplace, but because the profitability of producers rests largely on the latter, we are led to a situation where the public's average taste is pulled down in that the desires to which the producer must respond in this context consist of 'the primitive, unsophisticated desires, or variants of desires, which the most simple-minded segment of the consuming public shares with the rest' (Scitovsky 1976, p. 9). Thus mass production caters to conformity rather than eccentricity and the prime function of advertising here is to secure 'agreement' among the mob as to the nature and quantity of the limited number of things that are to be mass produced. Consumer free choice is free choice among those products that can be mass produced in this way. Advertising does not create demand in this perspective but molds it and steers it in certain directions that work for the benefit of producers.

Scitovsky has very little to say of a critical nature on the actual process of mass production. His real concern is with the effects of mass production on consumer *satisfaction*, for he believes that the present system of production caters to *comfort* rather than to *stimulation, pleasure* or *arousal* which are the real factors in the consumer's search for satisfaction. His most pertinent point here is that consumption of the same product at different times can lead to either stimulation (where consumption takes on a thrilling, novel character) or comfort (if one has got used to the experience and takes it for granted). Traditional economic theory, however, cannot explain this *change and variation* of consumer tastes because of the conventional view of the consumer as someone with set tastes, who pursues conscious actions (limited only by resources) to satisfy them. This approach is quite inadequate and has kept 'the profession from even considering the influences that mould the dominant lifestyle and push us all toward accepting and adopting it' (Scitovsky 1976, p. 11). For Scitovsky, the most important motive force of behaviour, 'man's yearning for novelty', is structurally denied within the context of mass production. Again it is a relational and dynamic view of consumption that provides the most fruitful leads as to why societal satisfaction does not necessarily rise with material progress and affluence.

Albert Hirschman (1982) has sought to refine Scitovsky's distinction between comfort and pleasure by focusing on a comparison between *durable* and *non-durable* goods. He notes that we draw much pleasure from the satisfaction of physiological needs (food, sex, sleep) and that much of this is achieved through the consumption of non-durables—items that are used up in the act of consumption. Because these needs are recurrent, comfort yields to discomfort at some time 'so that the pleasure-yielding trip back to comfort can once again be undertaken'. Food, for example, has a special ability to provide pleasure. Non-durables are both pleasure-intensive and—because the proof disappears in the eating—they are also disappointment-resistant. Hirschman (1982, p. 29) writes:

The Roman Emperors knew, so it seems, what they were doing when they took care to supply the masses with bread and circuses: *both* vanish once you have taken them in, without leaving behind a corporeal shape on which consumers can vent any disappointment, boredom or anxiety they may have suffered or may yet suffer.

This is not true of durable objects, which once we get used to them do not provide the pleasure that comes from the passage from discomfort to comfort. Objects such as refrigerators, washing machines, heating systems, and so on, which have become widely available in the modern age (and on which many status distinctions are based) have shifted the balance between pleasure and comfort towards the latter, and have contributed to a sense of *disappointment* towards our purchases.

Fred Hirsch, in *Social Limits to Growth* (1976) also takes up the central aspect of what he labels the 'paradox of affluence'. He explains the stagnation in the level of societal happiness in three ways. First, by the central role in affluent societies played by *positional* goods, competition for which, once basic material necessities have been taken care of, provides a major area of status ranking. These goods are scarce by their very nature (because they are highly valued) and because the conditions of their use would deteriorate if they were in widespread use. Scarcity here refers not only to physical limits to production but social limits to consumption: 'the limit is imposed on satisfactions that depend not on the product or facility in isolation but on the surrounding conditions of use' (Hirsch 1976, p. 3). For example, our enjoyment of natural beauty is dependent in part on limiting access, at any one time, to others who would adversely affect our experience of it. When access to scenic beauty is limited in some way then the social distance between those who have access and those who do not is great. When access is not limited, when anyone is able to 'enjoy' it, then overcrowding leads to a deterioration in the social value of that beauty. In this situation, there is no social distance between groups and hence no prestige or status in that consumption. Societies based on status ranking are continually producing new groups of socially scarce positional goods.

Second, Hirsch (1976, p. 84) argues that there is a commodity bias to contemporary society by which 'an excessive proportion of individual activities are channelled through the market so that the commercialised sector of our lives is unduly large'. He labels this as 'the new commodity fetishism'. There are two broad negative effects in relation to consumer satisfaction. One is the effect this has on the non-material and non-market sources of satisfaction. The tendency of any market society is to stress those things that can be bought and sold, whereas satisfaction seems to be more closely linked with areas of life that fall outside of this 'price-indexing'. The things that really make people happy seem to be non-material things such as autonomy, self-esteem, family felicity, tension-free leisure time, and good friendships. Commodities however are weakly related to these sources of satisfaction. The bad luck of consumers is that 'they derive utility from environmental characteristics that lie outside of the market to provide' (Hirsch 1976, p. 91).

The other effect of the 'new commodity fetishism'—and this is the third of Hirsch's broad explanatory factors behind the 'paradox of affluence'—is the nature of the satisfaction derived from goods within a market setting. Consumers derive utility from goods both from their embodied characteristics and from the 'environmental conditions' of their use. More precisely, the individual acquisition of goods takes place within a social context. It is the critical tension between individual consumption and its societal effects and contexts that is the key here. The market can only focus on its individual rather than its societal dimensions. In this process advertising emerges as a major culprit. Hirsch (1976, p. 109) writes:

The life depicted in the glossy magazines clearly is attractive to many of us, and no higher code of morality need be invoked to say that it ought not to be. The snag is that much of it is unattainable to very many of us at once, and its diffusion may then change its own content and characteristics. Which is to say that private goods have a public context, in the broad environmental conditions of their use; a context that their private marketing does not properly take into account. What is then wrong in the industrial system is not the delivery but the order: to meet consumers' *individual* wants . . . To the extent that marketing and advertising appeal to individuals to isolate themselves from these group or social effects—to get in ahead or to protect their positions—they are socially wasteful. They are then also socially immoral on the mundane level of the morality concerned with social stability and consistency. If all are urged to get ahead, many are likely to have their expectations frustrated.

Advertisements do not lie to us. They show the mediating role that commodities *could* play in the relation between individuals and expectations. The problem is they cannot play that role for all who want to attain it. And if all attain it then satisfaction is altered for all. Whereas individual consumption takes place in a social and ecological context, advertising stresses only the individual element and thus generates false expectations.

The works by Scitovsky and Hirsch represent an important advance in our understanding of the consumer culture but neither of them closely examines the role of advertising as it affects the process of consumption. For Scitovsky, advertising assures the mass 'agreement' that is needed for mass production, while for Hirsch advertising stresses individual interests at the expense of social context. For both, advertising is a small part of the process of want dissatisfaction and disappointment. The capitalist market provides the wider explanatory factor for this. There is no doubt that they are largely correct, but a failure to concentrate on the specific role of advertising weakens any insights into the overall process that could be gained from such a perspective. As such advertising remains a (weak) intervening variable in the analysis of satisfaction.

## The triple ambiguity: needs, commodities and advertising

William Leiss in *The Limits to Satisfaction* (1976) also examines the relationship between satisfaction and the market, and in later work with Stephen Kline has integrated advertising more fully into the analysis. Although Leiss's book is concerned very strongly with the *ecological* limits to growth, its most sophisticated reasoning is saved for the analysis of human needs as they are mediated by commodities. The key analytical concept is 'the high-intensity market setting', which is defined as 'a market economy in which there is a very large number of commodities available to large numbers of people, and in which many commodities are the result of highly complex industrial production processes involving sophisticated scientific and technological knowledge' (Leiss 1976, p. 7). It is within this setting that individuals strive for need-satisfaction. However, this becomes problematic as the setting itself works to make individuals increasingly confused as to the nature of their needs.

There are numerous dimensions to the problem. First, because 'craft knowledge' of products is impossible within this setting, individuals do not have complete or adequate information about the quality of goods. The 'free choice' of the market becomes little more than a 'grand experiment' in trying to match needs and commodities with arbitrariness replacing rationality as the basis of decisions. Such a situation leads to wants becoming shallower as products that are considered indispensable one day are replaced the next, so that—paradoxically—as we spend more time in consumption we become more indifferent to each want. In addition—and this again stems from the lack of craft knowledge—there are both physiological risks (poor nutrition, dependence on drugs, hyperactivity in children due to food additives, the carcinogenic properties of many widely used chemicals, and so on) and psychological risks inherent in the high-consumption lifestyle. The most important element of the latter is that 'each aspect of a person's needs tends to be broken down into progressively smaller component parts, and therefore ... it becomes increasingly difficult for the person to integrate the components into a coherent ensemble of needs and a coherent personality structure' (Leiss 1976, p. 28). The vast number of products produced for supposedly specific tasks encourages the individual to fragment his/her needs and subsequently his/her personality such that a greater effort is needed to hold the various parts together. This effort is translated into more time being necessary for consumption decision-making, simultaneous to that time contracting even further.

Leiss deliberately does not differentiate between the concepts of need and want, for he argues (Leiss 1976, p. 74) that such a distinction hides the fact that 'every expression or state of needing has simultaneously a material and symbolic or cultural correlate'. Any attempt to order needs in terms of biological or cultural aspects or in a hierarchical fashion, or by trying to identify true and false needs, is rejected as not recognising the absolutely fundamental characteristic of 'the material-symbolic correlate of human needing'.

This duality is reflected in the objects through which human needing is mediated. Drawing on the work of economist Kelvin Lancaster (1971), Leiss attempts to show that commodities in the high-intensity market setting are collections of *characteristics* rather than just a set of product *qualities*. Consumers have a direct interest in the former and an indirect interest in the latter. 'Rather than saying that people have an interest in food items *per se*, for example, we should say that they seek a bundle of characteristics such as nutritive content, convenience of preparation, packaging or portions, appearance and texture, and so forth' (Leiss 1976, p. 90). Consumers order their preferences directly in terms of characteristics and indirectly in terms of goods. Commodities themselves thus become highly complex material-symbolic entities.

In such a situation as the high-intensity market setting (based on mass production) there *cannot* be a direct correlation for all individuals and all goods between the former's wants and the latter's properties (Scitovsky's point). Attempts at matching individual's wants with goods are not likely to be very successful, especially when the individual is shifting preferences in different ways to hold the 'fragmenting' personality together, and where the precise characteristics of goods themselves are difficult to pin down. In the high-intensity market setting individuals are confused both about their wants and the goods these wants have to be matched with. Because this confusion stems from the nature of both needs and goods, Leiss labels this 'the double ambiguity' of needs and commodities. Ambiguity in consumption does not lead to *dis*satisfaction alone, but produces feelings of *both* satisfaction and dissatisfaction simultaneously.

Given the fluidity of the contextual setting, individuals may become progressively more confused both about the nature of their own wants and about what are the best ways of attempting to satisfy them. The steadily increasing complexity in the makeup of wants and goods may result in, among other things, an increasing degree of ambiguity in the attempted satisfaction of wants. The outcome of the consumption act may be an ensemble of satisfactions and dissatisfactions, whose components are not clearly identifiable, rather than a determinate experience of either satisfaction or dissatisfaction (Kline and Leiss 1978, p. 15).

For Leiss advertising is a part of this matching process of needs and commodities and intensifies the structural conditions of ambiguity in two ways. First, the contextual setting regarding the symbolic properties of goods becomes constantly fluid. The material and especially symbolic correlates of commodities are shifting as marketing strategies change and competition for a share of the market intensifies. There is no stability to the images of products in such a context and thus the matching of wants and goods becomes even more problematic.

Second, changing styles in the historical development of advertising contribute even more to this phenomenon. Through the course of twentieth-century advertising there have been two significant parallel developments; the shift from explicit statements of value to implicit values and lifestyle images; and a decline in textual material with a correlative increase in 'visualised images of well-being'. Modern advertising is characterised by the growing domination of *imagistic* modes of communication. This shift to images has two paradoxical effects. The use of visual stimuli and imagery increases, without awareness, the attention paid to advertising and builds *strong associational links* while at the same time it retains a significant degree of *ambiguity*. Within a context in which market-based knowledge provides almost all of the 'information' regarding the characteristics and qualities of goods, the possibility of successful matching of wants and goods becomes ever more problematical.

## Conclusion

I have attempted to show that an understanding of the social role of advertising involves an analysis of a number of interconnected relationships—those between person and object, use and symbol, symbolism and power, and communication and satisfaction. More broadly, I have examined material that shows that the manner in which people use goods in modern Western industrial societies is hugely influenced by the mediating institution of the *market*. In order to understand the usefulness of a product one must also understand its relation to other products—the use of *one* is subordinated to its position within a *system* of objects. The system of objects is itself an outcome of a process whereby goods are produced to be *exchanged* rather than to be *used* directly by the producers. In more traditional terms this is known as the subordination of use-value (what it does for people) by exchange-value (what it is worth). An adequate understanding of the use-value–exchange-value relation, then, is the starting point for an analysis of the other vital relationships I have outlined. This is attempted in Chapter 2, which locates 'the fetishism of commodities' as a useful concept to aid our understanding of advertising.

However, an understanding of the object world is only a part of the task we must undertake, for, as the analysis of Leiss in particular has shown, advertising is an important factor in the way people attempt to satisfy their needs through the consumption of products. In fact, as Kline and Leiss (1978, p. 18) note: 'it is not that the world of true needs has been subordinated to the world of false needs, but that the realm of needing has become a function of the field of communication'. An understanding of the communication industry that mediates needs is also a vital element in the understanding of the social role of advertising. This is attempted in Chapter 3 which revolves around how advertising supported media *valorise* time and the impact of this on the style and content of commercials and the effect of this on the satisfaction of needs. I will argue that in the realm of communication also, use-value is subordinated to exchange-value, such that it is the *double* subsumption of use-value to exchange-value that best helps us understand the social role of advertising in Western industrial society.

# 2 The fetishism of commodities: Marxism, anthropology, psychoanalysis

## Information and commodities

The economic and marketing literatures have been dominated by one concept in the discussion concerning advertising—that of *information* (Stigler 1961; Nelson 1974). The prevailing argument runs that as the modern marketplace has grown and become more complex, so consumers desire information about products to be able to make rational purchasing decisions. Advertising provides this information. To this end there have been numerous studies that seek to measure the 'amount' of information contained in advertising. However, their 'operationalisation' of what constitutes information has been rather narrow. The focus has tended to be on the *objective* features of the product world: what it does, how well it does it, what it is made of, its technical performance features, and so on (e.g. Pollay 1984). Information has largely been taken to refer to information about the *uses* of products. Depending on what precise operationalisation is used, advertising is concluded to offer substantial information (e.g. Howard and Hubert 1974) or little information of use to consumers (e.g. Sepstrup 1981).

This focus on performance features is a very narrow definition of what constitutes information about commodities. For consumers to have full knowledge about goods, some other vital information also needs to be known. Truly complete information about products would also involve information about how goods were made and who produced them. Information about the *relations of production* is as important as information about the performance features of the objects of production.

The importance of this type of information can be seen from both historical and contemporary sources. For example, Marcel Mauss, in his analysis of Maori gift-giving (1967), writes that it was believed that goods were made up of both natural raw materials and the 'life-force' of the person who produced it. The exchange of things in many cultures was literally an exchange of persons and is the reason why reciprocity is so important in many non-market exchange situations—people were literally giving a part of themselves to other people. In the process of objectification (see Chapter 1) in older societies, there is an 'organic unity' between people and the things in which labouring activity is objectified. In such a situation individuals can *only* think of themselves in terms of the external social world because they have 'deposited' a part of themselves in it. Paul Radin describes 'primitive' cultures in the following way:

Nature cannot resist man, and man cannot resist nature. A purely mechanistic conception of life is unthinkable. The parts of the body, the physiological function of the organs, like the material form taken by objects in nature, are mere symbols, *simulacra*, for the essential psychical-spiritual entity that lies behind them (in Taussig 1980, p. 37).

In such a context, part of the *meaning*, part of the vital *information* that people needed about the products was: who produced it; where it came from; and what its role is in social relations.

In our own society, the way that goods are produced and who produces them are also important in defining the meaning a product has for us and thus in defining its use-value to us. For example, in an age of increasing machine and factory production, the hand-crafted product is highly valued both symbolically and materially. In an age of mechanical reproduction people desire *human* production in the things they surround themselves with. We search for authenticity, it seems, in a flood of artificiality. (Walter Benjamin made a similar point with regard to the role of art in an age of mechanical reproduction.) Embedded in goods, as part of their meaning, then, are the social relations of their production. This is part of the information we require in order fully to understand the meaning of things.

Karl Marx, the most sophisticated and penetrating analyst of capitalism, understood this 'organic unity' between goods and social relations. In looking for the best way to unravel the system of capitalist production, he focused on one element as being the key to this understanding. The very first lines of Volume I of *Capital* (Marx 1976, p. 125) are as follows: 'The wealth of societies in which the capitalist mode of production prevails appears as an "immense collection of commodities"; the individual commodity appears as its elementary form. Our investigation therefore begins with the analysis of the commodity.' But why did Marx choose the commodity as the starting-point of his analysis? After all, his major *tour de force* is called *Capital*. Why not start there? Or why not start with labour, which plays such a fundamental role in the production of value? Marx, at one time or another, considered these other options. But after many years of deliberation, he chose the commodity as the starting point of his exposition. As we read *Capital* we can see why. Marx started with the commodity because he thought that if one can understand how the commodity was produced, distributed, exchanged and consumed, then one can unravel the whole system, because objectified in the commodity are the social relations of its production. They are part of the information that the commodity contains within itself. They are part of its communication features. If only we can penetrate down to this information, then we can understand and unravel the whole system of relations of capitalism. The materialist theory of history, then, is fundamentally a theory of the 'reading' of goods, an understanding that the social relations of production are *reflected* in goods.

However, in capitalism, there is a problem in terms of 'reading' goods. In fact, says Marx, the relations of production mask or hide the information embedded in goods about the process of production. There is a rupture in capitalism between the way things *appear* and their *real* or *actual* *meanings*. The commodity is the prime example of this (Marx 1976, p. 163): 'A commodity appears at first sight an extremely obvious, trivial thing. But its analysis brings out that it is a very strange thing, abounding in metaphysical subtleties and theological niceties.' Something occurs in the way that goods are produced and exchanged to render invisible the information embedded in goods about the social relations of their production. The search by Marx for why this occurs in capitalism led him to develop his theory of 'the fetishism of commodities'.

## Marx and the fetishism of commodities

I ended Chapter 1 with the claim that we needed to conceptualise properly the use-value–exchange-value relation in modern society. Marx provides the most developed discussion of this relation. Indeed, his writings provide the most adequate starting point for a study of societies operating within a capitalist mode of production. The identification of surplus-value as the dynamic element behind the movement of capitalist societies in their totality, together with the domination of the commodity-form lies at the heart of Marx's contribution to social theory and provides the framework for understanding much of the contemporary world. Marx never confronted the issues regarding symbolism, consumption and advertising that are of concern to us here. It is unfortunate that those Marx*ists* who have examined this area of contemporary society have tended to dismiss in a puritanical fashion, and out of hand, one of the most fundamental characteristics of human behaviour—the symbolic constitution of utility (see Chapter 1). While many of the overall conclusions derived from the specific Marxist critique of capitalism are indeed valid and correct, the form of the critique has tended to throw out the baby, the problem of symbolism in a more general context, with the bathwater.

This is especially disappointing in that one of the great concepts of the Marxian heritage, 'the fetishism of commodities', refers precisely to the relationship between people and products and to the relation between use-value and exchange-value. Unfortunately, where this has been applied to consumption and advertising, it has been used in far too general and loose a manner to be of very much analytical use (e.g. Debord 1970). The aim of this chapter is to examine closely the theory of fetishism and to see if it can provide the basis of a critical approach to the problems of advertising and consumption in Western capitalism. This means a reformulation, rather than a simple adoption, of the famous radical clichés.

Marx's theory of the fetishism of commodities is a very complex and difficult subject, but is central to an understanding of his overall project. Distinguishing between 'appearance' and 'essence' (real social relations), he thought that the uncovering of the latter was the minimum necessary condition for any scientific work. Norman Geras (1971, p. 71) has suggested that it is precisely this injunction that lies behind the theory of fetishism:

It is because there exists at the interior of capitalist society, a kind of internal rupture between the social relations which obtain and the manner in which they are experienced, that the scientist of the society is confronted with the necessity of constructing reality against appearances. Thus this necessity can no longer be regarded as an arbitrary importation into Marx's own theoretical equipment or something he merely extracted from other pre-existing sciences . . . [It is] seen to lead, by a short route, to the heart of the notion of fetishism.

It is important to stress here that appearance does not mean illusion. Appearance is a dimension of reality, the form in which essence shows itself.

In *Capital*, Marx is specifically concerned with delving beneath the appearance of generalised commodity production. To do this he distinguishes between the use-value and exchange-value of commodities. He claims that, as far as the former is concerned, there is no disjuncture between appearance and essence: 'So far as it (the commodity) is a use-value, there is nothing mysterious about it.' The mystery of the commodity flows instead from its form, its exchange-value, and it is the unraveling of this side that will give an answer to the problem of the 'fetishism of commodities'.

What does it mean to 'make a fetish' of something in this context? It means to invest it with powers it does not have in itself. It is not that we see powers in things which are not present (that would be pure illusion) but that we think that the powers a product does have belong to it directly as a thing, rather than as a result of specific human actions that give it the power in the first place. For example, if we were to think that money actually has value (of which it is merely a representation) as an inherent quality, without recognising that its value is only the result of a monetary system created by humans, then we would be fetishising money. Similarly with capital. If we think that capitalism is productive in and of itself, regardless of its relationship to other elements in the process of production (such as labour) then we would make a fetish of capital. (G. Cohen (1978) argues that in fact capitalism manifests these fetishisms as well as commodity fetishism.)

In short, fetishism consists of seeing the meaning of things as an inherent part of their physical existence when in fact that meaning is created by their integration into a *system* of meaning. The mind does not create the fetishism (as in other forms of it) but registers it in a mistaken fashion. For Marx commodity fetishism consists of things seeming to have value inherent in them when in fact value is produced by humans: it is to *naturalise* a *social* process. Thus things *appear* to have value inherent in them. The *essence* however is that humans produce value.

There are two major dimensions that need to be examined when looking at *how* fetishism arises. The first of these is the exchange of commodities in the capitalist marketplace. The second concerns the structure of the capital–labour relationship centered around the wage relation. I will deal with each of these in turn.

Labour must be performed in all societies if they are to survive, and as they evolve there has to be a *social division of labour*. The distribution of total social labour cannot be avoided—only the form of its distribution can vary. The manner in which this distribution operates in market society lies at the root of the fetishism of commodities (Marx 1934). Since generalised commodity production entails that production is carried on by private individuals or groups of individuals labouring *independently* of each other, the social character of production is manifested only in exchange. The *market* acts as the distributing force of the total labour of society and its only socially unifying element. The equalising factor in the exchange of different use-values is *abstract human labour*. However, the workings of capitalist society work to mask this feature of exchange-value. It is at this vital point of the argument however that Marx (1976, p. 167) lapses into an empirical detour from its logical basis.

What initially concerns producers in practice when they make an exchange is how much of some other product they can get for their own: in what proportion can the products be exchanged? As soon as these proportions have attained a certain customary stability, they appear to result from the nature of the products so that for instance, one ton of iron and two ounces of gold appear to be equal in value.

It seems, then, that the naturalisation of value in the commodity is not only the result of the structure of relations of market society, but of a process over time. Consequently, what is a 'social relation between men . . . assumes here, for them, the fantastic form of a relation between things' (Marx 1976, p. 165).

It is important to stress that the fetishism of commodities does not result from their *social* form. As Leiss (1976) says: 'the division of labour has stamped the products of human activity with a social character as far back as our anthropological researches permit us to go'. Cohen (1978, p. 119) agrees with this.

Mystery arises not because there is a social form but because of the particular form it is . . . mystery arises because the social character of production is expressed only in exchange, not in production itself. The product lacks social form anterior to its manifestation as a commodity. The commodity form alone connects producing units in market society.

Marx uses other modes of production as comparisons to illustrate commodity fetishism. Thus, in feudalism, social relations are manifested directly through 'producing units'.

Here, instead, . . . we find everyone dependent—serfs and lords, vassals and suzerains, laymen and clerics. Personal dependence characterises the social relations of material production as much as it does the other spheres of life based on that production. But precisely because relations of personal dependence form the given social foundation, there is no need for labour and its products to assume a fantastic form different from their reality. They take the shape, in the transactions of society, of services in kind and payments in kind. The natural form of labour, its particularity—and not, as in a society based on commodity production, its universality—is here its immediate social form (Marx 1976, p. 170).

The social reality of oppression is directly visible here. In capitalism however, only commodities are *immediately* social, production relations are only indirectly so. Fetishism is manifested in exchange within capitalist market relations. Cohen (1978, p. 120) writes:

Social relations between things assert themselves against material relations between persons who lack *direct* social relations. It appears that men labour because their products have value through which they relate, and which therefore regulates their lives as producers. They are thus in a quite specific sense alienated from their own power, which has passed into things.

In feudalism, these social relations are expressed directly and 'not disguised as social relations between things, between the products of labour' (Marx 1976, p. 170). Thus products become social before circulation in feudalism and not only in their actual circulation and exchange as in capitalism. The market is necessary to link people's labour 'behind their backs'. Marx (1976, pp. 165–6) writes:

Since the producers do not come into social contact until they exchange the products of their labour, the specific social characteristics of their private labours appear only within this exchange. In other words, the labour of the private individual manifests itself as an element of the total labour of society only through the relations which the act of exchange establishes between the producers. To the producers therefore, the social relations between their private labours appear as what they are, i.e. they do not appear as direct social relations between persons in their work, but rather as material relations between persons and social relations between things.

One may ask here what the fetishism consists of, for Marx is saying that the relations appear as what they really are. If consciousness is reflecting reality, what is false or mystified about it? Remember that, according to Marx, in feudalism products are social directly, in production, whereas in capitalism they become social after production. They become social only in relation to other commodities. What is reflected in consciousness here is the social reality behind commodity *relations*. Rose (1977) calls this the reality of the *visible*. What is hidden is the social reality of the *invisible*, that is, the social reality of commodity *production*. The fetishism thus consists in *naturalising* properties in commodities which are in fact social: it is to see historically specific social relations as eternal and natural. Lichtman (1975, p. 71) writes: 'We grasp our powerlessness in this society and this aspect of our awareness is a reflection of the real fact of our exploitation. But we grasp this powerlessness as a permanent, inexorable fate, rather than a historically transformable situation.' In such a society the economy seems to move by its own laws and of its own volition. It is independent of human control. Such a society would also subscribe to an almost religious belief, that a free functioning of the market would lead to the greatest human welfare. Freed from human control, the marketplace would work its 'magic' in beneficial ways for its human parishioners. Fetishism thus operates to conceal the possibility of a society in which labour is consciously and rationally distributed in accordance with the self-determined needs of people.

The second broad explanatory feature of the theory of fetishism is based upon the analysis of the wage relationship. Whereas the fetishism explicated in Chapter 1 of *Capital* is not an illusion, having a basis in *a* reality, wage-labour and its accompanying relations are based upon illusion. But it is an illusion built upon the first stage of commodity fetishism just described and thus extremely difficult to expose. At the level of circulation, it seems that what we have is an exchange of equals—the worker's labour for wages. The problem is, if everything exchanges for its *equivalent*, how can generalised commodity production based on wage-labour produce a *surplus* or a *profit*? Marx's answer to this is that, in the wage relation, the equivalence is only an illusion based on the first stage of commodity fetishism—the *naturalisation* of value in the commodity. The vital distinction made by Marx is between *labour* and *labour-power*. The use-value of labour-power is labour. The latter creates more value than the value of the former. The capitalist, however, only pays the worker the value of the reproduction of labour-power (what it costs for workers to be fit and able to work—the socially determined level of the means of subsistence). This is less than the value created by labour-power. Thus, in production, the worker works both *necessary* labour time (in which value is created equalling the cost of labour-power, that is, the wage) and *surplus* labour-time (in which value is created for appropriation by capital). But because the objectification of human labour in products is masked by the market system of generalised commodity production, the worker is unable to make the distinction between necessary and surplus labour-time, and thus cannot penetrate to the heart of capitalist exploitation. Again, Marx is explicit on what causes this mystification, for he believes that at root the exploitation of the worker is the same as the oppression of the slave or the serf. Whereas in the latter two cases (the serf especially) the division between necessary and surplus is manifested *objectively* without mystification, the system of generalised commodity exchange *masks* this objective feature in the case of the worker (see Marx 1952). He writes:

The exchange of equivalents, the original operation with which we started, has now been turned around in such a way that there is only an apparent exchange . . . The relation of exchange between capitalist and worker becomes a mere semblance belonging only to the process of circulation, it becomes a mere form, which is alien to the content of the transaction itself, and merely mystifies it (Marx 1976, pp. 729–30).

The wage-form also gives rise to other appearances, that is, that workers are 'free' to dispose of their own labour-power as they see fit.

All the notions of justice held by both worker and capitalist, all the mystifications of the capitalist mode of production, all capitalism's illusions about freedom, all the apologetic tricks of vulgar economics, have as their basis the form of appearance . . . which makes the actual relation invisible and indeed presents to the eye the precise opposite of that relation (Marx 1976, p. 680).

Fetishism then manifests itself in both reality and illusion, and is a major factor in how capitalism as a system of economic relations produces its own shroud of mystification around social praxis.

Marx's analysis here is fundamental to our own understanding of how goods communicate information about social relations and operate within a social context. The mystification or the fetishism that Marx refers to does not only exist in the realm of consciousness and ideas—the misrepresentation about production and consumption is embodied in material objects themselves.

The problems of capitalist society are clearly highlighted when Marx turns to a vision of society in which there is no fetishism and (unlike feudalism) no oppression. He presents a form of market socialism in which there is no capital–labour relation because he envisions 'an association of free men, working with the means of production held in common'. Moreover, while there will be a social division of labour with regard to tasks, these workers will expend 'their many different forms of labour-power in full self-awareness as one single social labour-force'. The market does not determine the distribution of social labour which instead is determined 'in accordance with a definite social plan'. Democratic discourse about social needs and common ownership of the means of production means that 'the relations of the individual producers, both towards their labour and the products of their labour, are here transparent in their simplicity, in production as well as distribution' (Marx 1976, p. 172).

What I have presented in this section has been what Marx believed about the capitalism of his day. In a later section of this chapter I will extricate and expand upon the elements of this theory that can help us fully understand the phenomenon of advertising in advanced capitalist societies. Before I do that, however, a serious challenge to the applicability of Marxian concepts to the study of consumption has to be met. In recent years there has arisen a critique claiming there is something inherently flawed in the way Marx conceptualised the relationship between use-value and exchange-value that prevents any approach based on his work from fully understanding the symbolic element in utility and thus in consumption in general, even its capitalist form. This attack has found its most sophisticated expression in the writings of Marshall Sahlins and Jean Baudrillard.

## Marx attacked: the naturalisation of use and the fetishism of exchange

Sahlins (1976, p. 127) claims that although Marx recognised quite clearly that humans are always social beings, the paradigm of the materialist conception of history was 'never fully symbolic', and that the tension between cultural and natural moments in materialist theory was resolved by dissolving the former. The cultural aspect is clear from the beginning of Marx's thought for people know themselves through the transformation of nature by their own *activity*. Nature is experienced as humanised nature, as socially relative, dependent on the purpose of society. It was this epistemology based on practice that separated Marx from the contemplative materialism of Feuerbach. According to Sahlins, Marx recognises here that 'the entire cultural superstructure figures in the production of economic categories'. Indeed Marx (1956) recognised quite explicitly that the human transformation of nature is not simply the reproduction of physical necessity but the reproduction of a 'definite mode of life'. In distinguishing between humans and animals, Marx (1964) writes: 'Man therefore also forms things in accordance with the laws of beauty'. Sahlins is quite happy with this cultural Marx who recognises the 'social constitution of the material logic'.

However, there is a second aspect of materialist theory which robs the material logic of its cultural impetus and in which culture now appears as the *consequence*, rather than the structure, of productive activity. Work and the natural reproduction of society relegate the cultural sphere to a secondary level. The passages that refer to this aspect of materialism are well known. For example:

The production of ideas, of conceptions, of consciousness, is at first directly interwoven with the material activity and the material intercourse of men, the language of real life. Conceiving, thinking, the mental intercourse of men, appear at this stage as the direct efflux of their material behaviour (Marx 1956, p. 47).

It seems that for Marx, the symbolic is displaced from production only to reappear as 'phantoms' in the brains of men, 'sublimates of their material life process'. Although Sahlins admits that there is some inconsistency on this point in Marx's work, he believes that the material constitution of the social logic, rather than the social constitution of the material logic, becomes the dominant moment of historical materialism. What we have here is Sahlin's wider culturalist challenge to the materialist theory of society, and I will return to it in the next section in defence of Marx. The crux of the matter is that, for Sahlins, Marx has no answer to the question of why a society chooses the specific set of goods it produces, rather than another set. In other words: what determines the needs that determine production?

There follows on this a second critique of Marx, although by an ingenious slight of hand Sahlins includes it under the first, for he goes on to extend the critique not only to production (the nature of the goods to be produced) but to *consumption* (the manner in which they are used), and specifically to the Marxian analysis of the use-value–exchange-value relation. According to Sahlins there is a crucial flaw in Marx's approach that weakens its critical thrust: Marx assumed that the 'mysterious' element of the commodity was a function only of exchange-value, and that there was nothing mysterious about use-value. For Marx, use-value is 'perfectly intelligible: it satisfies human needs'. Sahlins (1976, p. 15) comments:

But notice that to achieve this transparency of signification by comparison with commodity fetishism, Marx was forced to trade away the social determination of use-values for the biological fact that they satisfy 'human wants'. This in contrast to his own best understanding that production is not simply the reproduction of human life, but of a definite way of life.

If this is correct then it seems that Marxism offers a poor basis on which to erect a critique of the consumer culture, for the idea of the symbolic constitution of utility is indispensable for a full understanding of such societies.

Jean Baudrillard, too, has focused on the same criticism of Marx. It was stressed earlier (Chapter 1) how for Baudrillard it is the integration of signs (objects) within a symbolic code that gives them whatever meaning they may have (this includes their utility). Thus there is no meaning inherent in the physical constitution of any object. Baudrillard (1981, pp. 130–1) argues, however, that because Marx linked fetishism only to exchange-value, and consequently within the dynamics of a sign system, use-value lies *outside* of this determination by the code. Use-value does not appear in Marx as a relation.

So it appears that commodity fetishism . . . is not a function of the commodity defined *simultaneously* as exchange-value and use-value, but of exchange-value alone. Use-value in this restrictive analysis of fetishism appears neither as a social relation nor hence as the locus of fetishisation. Utility as such escapes the historical determination of class. It represents an objective, final relation of intrinsic purpose which does not mask itself and whose trans-parency, as form, defies history (even if its content changes continually with respect to social and cultural determinations). It is here that Marxian idealism goes to work; it is here that we have to be more logical than Marx himself. For use-value—indeed utility itself—is a fetishised social relation, just like the abstract equiv-alence of commodities. Use-value is an abstraction. It is an abstraction of the *system of needs* cloaked in the false evidence of a concrete destination and purpose, an intrinsic finality of goods and products.

What I understand by Baudrillard's contention that use-value is a fetishised social relation is that, through the manipulation of the symbolic code, any object can take on any symbolic meaning regardless of its physical constitution. Thus an automobile could be elegant, sophisticated, exciting, youth-ful, manly, feminine, and so on. There is nothing inherent in the object as such to give it an intrinsic meaning and depending on its place in a sign system it can take any one of these meanings. For Baudrillard, use-value itself is a form of equivalence and as such is capable of being manipulated within a system of *exchange*. Marx, it is claimed, did not recognise this relational aspect of use-value.

Thus the reading advanced by Sahlins and Baudrillard argues that Marx was *forced* to trade away the symbolic element of use to make comprehensible his theory of com-modity fetishism. As far as I understand it, both of them want to claim that Marx believed that for any object there is only one use, one meaning, inherent in its physical property and which therefore cannot be manipulated symbolically in a code or in culture. If such is the case, then there can be no Marxian basis for the analysis of consumption, and thus of advertising, which is nothing more than the manipulation of signs. As William Leiss (1978, p. 42) writes on this point:

A theory that ignores the interpenetration of the concrete material and cultural (symbolic) determinants in the satisfaction of needs, restricting itself entirely to its formal structure (the commodity-form under capitalist relations of production) will remain unable to explain processes of social change in precisely that kind of society which the theory pretends to have as its object of analysis—a society where the self-understanding of persons has been formed under conditions of fully developed capitalist market relations.

## Marx defended: the symbolism of use and the mystery of exchange

Before attempting an alternative reading of Marx, I wish to clarify precisely what the issue is and what it is not. Sahlins' sleight of hand was mentioned above. It consists of this: because there is no explicit cultural logic in Marx's writings (which may well be true) it follows from this—and the section on fetishism seems to say—that there is no cultural/ symbolic logic to consumption. Because production is governed by a material logic, so, too, is consumption. Yet the claims for the naturalisation of use and the symbolic constitution of utility refer only to production. It is unclear precisely what Sahlins's point is. For others, however, it is obvious that the issue is consumption. Kline and Leiss (1978, p. 13) write:

We agree with Sahlins that all utilities in all cultures are symbolic. In a society like ours, where large numbers of people participate daily in extensive market exchanges, there is a *double* symbolic process at work. One facet of it is the symbolism consciously employed in the manufacture and sale of the product, including the imagery employed in the advertising designs. The second facet is the symbolic association employed by consumers in 'constructing' lifestyle models.

It is this aspect of the symbolisation process (focusing as it does on advertising) that is of interest here. As such, I will restrict myself in this section to the issue of the symbolic constitution of utility in *consumption*.

In what follows the argument will be constructed of four parts: (1) a distinction has to be made between 'mysterious' and 'symbolic'; (2) Chapter 1 of *Capital* will be reinterpreted with special emphasis being placed on Marx's comments on use-value; (3) the other aspects of what Sahlins calls the cultural moment of Marx's writings will be reintegrated into the structure of the argument; (4) the broader question of the material determination of the cultural aspect of human behaviour will be addressed through the concept of 'partial necessity'.

Marx states that use-value is not mysterious but exchange-value is. Sahlins claims that this ignores the symbolic aspect of the symbolic material duality of commodities. Is this indeed the case? To answer this question, we need to closely examine what 'mysterious' and 'symbolic' actually mean and what is the distinction between them. It is quite clear that, for Marx, commodity fetishism and the mystery of the commodity concerns the *false* appearance of the commodity as possessing value in itself rather than as the result of labour. The theory of fetishism is indeed a theory of *mystification*. The symbolic constitution of utility, on the other hand, is not defined as a relation of falsification, as the *misrepresentation* of objective reality. 'Symbolic' in this instance refers to the giving of meaning to something that has no meaning separate from this symbolism. For instance, attributing status to objects is not necessarily false but is a location of them as part of a symbolic/cultural code. If people believe that attribution to be true and act upon it, there is no recourse to other inter-pretations of reality to disprove it. This, of course, is not to deny that symbolic processes can be placed within structures of mystification, as I will argue later in this chapter. Mystifica-tion is distinguished from symbolism because the former seeks to give false meaning to something that already has meaning. The material/symbolic duality of commodities is their content and hence by definition cannot be false. Thus use-value is not mysterious in that there is no deeper meaning being hidden. Exchange-value is mysterious precisely because it hides a deeper reality. If mystification and fetishism are connected to exchange-value, there is nothing to stop use-value from having a range of possible (non-false) symbolic attributes.

At the present stage, however, we do not even need to go this far, for all that has to be shown is that Marx did not conceive of use-value as a natural relation but as the effect of social relations. There are a number of passages from Chapter 1 of *Capital* that can illuminate this. For example:

The commodity is, first of all, an external object, a thing which through its qualities satisfies human needs of whatever kind. The nature of these needs, whether they arise, for example, from the stomach, *or the imagination*, makes no difference ... Every useful thing is a whole composed of many properties; it can therefore *be useful in various ways* (Marx 1976, p. 125, emphasis added).

Two points can be made here. First, imaginary needs imply a variability in the relation between people and objects based on a symbolic mediation. Possession of a pot could be sign of status or of low ranking. Second, Marx states quite explicitly that an object can have various uses (that is, more than one). Thus a pot can be used to hold various substances (either water or ceremonial blood, for example). It can also be used to break over someone's head in a fight. In addition he writes: 'The labour of the individual producer acquires a two-fold social character. On the one hand, it must, as a definite useful kind of labour, satisfy a definite social need.' But perhaps the most forceful statement of the variability of utility can be demonstrated by looking at the words that Marx (1976, p. 176) puts into the commodity's mouth. 'If commodities could speak, they would say this: our use-value may interest men but it does not belong to us as objects.' Thus it is precisely the *relationship* between people and products that defines use-value. Products are useful *to us*, not in and of themselves. Use-values are realised only in consumption. There are even more explicit statements if we look elsewhere. For example, in the *Contribution to the Critique of Political Economy* Marx (1970, p. 28) writes:

A use-value has value in use, and is realised only in the process of consumption. One and the same use-value can be used in various ways. But the extent of its possible applications is limited by its existence as an object with distinct properties... Although use-values serve social needs and therefore exist within the social framework, they do not express the social relations of production. For instance, let us take as a use-value a commodity such as a diamond... Where it serves as an aesthetic or mechanical use-value, on the neck of a courtesan or in the hand of a glass cutter, it is a diamond and not a commodity.

There are many other examples that can be used. I do not want to claim that by themselves these passages prove that Marx did not naturalise use but, taken in conjunction with the distinction between symbolic and mysterious, I believe it shows that Marx was not *forced* to naturalise use for the sake of the coherence of fetishism and that rejection of a Marxian theory of advertising and consumption is premature. The mystery of fetishism is false. The symbolism of use-value not necessarily so. Use-value can thus be seen as the result of a social mediation.

From such a perspective, some of the examples from Marx's 'cultural moment' can be integrated without contradiction. The production of a 'definite mode of life' has already been mentioned: and in *Capital* (Marx 1976, p. 275) when discussing the reproduction of labour-power, he writes:

The number and extent of his so-called necessary requirements, as also the manner in which they are satisfied, are themselves products of history, and depend therefore to a greater extent on the level of civilisation attained by a country; in particular they depend on the conditions in which and consequently on the work habits and expectations with which, the class of free workers has been formed. In contrast, therefore, with the case of other commodities, the determination of the value of labour-power contains a historical and moral element. Nevertheless, in a given country at a given period, the average amount of the means of subsistence necessary for the worker is a known datum.

What is Marx recognising here if not the cultural and historical determinants of production? But he then goes on to say that he is *assuming these as a given, as a constant*, in his attempt to show where surplus-value is produced and by whom. Sahlins is right in that Marx does not answer in detail the question of why some sets of goods are produced. Marx was aware of it and posed it directly (Marx 1973, p. 528): 'These questions about the *system of needs and the system of labours*—at what point is this to be dealt with?' He did not answer it because it was not his central concern. Sahlins, however, takes the silence to mean that Marx substituted the material constitution of the social logic for the social constitution of the material logic. I do not believe that Sahlins has made his case strongly enough to warrant this conclusion.

If further proof be needed for the cultural/symbolic element of utility in Marx, we need only look to *Wage Labour and Capital* where Marx (1952, pp. 32–3) talks about the *relative* nature of satisfaction and needs:

A house may be large or small; as long as the surrounding houses are equally small it satisfies all social demands for a dwelling. But let a palace arise beside the little house and it shrinks from a little house to a hut. The little house shows now that its owner has only very slight or no demands to make; and however high it may shoot up in the course of civilisation, if the neighbouring palace grows to an equal or even greater extent, the occupant of the relatively small house will feel more and more uncomfortable, dissatisfied and cramped within its four walls . . . Our desires and pleasures spring from society. We measure them, therefore, by society and not by the objects which serve for their satisfaction. Because they are of a social nature, they are of a relative nature.

What clearer indication could we need that Marx recognised the symbolic constitution of utility?

Although this part has relied in large part on citations from Marxian passages, the aim was not simply one of providing alternative 'evidence', of seeking to argue by virtue of the method of 'duelling texts'. This is never enough when discussing Marx for, in the vast corpus of his writings, one is always able to find fragmentary contradictory passages. The vital issue is formulating an adequate theoretical framework for dealing with the issues at hand. The aim of this section is to show that one can have a reading of Marx that does not force one into naturalising use-value and which does not thus force one into the role of material determinist.

The fundamental issue, however, cannot be avoided, for what Sahlins presents is nothing less than an idealist challenge to the materialist 'orthodoxy'. Baudrillard is especially strong on this point and his argument for the monopoly of the code is an attempt to break with any materialist determination of the social world. Any object can take any symbolic meaning: the material/symbolic correlate is broken in favour of the latter. Sahlins does not go quite so far, still maintaining the duality and its interrelation (Sahlins 1976, p. 208): 'The material forces taken by themselves are lifeless... The material forces become so under the aegis of culture.' Noting the wide variety in the patterns of human culture and that different organisms inhabiting the same ecological space interact differently with nature, he claims (Sahlins 1976, p. 209) that nature 'rules only on the question of existence, not on specific form... licensing indiscriminately (selecting for) anything that is possible'.

Now in arguing that Marx did not naturalise the concept of use-value and did not link goods with one intrinsic meaning, one should seek to avoid the extreme culturalist position adopted explicitly by Baudrillard and Sahlins. Certainly Marx cannot be placed at this extreme.

The usefulness of a thing makes it a use-value. But this usefulness does not dangle in mid-air. It is *conditioned* by the physical properties of the commodity, and has no existence apart from the latter... Use-values are only realised in use or in consumption. They constitute the material content of wealth, whatever its social form may be (Marx 1976, p. 120, emphasis added).

(The Moscow English edition of *Capital* translates the crucial word as 'constrained'.) Thus the meanings of a particular product are not open-ended and infinite, but neither are they unique, and I believe that Marx would not have claimed they were so. But this does not mean that they are not determined, not objectively given, for if they are not infinite then there is some boundary to the range of meanings available in any contextual setting. Therefore, as long as meanings are not infinite, you *can* have and *must* have a materialist theory of meaning. Our present epistemologies of determination and contingency cannot quite grasp this *partial necessity*, that meanings are developed and used not in an abstract manner (in which anything is possible as there are no laws of the physical world constraining action) but as *socially concrete*. Concretely, a restriction always appears in as much as any one of a range of meanings will have priority over others. David-Hillel Ruben (1979, p. 58) writes of Marx, concerning this notion of partial necessity:

Marx quotes in the 'Introduction' to the *Grundrisse* Spinoza's dictum that *determinatio est negatio*. When something is determined to be something, or to act in some way, certain alternatives are closed off to that thing. Just as acorns are determined to become oaks and not beech trees, so also late capitalism is determined to develop a monopoly stage and not petty commodity production. What physical necessity offers is a way of seeing the world with restricted possibilities and options, and sets the task of tailoring actions to fit in with the physical necessities that do make some things impossible . . . Physical possibilities, impossibilities, and necessities, both natural and social, set the parameters of rational action.

While recognising that Ruben slips between organic and social conceptions of necessity here, his central point is fundamental. Although in any social setting there are a range of possible meanings and thus of courses of action, concretely a restriction always appears, if not on the number of meanings then on their priority. Thus, in any social setting there is a qualitative texture of restriction on the possibilities.

It is this relation between freedom and necessity that Sartre (1976) seeks to capture in his concept of the *practico-inert*. The social context within which people attempt to attain meaning is not an abstract world—it is a socially concrete world. Objectification consists of human activity becoming externalised and embedded in the material world. History then bears on the present in the form of the social world in which praxis takes place.

Through trans-substantiation, the project inscribed by our bodies in a thing takes on the substantial characteristic of the thing without altogether losing its original qualities. It thus possesses an inert future within which we have to determine our own future. The future comes to man through things in so far as it previously came to things through man (Sartre 1976, p. 178).

The domain of the practico-inert is not limited just to objects, but includes language, culture and institutions. The past, captured in this materiality, acts as a constraint on the present and the future because humans have to interact with this 'inert' realm on its own terms.

## The theft of meaning

I started this chapter with a concern with the kind of *information* available through the market about the *production* of goods. Marx's analysis of the structure of social relations showed how this leads to *misinformation* about the way capitalist society functions. The focus particularly on the way the process of production is hidden in the objects of production was vital. The question remains, however, whether this is still a useful way to examine the capitalist market. Marx, after all, wrote about nineteenth-century capitalism and the twentieth century has seen many changes in the way goods are produced that might lessen the 'fetishism'. I wish to argue in this section that fetishism still provides the basis for understanding the *mystification* that capitalism produces about itself and the meaning of goods. To accomplish this, however, means that we have to extend Marx's original vision concerning commodity fetishism. Particularly, we have to integrate advertising into the context within which the use-value–exchange-value relationship is formed. I will seek to show in this section how mystification reaches today also into the realm of use-value such that the symbolic processes of capitalism concerning the discourse through and about goods are largely based upon structures of *falsification*. This extends the argument that in Marxian analysis use-value is not naturalised, although the economic conditions did not exist in the nineteenth century for Marx himself to develop this particular view. What follows, however, is a logical extension of the foundation he established.

There are two major domains in which people come into contact with goods—as producers and as consumers. I will deal with each of these in turn. One of the fundamental characteristics of capitalist commodity production is the sale by workers to capitalists of their *labour-power* (their capacity to labour) as a commodity. They enter into the process as just another (although vital) *means* of production. By selling their labour to employers, workers have thus lost control of their activity—in the realm of work our activity is alienated from us and belongs to someone else. Control of labour has been transferred to the owner of the means of production, the capitalist. However, it is interesting to ask what else workers have lost over the course of time by the sale of their labour-power. Most importantly, they have lost *access* to knowledge of the process of production. In this context, control is knowledge.

The best and most sophisticated historical account of the degradation of labour under capitalism is Harry Braverman's *Labour and Monopoly Capital* (1974). Braverman starts his analysis by discussing the specificity of human labour and its potential for utilisation as labour-power. Because labour is not an instinctive activity (as in animals) but is preceded by a *conception* of the action, it is not tied to one particular kind of activity but can perform many varied and complex tasks. However, at the same time, there is a potential for the *unity* of this process to be dissolved. Conception can be achieved by one and executed by another. However, labour-power cannot be separated from the owner of the labour-power so to use that capacity to labour involves an appropriation and control of the owner of that labour-power.

Thus for humans in society, labour power is a special category, separate and inexchangeable with any other, *simply because it is human*. Only one who is *master of the labour of others* will confuse labour power with any other agency for performing a task, because to him, steam, horse, water or human muscle which turns this wheel are viewed as equivalents, as 'factors of production'. For *individuals who allocate their own labour* (or a community which does the same) the difference between using labour power as against any other power is a difference upon which the entire 'economy' turns. And from the point of view of the species as a whole, this difference is also crucial, since every individual is the proprietor of a portion of the total labour power of the community, the society and the species (Braverman 1974, p. 51).

Capitalist relations of production have transformed the historic unity of conception and execution (the 'organic unity') into a situation where the working class fulfils only the latter while the capitalist class concentrates control of the former in its own hands. Marx writes (1976, p. 799):

all means for the development of production undergo a dialectical inversion so that they become means of domination and exploitation of the producers; they distort the worker into a fragment of a man, they degrade him to the level of an appendage of a machine, they destroy the actual content of his labour by turning it into a torment; they alienate [*entfremden*] from him the intellectual potentialities of the labour process in the same proportion as science is incorporated in it as an independent power.

In the early history of capitalism, workers held and controlled much of the knowledge of the labour process and organised the productivity to their own pace and created social relations of their own choosing. The 'irrationalisation' of this in terms of the efficient mobilisation of labour for profit maximisation led to the movement of 'scientific management' as systematised by Frederick Taylor. 'Taylorism' involved three explicit principles:

1. The disassociation of the labour process from the skills of the worker in that management assumes the 'burden of gathering together all the traditional knowledge which in the past has been possessed by the workmen and then of classifying, tabulating and reducing this knowledge to rules, laws and formulae'. (Taylor, cited in Braverman 1974, p. 112).
2. Access to and the concentration of this knowledge within management so that conception is divorced from execution. Braverman (1974, p. 118) writes:

Both in order to ensure management control and to cheapen the worker, conception and execution must be rendered separate spheres of work, and for this purpose the study of work processes must be reserved to management and kept from the workers, to whom the results are communicated only in the form of simplified instructions which it is thenceforth their duty to follow unthinkingly and without comprehension of the underlying technical reasoning or data.

3. The use of this knowledge by management to lay out, control and separate the labour process into its constituent elements. Management systematically preplans and precalculates all the elements so that the labour process now exists completed only in the realms of management, and not in the minds of workers who view it in a particularistic and fragmented manner.

Conception and execution are not only separated, but become hostile and antagonistic 'and the human unity of hand and brain turns into its opposite, something less than human'. One result of this is that a whole host of new occupations are created whose central concern is the flow of paper rather than the flow of things. Thus, while knowledge and control of the production process is concentrated in the hands of management, the working classes gain only in ignorance of their own activity. A group of managers and engineers have been created who continually fragment the labour process and return it in an alien and separated form to the working class, who are robbed of the potential to view the labour process in total.

Braverman's argument is a general analysis of labour relations under capitalism. But consider also the individual case. What does an individual worker know of the product he/she has a hand in producing? The specialised division of labour ensures that the worker will have only partial knowledge of only one part of the production process. Where the product comes from and where it goes remains a mystery to the 'direct producers'. This specialisation is exacerbated in the modern age by different parts of one product being produced in many different factories in many different countries. The worker thus from his/her position as a material factor of production cannot see the whole process of the production of commodities. It is *structurally impossible* for this to take place in a consistent or total manner. The structures of capitalist property relations work against acquisition of such knowledge.

Moreover, the number of workers engaged in industrial production has been declining through this century as capital-intensive investment (in technology) decreases the reliance on human labour. The new service and clerical industries are supports of the system of industrial production, although the same process of scientific management is visible there also. The only time the vast majority of people come upon products thus is in the marketplace where completed products magically appear with great regularity. The only information we have of these products is what the marketplace (through advertising) provides us. The only independent information we can gain of products is provided by consumer magazines which focus largely on *performance* features. Moreover, exchange in the market is the only time that we have a *social* dimension to the production and distribution of products. The marketplace is the dominant institution that allocates social resources in various directions.

What *exactly*, then, is hidden? As Marx (1976, 163) says: 'A commodity appears at first sight an extremely obvious, trivial thing. But its analysis brings out that it is a very strange thing, abounding in metaphysical subtleties and theological niceties.' Marx did not see the consumer society emerge, but he did spot the first form of this peculiar feature in a market economy, remarking that the objectified forms for what is produced and consumed there have an 'enigmatic' or 'mysterious' character: Although marketed goods have a richly-textured social composition, involving a co-ordinated production, distribution, and consumption system on a global scale, their social character is not immediately apparent. Thus commodities are 'sensuous things which are at the same time supra-sensible or social': A unity of features that we can see, touch, and smell, on the one hand, and of those (the complex but hidden social relations orchestrated by the market economy) that remain out of view, on the other. Commodities are, therefore, a unity of what is revealed and what is concealed in the processes of production and consumption. Goods reveal or 'show' to our senses their capacities both as satisfiers of particular wants and as communicators of behavioural codes. At the same time they draw a veil across their own origins: products appear and disappear before consumers' eyes as if by spontaneous generation, and it is an astute shopper indeed who has any idea at all about what most things are composed of and what kinds of people made them.

Marx called the fetishism of commodities a disguise whereby the appearance of things in the marketplace masks the story of who fashioned them, and under what conditions. Were it thought to be important for us to hear this story, our being deprived of it would constitute a systematic misrepresentation or distorted structure of communication within the world of goods itself.

What commodities fail to communicate to consumers is information about the process of production. Unlike goods in earlier societies, they do not bear the signature of their makers, whose motives and actions we might access because we knew who they were. Specifically, the following kinds of information are systematically hidden in capitalist society: the process of planning and designing products; the actual relations of production that operate in particular factories around the world; the conditions of work in factories; the level of wages and benefits of workers; whether labour is unionised or non-unionised; quality checks and the level of automation; market research on consumers; the effect on the environment of producing goods through particular industrial processes; the renewable or non-renewable nature of the raw materials used; and the relations of production that prevail in the extraction of raw materials around the world. *All* of these things constitute part of the meaning (information) that is embedded in products.

Information such as the above, if available to people, would affect their interaction with goods because products are the objectification of *human* activity. Our interaction with products is also an interaction between people. Consider how consumers would react if the following kinds of meaning were associated with particular commodities: that a product was produced by child labour in a Third World dictatorship; that raw materials were mined by young children; that a product was produced by someone working eighteen hours a day for subsistence wages in nations such as Korea or Taiwan; that making a product used up scarce non-renewable resources or destroyed traditional ways of life for whole people (as in the Amazon region); or that a product was produced by scab labour. All these things, I believe, would severely impact on the meaning of consumption, on the *way* we buy. Even the conditions of *exchange* embed themselves into the meaning of things (for example, the sentimental gift). Meaning is always more than just the product as a purely material object. Its use-value is socially determined.

Moreover, we know that when this type of information becomes available, it becomes an important factor in terms of consumers' perception of products. For instance, the publicity surrounding the marketing of powdered baby milk by Nestlé in Kenya which resulted in a large number of infant deaths became part of the meaning of all Nestlé products. This resulted in many consumers' boycotting their products. Also, the revelation of the reactionary racial views of Adolph Coors (owner of Coors breweries), once known, led to a concerted effort by minority groups to effect a large-scale boycott of the product in the marketplace. The meaning of products in these cases was extended beyond the meaning only to be derived in the market. But the structures of capitalist social relations outlined in this chapter ensure that the full social significance of products will not be known in a *systematic* manner. The *real and full* meaning of production is hidden beneath the *empty appearance* in exchange. Only once the real meaning has been systematically *emptied* out of commodities does advertising then *refill* this void with its own symbols. Thus when products appear in the marketplace, although we may well be aware of them as products of human labour, because there is no specific social meaning accompanying this awareness, the symbolisation of advertising appears as more real and concrete. *The fetishism of commodities consists in the first place of emptying them of meaning, of hiding the real social relations objectified in them through human labour, to make it possible for the imaginary/symbolic social relations to be injected into the construction of meaning at a secondary level. Production empties. Advertising fills. The real is hidden by the imaginary.* The social significance of the marketplace is only possible after the social significance of production disappears beneath the structure of capitalist property relations. The hollow husk of the commodity-form needs to be filled by some kind of meaning, however superficial.

It is for this reason that the 'triviality' of advertising is so powerful. It does not give a false meaning *per se* to commodities, but provides meaning to a domain which has been emptied of meaning. People need meaning in their interaction with goods. Capitalist social relations break the traditional 'organic unity' between producers and goods. At the same time capitalism weakens other institutions that could have filled this void (family, community, religion). Advertising then derives its power because it provides meaning that is not available elsewhere. Its power stems from the human need to search for meaning and symbolism in the world of goods. (Chapter 6 provides a more detailed discussion of this point.)

In seeking to extend the discussion of fetishism in advertising in this way I believe that I have not departed from the logical scheme that Marx identified as the dynamic of capitalism. However, the argument just developed does mean that we have to rethink the relationship between the 'symbolic' and the 'mysterious'. Marx recognised the variability of use-value but not its mystery. The introduction of the messages of advertising into this discourse and the increasing split between mental and manual labour throughout this century force us to rethink the relation between symbol and mystery. In the modern age, use-value (defined as the symbolic constitution of utility) is stuck within *systematic structures of mystification* concerning the world of goods. It is not just that the ideology surrounding goods is couched in mysterious terms (this is the case with all types of religious belief) but that in modern society the mysticism arises not from the realm of ideology but from the realm of production directly. The mystery of modern symbols is manifested in consumption but is rooted in the structures of industrial production.

From this perspective we can see the mistake that perceptive commentators such as Sahlins and Baudrillard make: they have succumbed to the mystification of commodity fetishism—they make a fetish out of consumption. What they see are vast proliferations of commodities capable of taking and reflecting multiple symbolic forms and they look exclusively to consumption to explain this multiplicity, forgetting the deeper reality of commodity production. In separating commodities from their *material* basis in production, they drift off into the idealist 'iconosphere' of the 'code' or 'culture'.

## Fetishism and magic

Marx's coining of the mystification of exchange-value as 'fetishism' was not the first use of this term to refer to the relationship between people and things. He derived the term from the early anthropological writings. The word itself is of Portugese origin, being a corruption of *feitiço*, meaning an amulet or charm (such as relics of saints, charmed rosaries, and crosses). A manufacturer or seller of these was called a *feiteceiro* and, in the African Portugese colonies in the late nineteenth century, it was used to describe a maker of charms, as well as the more modern meaning of sorcerer or wizard. The word itself means 'magically active' according to W. Hoste (1921), although the famous English anthropologist Edward Tylor writes that it derives from the Latin *factitius* and means 'magically artful'. At the time of the European 'voyages of discovery' (1441–1500), when Portugese sailors found the natives apparently 'worshipping' or paying reverence to objects, they termed these *feitiços*.

Much of the early anthropological work concerning Africa consisted of accounts by missionaries, travellers or colonial military officers. Unfortunately, the unsystematic and biased nature of these early accounts renders them unreliable for serious students. However, their appearance did stimulate a fresh interest among scholars who needed relevant examples to illustrate various theories on the origins of human culture, and especially the origins of religion. In 1760 de Brosse, in his *Du culte de dieux fétiches*, remarked that fetishism was the first stage of general religious development, with monotheism, the belief in the one God, being the second and last stage. (Marx's source for the term 'fetishism' is de Brosse.) His definition of a fetish is 'anything which people like to select for adoration'. Most importantly, he believed that these fetishes were worshipped on account of the powers that they were believed to possess in and of themselves alone.

August Comte, the 'father of modern sociology', slightly modified de Brosse's theory and located fetishism as the first of three stages in the development of religion (followed by polytheism and monotheism). Fetishism here describes a necessary stage in the development of all religion, in which all material bodies are supposed to be animated by souls essentially similar to our own. This theory was generally accepted until the middle of the nineteenth century when Tylor (1871, p. 230) proposed that Comte's theory should more properly be labelled as animism and that the term 'fetishism' should be restricted to the 'doctrine of spirits embodied in, or attached to, or conveying influence through certain material objects'. Tylor is especially concerned to distinguish the spirit and the material object in which it is located. Fetishism is seen here as the practice by which objects become the temporary home of some spirit which if worshipped and appeased can have a beneficial influence on the worldly existence of the owner of the fetish. There is nothing intrinsic in the object that qualifies it as a fetish and the imposition of a spirit takes place within a religious (and ritualistic) context by the performance of a priest or fetish-man. Once this spirit is installed in the object then it is treated as being able to see, hear, understand and act. However, this is not a case of blind faith, for the fetish must pass the test of experience. If it fails it will be discarded.

In a move which extended the concept even further, Herbert Spencer (1879) considered fetishism as an extension of ancestor worship, by which the spirits of the dead inhabit objects and places of 'striking or unusual aspect'. Fetishism has also been used to describe the capture or embodiment of *natural forces* in an object, whereby things such as an eagle's talons or the claw of a leopard become valuable fetishes because one may avail oneself of the powers inherent in these objects. In summary, then, it can be seen that until the end of the nineteenth century the term 'fetishism' was very loosely applied and covered phenomena as disparate as animal, nature and spirit worship.

Much of the later work in this area has tended to accept this fuzzy and confused terminology regarding fetishism. As a result of this confused usage, recent anthropological writings have criticised and tended to drop the term from their analytical vocabulary. Indeed, the use of fetishism has caused such a conceptual muddle that an 'anthropological com-mittee' suggested that the word 'fetish' be retained for 'a limited class of magical objects in West Africa' (Parrinder 1961, p. 9). For our purposes here it is important to distinguish the *level* of everyday activity to which the term fetishism should apply.

Fetishism is not a *total* spiritual belief system: rather, it is *part* of a much larger one. In all societies where the term has been applied, there are different levels of spiritual belief and an acceptance of the powers of the fetish should not blind us to the possibility that its user may also have belief in a higher spiritual power, such as a supreme being. There is no denial of God but merely an indifference to him as regards the conduct of everyday life. It is the vast number of spirits in the air that affect physical human conduct and it is to their influence that attention is directed. Thus, for Rattray (1927, p. 23), 'a fetish is an object which is the potential dwelling-place of a spirit or spirits of an inferior status, generally belonging to the vegetable kingdom'. The location of one of these lesser spirits in an object is the result of ritual and religious activity. As Rattray (1927, p. 90n) says: 'the African with his charm or fetish is infinitely more logical and sensible in his ideas and application of such than is the European with his or her mascot. The African knows why his *suman* should have power and whence that power is derived. We do not.' Thus, almost anything, however small or insignificant, can be considered for use as a fetish, but when the spirit is supposed to have abandoned the material object, it will be thrown away, 'a perfectly empty and useless object'.

What exactly does the fetish *do*? Rattray (1927, p. 23) in his definition of the fetish writes that it is 'directly associated with the control of the power of evil or black magic, for personal ends, but not necessarily to assist the owner to work evil, since it is used as much for defensive as offensive purposes'. For Tylor (1871, p. 245), their purposes include guarding against sickness, bringing rain, catching fish, catching and punishing thieves and making their owners brave: 'there is nothing that the fetish cannot do or undo, if it be but the right fetish'. For Hoste (1921), fetishes serve many ends: they protect against evil spirits as well as detecting them; they cure disease; they are 'an incentive to affection'; and they predict when to do certain things (such as journeys). Nassau (1904) has an interesting chapter on the fetish in daily life and its role in hunting, fishing, planting and love-making. The latter of course is especially pertinent for a study of modern advertising and the examples that Nassau gives could in fact be taken from network television. Rattray (1927) also has an illuminating chapter on the fetish and its everyday use. For example, the following words are chanted as the object is being turned into a fetish: 'if anyone poisons me, let it have no power over me; if anyone invokes my name in connexion with an evil name, do not let it have any power over me' (Rattray 1927, p. 14). In summary then, we can see that the work of the fetish takes place at an everyday, daily level. Its effects are short-term and immediate and concern the practical welfare of its possessors. It does not operate at a higher spiritualistic or vague futuristic level, for which other spheres of religion are more appropriate.

## The devil and commodity fetishism

In the last section, I examined some traditional modes of belief concerning the person–object relation. An interesting question to consider from this perspective is what happens when the 'old' fetishisms come into contact with the 'new' fetishisms of capitalist commodity relations. The result is the development of practices representing a blend of old fetishisms with other elements, devised in response to pressures exerted on traditional societies in the twentieth century by market forces operating on a global scale. Michael Taussig (1980) has studied in detail two such cases in South America. There some traditional societies have called upon a mixture of folklore and Christian doctrine to construct an adequate representation for themselves of what has happened to their way of life, particularly in the domain of producing goods. In the two cultures studied by Taussig (in Colombia and Bolivia), it is held that the devil is responsible for visiting such severe stresses upon them.

Among the Bolivian tin-miners, the mythic structure of explanation says that people have been seduced away from their traditional agricultural pursuits by the promise of great wealth to be gained by labouring in the mines. But the mineowner is actually the devil, and it is he who deludes the workers into accepting this bargain. To protect themselves against the resultant misfortune and death occurring in the mines, the workers adapted peasant sacrifice rituals to their new situation, seeking to propitiate the devil-owner with gifts and ceremonies, chewing coca together and offering it to the icon that represents the devil-owner (Taussig 1980, p. 143):

His body is sculptured from mineral. The hands, face, and legs are made from clay. Often, bright pieces of metal or light bulbs from the miners' helmets form his eyes. The teeth may be of glass or crystal sharpened like nails, and the mouth gapes, awaiting offerings of coca and cigarettes. The hands stretch out for liquor. In the Siglo XX mine the icon has an enormous erect penis. The spirit can also appear as an apparition: a blond, bearded, red-faced *gringo* wearing a cowboy hat, resembling the technicians and administrators . . . He can also take the form of a succubus, offering riches in exchange for one's soul or life.

In both cases materials from older fetishistic practices were adapted and transformed, in order to provide a workable representation of what was happening to the relation between human agents and the material world upon the introduction of wage labour. The personification of the agent who is behind these changes (the devil) is anchored in the idea of the seduction of material wealth to be gained by accepting the rules of the game in a market economy founded on working for wages and producing sugar or tin for world markets.

What prompts cultures to create such representations is the need to supply a coherent account (however implausible it may appear to outside observers) of changes that have a major impact on established ways. In these cases social relations orientated around long-standing modes of production—subsistence agriculture, extended family or kinship groups, barter exchange—began to dissolve as private capitalists and market economics took control. But what is *visible and tangible* among these new events? Not capital investment decisions, international stock-exchange fluctuations, or profit targets set by multinational corporations for their operations in foreign countries; rather, what is visible is loss of access to land, cash wages determined and paid by strangers, radically different types and conditions of work, breakdown of kin groups, and so forth. For the indigenous peoples of Columbia and Bolivia in recent times, just as for

European and other populations earlier, structures of life and experience familiar to countless generations suddenly disintegrated before their very eyes. It is hardly surprising that they should suspect the devil of having a hand in it.

For the material world and activities that sustain life, including the ensemble of objects produced from its resources, no longer make sense when assayed by the accepted standards of judgement. The communication lines running through the world of goods snap, so to speak. In the course of becoming predominant, a market economy unravels and discards not only specific things, habitual routines, and norms, but also the integument holding them together, the sense of a collective identity and fate. At first no new means for binding together our experience of the material world is proffered. It appears only as an 'immense collection of commodities'.

**Fetishism and sexuality**

The area in which there is the most substantial sustained body of literature on fetishism is undoubtedly Freudian psychoanalytic theory. It is also the area in which the term has been applied with the most beneficial results. The clinical usage of fetishism has its basis in Freud's theory of ego development and infantile sexuality, especially as concerns the phallic-genital-oedipal stage. Much of the literature uses this as the starting point and within this framework, the theory of fetishism is part of the theory of 'sexual perversion' in general, including also transvestism, transsexuality, sadism, and so on. It is also a strictly *male* phenomenon and refers to situations whereby sexual satisfaction is impossible to obtain without a non-genital part of the body or some inanimate object being present and attended to.

Fetishism is regarded as a 'perversion'—an *abnormal* development of the sexual instinct. As such it is useful to consider what is *normal* within this theoretical context. Freud (1953) posits an intimate connection between infantile sexuality and the development of normal sexuality at, or following, puberty. Infantile sexuality is the transformation of an instinct through various developmental stages in the first four or five years of life. The particular instinct that Freud is discussing can be labelled 'libido', which in the early years is connected with other functions of life. The first occurrence of this is breast feeding, the need for nourishment. However, the infant repeats this when there is no need for nourishment and this 'pleasure sucking' is the first form of sexual satisfaction. The second stage is the anal stage and is connected with the process of excretion. The third period is called the phallic stage and it is here that the first differentiation between the sexes occurs. For the male in this period, the sexual urge towards his mother increases and the boy's love for her becomes incestuous. As a result, he becomes afraid of his rival, the father. This Oedipal stage is characterised by castration anxiety whereby the fear is that the father will remove the offending sex organ of the boy. Consequently, the boy represses his incestuous desires for his mother and his hostility to his father and the Oedipus complex disappears. For the female, the girl's first love object is also the mother, but when she notices that she does not possess the noticeable external genitals of the male, she feels castrated and blames the mother. The girl begins to prefer the father but this is mixed with envy because he possesses something she does not have and leads to penis envy. Gillespie (1964, p. 127–8) sums this up as follows:

During the first few years of life the child normally undergoes a process of psychological development which differs in many ways from the normal adult sexuality, and especially in its earlier phases, possesses a number of characteristics which, when they occur in adults are regarded as perverse . . . There is a gradual increase in genital interests which culminates in the oedipal stage of development. This is followed by the rather puzzling 'latency period' when there is a recession of sexual activity, during which the 'shades of the prisonhouse begin to close upon the growing boy'; a period when the instinctual impulses become bridled by increasing conformity to outside pressures and inner defences against impulses. The onset of puberty upsets the equilibrium established in the latency period through a biologically determined increase of the instinctual forces, aggressive as well as sexual. The stormy period of adolescence *normally* leads to transformations of psychosexuality of such a kind that the sexual impulse becomes concentrated in a heterosexual, genital drive directed towards non-incestuous objects.

This, then, is the normal model of heterosexual development of which fetishism is a deviation or 'perversion'.

The classic work in this field is Freud's 1927 essay titled simply 'Fetishism'. Here he states categorically that the fetish of adulthood is a *penis substitute*.

It is not a substitute for any chance penis, but for a particular, quite special penis that has been enormously important in early childhood but was afterwards lost. That is to say: it should normally have been given up, but the purpose of the fetish precisely is to preserve it from being lost. To put it plainly: the fetish is a substitute for the woman's (mother's) phallus which the little boy once believed in and does not wish to forgo.

This belief, then, is at the expense of a *denial* of reality and the 'token triumph over the threat of castration and a safeguard against it'. The fetish is activated by the trauma of seeing the female genitals and is an attempt to ease the castration anxiety this causes. The fetish is the penis that the mother must have if the anxiety is to be resolved. It is the *imaginary* penis of the mother. Freud (1953, Vol. 21, p. 206) writes:

Probably no male human being is spared the terrifying shock of threatened castration at the sight of the female genitals. We cannot explain why it is that some of them become homosexual in consequence of this experience, others ward it off by creating a fetish, and the great majority overcome it.

Subsequent work in this area has sought to answer this problem posed initially by Freud by concentrating on the process of the splitting of the ego and events that might lead to an abnormal development of the sexual instinct. The post-Freudian development of this concept has not sought radically to alter its content but basically to extend it to disturbances in ego development in the pre-oedipal stage that magnify the contradictions of the phallic stage.

In the psychoanalytic literature, fetishism is treated as strictly an adult male phenomenon which manifests the traumas of childhood. Its major effect is that for the fetishist any kind of sexual activity with females is *impossible* to engage in without the fetish being present, for it is only that which prevents the outward manifestation of the castration anxiety (impotence) that would be caused if the reality of the penisless female were to be directly perceived. Without the fetish, the fetishist cannot engage in heterosexual sexual activity, for it represents the lost phallus of the mother by which the castration anxiety is overcome. The fetish thus has no power, it does not do anything. It merely completes the scene: it becomes a sign without which the semiological consummation of sexual activity is literally impossible. Social relations thus are mediated *through* the fetish. It completes the scene and without it there can be no action. It makes possible the continuance of social life. Given the phase-specific castration anxiety lying behind male fetishism it should not be surprising that there is not one accepted case of female fetishism (see Bak 1974).

Within Freudian theory, then, fetishism is connected to the development of sexuality in all the early oral, anal and phallic stages and especially to castration anxiety in the Oedipal period. All males go through this process, but depending on events during this there can be a healthy or unhealthy consequence. The healthy consequence is the development after puberty of heterosexual activity whereby the male can relate to the female in an unmediated manner and achieve satisfaction therein. The unhealthy consequence is the development at puberty of heterosexual activity whereby the male can relate to the female only through the mediation of an inanimate object which has the effect of seeing the woman as a phallic woman, and thus denying her natural sexual definition. The latter is a real need *falsely* fulfilled by distorting reality. The former is real, the latter mystified. At the heart of this lies a real, natural and universal need (sexual satisfaction). It is the manner of its satiation that defines whether it is healthy or unhealthy.

## Conclusion

I attempted in this chapter to come to a proper understanding of the relationship between use-value and exchange-value. The analysis of the work of Marx on this point and the addition of advertising to the more general concept of fetishism provides, I believe, the most advanced conceptualisation of this relationship in modern society. Particularly here, I was concerned with demonstrating the manner in which use-value is subordinated to the strictures of exchange-value. Thus before we can understand the 'content' of advertising, we must contextualise it concretely in the modern economy. The symbolisation of commodities is not merely about how goods are consumed—it is also about how goods are produced. The use-value–exchange-value relation shows the manner in which the domain of appropriate symbolisation and meaning is narrowed in the capitalist marketplace and the role of advertising in this process.

The 'fetishism of commodities', then, provides a broad framework for an understanding of the modern relationship between persons and objects. However, the concept of fetishism is a very rich one indeed. Its use in anthropology and psychoanalysis provides us in addition with a very specific description of some 'problematic' person–object relations. The intriguing question that derives from this genealogical exploration of the concept is whether or not it is a useful way to examine the relations between persons and objects as they exist in advertising in the modern age. I attempt to answer this question in Chapter 5 and the conclusions to be derived from this are outlined in Chapter 6. However, before we arrive at a point where we can attempt an empirical study of advertising, we still need to lay the groundwork by filling in the material context within which it is located. The domination of use-value by exchange-value in the general economy is the first and more general context for an understanding of the person–object relation. A more specific realm in which the material context shapes symbolic content and style is the *communications industry*. There, too, the search for exchange-value (profits for media investors) dominates the search for meaning (use-value). A materialist analysis of the communications industry and the relation of that to various dimensions of the person–object relations as represented in advertising is conducted in the next chapter.

# 3 The valorisation of consciousness: the political economy of symbolism (with Bill Livant)*

The previous chapter sought broadly to contextualise the institution of advertising within the framework of the economy in general and to see the way in which the system of exchange-value constrained the system of meaning within which commodities could be located. In this chapter I will focus more specifically on the material context provided by the commercial communications industry for the construction and consumption of advertising messages. This is a vital issue because, as was demonstrated in Chapter 1, advertising plays a key role in the definition and satisfaction of needs in a consumer society. This is not because advertising 'creates' (false) needs, but because 'the realm of needing has become a function of the field of communication' (Kline and Leiss 1978, p. 18). In particular, then, there is a need to understand the role of advertising within the modern communications industry. The major focus in what follows is on the commercial media, especially commercial (advertising-supported) television. I will argue that in the realm of communication also, exchange-value subordinates use-value.

---

* The ideas contained in this chapter were developed jointly by Bill Livant and myself. It has become impossible to separate his contribution from mine. Bill did more than just inspire these ideas: much of the language here is drawn directly from his unpublished writings and his correspondence with me. Although for the sake of stylistic consistency with the rest of the book I continue to use 'I', this chapter should be regarded as truly collaborative work.

## Use-value, exchange-value and the study of the media

The first objective here is to reach a proper understanding of the media of modern capitalism. Although communications as a discipline is relatively young, we can already identify some major differences in the way that this problem has been conceptualised. The early study of the media focused on its seemingly omnipotent power over passive populations and was linked with the analysis of propaganda. From the late 1930s the assumptions of media power were questioned from an empirical basis by the work of Paul Lazarsfeld and his colleagues in what came to be known as the 'effects' approach to the media. Focusing on short-term message effects and only looking at *changes* of attitude as indicative of media influence, this approach concluded that the media were in fact not very important elements of modern society and that whatever power they exercised was mediated through opinion leaders within communities. The belief that media did not do a great deal to people diverted attention instead to the question of what people do with media. This concern was the basis for the establishment of the 'uses and gratifications' approach to media. In the mid 1960s, the dominant 'effects' paradigm came under criticism from a couple of different sources. In the United States media researchers began to question the conclusion that the communications industry has little effect on social life and changed the focus from attitude change to attitude *formation*—that is, the media might not be able to change people's minds on issues but what is the role of media in forming those opinions in the first place? Working within the broad framework of the 'social construction of reality' the media in this perspective were seen as offering 'windows' to the world in the process by which people came to understand the world. The schools of agenda-setting and cultivation analysis emerged from this re-examination.

In Europe the reaction against the dominant 'effects' paradigm took a different direction. Theorists, working within the rubric of critical social thought, broadened out the terms of the discourse surrounding media analysis. In addition to asking questions about the role of media in constructions of social reality, the critical approach also asked questions about the relationship of the media to other institutions of society such as economics and politics. It was the link with wider structures of social *power* that proved the most useful to explore. 'Ideology' became the key descriptive and analytic term by which to understand the role of the media. This perspective has produced an enormous body of literature centring on two crucial questions: first, what is the content of media ideology and what is its relationship to existing structures of power and privilege; and second, how is this ideology produced within the organisational and occupational framework of media industries?

Despite the enormous contribution made by these studies, there has been an increasing recognition in recent years that the critical perspective on communications has failed to penetrate to the core understanding of its place in advanced capitalism, and that the traditional concepts of base and superstructure, and so on, are not enough to explain the dynamic changes that are taking place in mass media. As Russell Jacoby (1980, p. 31) writes more broadly about critical analyses of cultural issues: 'If none of these concepts have been wrong, none have grasped the specificity of the phenomenon'. At a time when mainstream writers were identifying a communications revolution and the development of an 'information society', there was clearly a need to address specifically from a materialist perspective the growing importance of mass media issues.

The attempts to establish new critical perspectives on communications have occurred in two major ways. First, in studies that seek to establish communications as another *industrial* process, producing commodities for sale in the expanding marketplace and concentrating on the manner in which the extraction of surplus value affects the content of cultural commodities. The best representative of this approach is the British communications theorist, Nicholas Garnham. He writes:

So long as Marxist analysis concentrates on the ideological content of mass media it will be difficult to develop coherent political strategies for resisting the underlying dynamic of development in the cultural sphere in general which rests firmly and increasingly upon the logic of generalised commodity production. In order to understand the structure of our culture, its production, consumption and reproduction and of the role of the mass media in that process, we need to confront some of the central questions of political economy in general (Garnham 1979, p. 145).

For Garnham, the central feature of modern communications is the manner in which it has become the latest sphere in which capital can most profitably reproduce itself, so that spheres of activity that have traditionally been outside the realm of commodity production are increasingly drawn in—a process of the industrialisation (or commodification) of culture.

The second major attempt to break with traditional critical analyses of mass media was inaugurated by Dallas Smythe in both his seminal 1977 article and his book *Dependency Road* (1980). For Smythe, Marxism has had a 'blindspot' about communications, concentrating on the concept of ideology instead of addressing the issue of the *economic* role of mass media in advanced capitalism. Smythe gives two original formulations to this problem. First, he argues that mass media produce *audiences as commodities* for sale to advertisers. The programme content of mass media is merely the 'free lunch' that invites people to watch. It is the sale of their audience-power to advertisers, however, that is the key to the whole system of capitalist communications. Second, he claims that advertisers put this audience-power to work by getting audiences to self-market commodities to themselves. Audiences thus *labour* for advertisers to assure the distribution and consumption of commodities in general. Whilst one cannot overestimate the enormous contribution that Smythe has made to a proper understanding of the political economy of communications, the stress on audience labour for the producers of commodities in general also tends to deflect the specificity of the analysis away from communications—the process is externalised from mass media to the ensuing consumption behaviour of the audience. Ultimately, Smythe was concerned with drawing attention to the place of communications in the wider system of social reproduction and the reproduction of capital.

Clearly, the attempts by Garnham and Smythe were motivated by a sense of dissatisfaction with existing mainstream and critical media studies. But what *precisely* were they attempting to break with? Examined more closely I think we can see that they were both attempting to break with *message-based* analyses of communication: in other words, to break with *symbolism* as the starting point. At a more fundamental and deeper level we can see that they were trying to break with a *consumer* model of communications. As Livant (1979) notes, the vocabulary of media analysis revolves around the relationship of audiences to messages. Audiences are largely defined by the messages they receive and consume.

There are good reasons why the attempts by Garnham and Smythe to forge new analyses of communications took this direction. Livant (1981b) claims in fact that the whole field of media sociology has been fixed on messages as the central factor in the study of mass communications. Practically every study, both radical and mainstream, focuses on these messages—their composition, flow, production, reception, behavioural effects, and so on. Similarly, discussion of the impact of the new communications technology, which it is claimed will increase the number of channels available to the audience, is nothing less than a discussion of messages, for a channel is fundamentally a flow of messages. Even the global debate on the 'new world information order' is cast in terms of messages and their movement and flow: 'Students of mass communications, despite their many vigorous differences, share an *immense underlying agreement*—mass communications are about *messages*, messages, messages' (Livant 1981b, p. 11).

But what specifically about message-based analyses had to be overcome? What did the break with 'ideology' entail? Garnham's and Smythe's attempts were directed against the 'cultural studies' approach to media which concentrates on analysing *systems of meaning*. In fact it is this stress on *meaning* that unites the diverse efforts to focus on the manufacture, transmission, reception and use made of messages. The analysis of messages historically has been a study of the meaning of those messages. It underlies the study of ideology (advertising, political, hegemonic), and the semiotic approach to mass media, as well as the ethnographic focus of the Birmingham School's study of culture.

What, then, is the relationship between meanings and messages? Clearly there is no one-to-one connection between meaning and message. Messages do not have only one meaning. This can be no more true for messages than it is for commodities (see Chapter 2). Indeed many of the studies in the critical tradition have stressed the context-specific nature of the derivation of meaning from messages. Meaning is the qualitative specificity in context of a message. In consuming messages we consume meaning. The use-values of messages are their meanings (in context). Just as in the consumption of a physical object, the use-value is the meaning derived from it *by the consumer*. This meaning can come either from 'the stomach or from fancy'. The use-values of messages are their meanings. The existing study of communication then, both mainstream and critical, has been the study of use-values. However, within the sphere of commercial mass media, messages have both a use-value *and* an exchange-value. More precisely, the use-values of messages are integrated within a *system of exchange-value*. To understand use-value we have to contextualise adequately its relation to exchange-value. This means a switch in focus from the question of the use-value (meaning) of messages, not because the understanding of meaning is unimportant, but because we can only understand it within its concrete specificity once we fully understand the conditions created by exchange-value. If meaning is the *content* of messages (their use-value), then we need to abstract from the contents of communication to the *form of value* that constrains it.

The need to break with messages as the starting point becomes clearer when we consider historically how mass media arose. Raymond Williams (1974, p. 25) writes of the beginnings of radio:

In broadcasting, both in sound radio and later in television, the major investment was in the means of distribution, and was devoted to production only so far as to make the distribution technically possible and then attractive. Unlike all previous communications technologies, radio and television were *systems primarily designed for transmission and reception as abstract processes, with little or no definition of preceding content*. When the question was raised, it was resolved, in the main, parasitically. There were state occasions, public sporting events, theaters and so on, which would be communicatively distributed by these new technical means. *It is not only that the supply of broadcasting facilities preceded the demand; it is that the means of communication preceded their content.*

In addition, the major actors who came to shape the structure of American broadcasting soon realised that profitability lay in something other than messages. In the late 1920s relations between networks (CBS and NBC) and affiliates were based upon two different types of programme: for programmes that were sponsored by an advertiser, the network paid the affiliate to carry them (the network paying for access to the audience of the affiliate); for programmes that were un-sponsored, affiliates paid the network. At a time when unsponsored programmes outnumbered sponsored shows, this involved smaller stations in considerable expense. Thus while both networks sold audiences to advertisers, they also sold messages to affiliates. It was William Paley's grasp of the implications of this, as president of CBS, and the way in which he changed the context of network–affiliate relations that proved vital to the evolution of the industry. David Halberstam (1979, p. 40) writes of Paley:

The critical years were the early ones. What he had from the start was a sense of vision, a sense of what might be. It was as if he could sit in New York in his tiny office with his almost bankrupt company and see not just his own desk, or the row of potential advertisers outside along Madison Avenue, but millions of the American people out in the hinterlands, so many of them out there, almost alone, many of them unconnected to electricity, people alone with almost no form of entertainment other than radio. It was his sense, his confidence that he could reach them, that he had something for them, that made him different. *He could envision the audience at a time when there was in fact no audience.* He not only had the vision, he knew how to harness it, he could see that the larger the audience, the greater the benefit to the network, because it would mean that many more advertisers would want to participate. If the larger audiences meant better advertisers, then it also meant more money, which meant better programs, which meant larger audiences, and which meant that more stations would want to affiliate with CBS.

Paley chose an ingenious strategy to attract affiliates. He started to give away, *free*, the unsponsored programming.

The affiliates could plug into CBS at any time without cost. CBS of course wanted something in return—an option, with two weeks notice, on any part of the affiliates' schedule for sponsored network shows. Whereas NBC had to negotiate with each station individually, many of whom were stubborn in allowing network programming at a time that they wanted to use, CBS could *guarantee* an advertiser coast-to-coast audiences. Affiliates swarmed to CBS. The very announcement of this idea almost doubled the number. As Livant (1981b, p. 3) remarks:

Paley's 'new idea' was precisely that in order to sell audiences, you had to *stop* selling messages. This is precisely what NBC had not grasped . . . NBC had the old idea. The new idea could not simply be added on to the old idea. It had to overcome it; it had to break the set that the object of commerce by the media is messages.

The industry itself had made the break with messages fifty years ago. Paley was interested in selling audiences, not in selling messages. This does not mean that he was not interested in messages, but that he was interested in how messages fit into the structure of the exchange-value of audiences.

## The value form of time in commercial media: absolute and relative surplus-value

We need, then, to comprehend properly the system of exchange-value within which the commercial media are based. To do so we need to understand the economic logic of the commercial communications industry and to answer three related questions: (1) what is the commodity-form sold by commercial media; (2) who produces this media commodity and under what conditions; (3) what is the source of value and surplus-value in this process? Once we have answered these questions we can then formulate an adequate context within which we can understand the role of advertising and advertising messages. I will address each of these questions in turn.

*What is the commodity-form sold by the commercial media?* From the foregoing analysis it seems clear what commodity broadcasting is based upon. Media sell *audiences* to advertisers. We need, however, to pin down specifically what about audiences is important *for the mass media*. For all his emphasis on communications, Smythe does not ask this question directly. For him it is audience-power put to work for *advertisers* that is important. There is no doubt that this is what advertisers are interested in, but it does not mean that the media are interested in the same thing. If we ask what advertisers buy with their advertising dollars, many of the confusions can be avoided. The obvious answer is that advertisers buy time. The question that is not often asked is 'whose time?'. The answer is not difficult to supply: *audiences' time*; more precisely, audiences' *watching time*. That advertising rates are determined by the size and demographics of the audience is ample confirmation of this. When media sell 'time' to a sponsor, it is not abstract time that is being sold but the time of particular audiences. Further, this is not (as Smythe contends) time spent in self-marketing and consuming advertisers' commodities, but rather time spent in watching and listening—*communications-defined time*. When an advertiser buys an audience, he/she buys their watching time. That is all the media have to sell. They can make no guarantees as to the purchasing acts of the audience. What they sell (because they own the means of communication) is what they control—the watching time of the audience.

This is an important point to clarify and resolve. For Smythe the commodity that is sold as an audience is in fact (subjective) audience-power used by advertisers in the realisation of value. I argue instead that the commodity is the (objective) watching time of the audience. The issue is *what is exchanged*, not how it is used. If Smythe were correct, advertisers who see a *drop* in their sales during a campaign (which must happen to some advertisers if market share is the thing that is affected by advertising) should be able to go back to the seller of the commodity audience-power, the media, and ask for their money back on the basis that they have been sold a defective product, for audience-power was not utilised in the realisation of value for *their* commodities. Clearly relations between advertisers and media do not operate in this way.

Media sell *potential* audience-power, but the only thing they can guarantee is the *watching activity* of the audience. How advertisers utilise that watching activity in the construction of commodity meaning is their own responsibility. It is instructive to note that the only instance in which the advertiser seeks compensation from the media is if the size of the audience watching is not as high as the price for that time indicates. In such a situation advertisers can ask for 'make goods'—more spots on other programmes—as compensation.

Most critical analyses of advertising have been stalled around these points. The watching time of the audience has been quite correctly characterised as the *domination* of 'free time' by capital to aid in realising the value of commodities in general. For example, the work of Stuart Ewen and Paul Baran and Paul Sweezy concentrates on this point. So too does Smythe's work. It is the functional role of advertising in creating demand for commodities that becomes vital. I do not want to deny the importance of this approach; but the discussion of audiences should not stop here. As Livant (1979, p. 103) remarks, the audience as a market is the first form of organisation of this commodity, *but not the last*.

The recognition of watching time as the media commodity is a vital step in the break with message-based definitions of media and audiences. It makes the problem an *internal* one to mass communications. The accumulation dynamic of media is located *in* mass media. Indeed the first break by Smythe was illusory. It led to a dead end, for it did not make a sufficient break with a message-based analysis of mass communications. The key to the whole process for Smythe is that the audience receives *consumerist ideology*. No matter how much he stresses the oppositional activities of audiences in constructing alternative lifestyles, Smythe has unsuspectingly fallen victim to his own blindspot. Once again the issue becomes the construction of *meaning*. Audiences may accept or reject commercial messages, but it is this *subjective* element that is vital. Smythe has drifted back to the use-value of messages. Contrary to this, I believe, is the focus on watching time that signals the real break in the attempt to establish an audience-centred theory of mass communications from a materialist perspective based on the analysis of exchange-value.

*Who produces this media commodity and under what conditions?* It is the working through of this question that lies at the heart of the break with message-based definitions. However, this question has been given a curious answer that has stalled a proper understanding. Networks consider themselves as the producers and sellers of audiences (Bergreen 1980; Reel 1979, pp. 4–5), and critical thinkers have tended to take this at face value, accepting the notion that because networks *exchange* audiences, that they also *produce* them. It is surprising to find this confusion in the writing of Marxist critics on the topic of *communication*, since they do not make this error in writing on the motor-car industry or petrochemicals, or indeed on communications hardware itself. In such cases a critical view sees that it is labour and nature which produce wealth, but labour alone which produces *value*. In such cases, we are able to cut through the main myth of capitalist society: 'the productivity of capital' (Marx 1976). But this critical judgement seems to be lost when it comes to communications. There, in the guise of message-making magic, the myth of the productivity of capital still befuddles us.

To avoid this trap we have to distinguish several common confusions. First, we must distinguish the production of *messages* from the production of *audiences*. The staff in the CBS newsroom produces news. The viewer, watching it, does not produce the news. But he/she does participate in producing the commodity audience-time, as does the CBS staff. Networks could produce messages that no one might watch. In that case a message could be produced without producing an audience. If no one watches the evening news, CBS would barely be able to give away that time, let alone sell it. The commodity audience time is produced by both the networks and the audience.

Second, therefore, we have to distinguish between the *production* of audiences and their *exchange*. There is a lot of talk in the industry about the media's producing audiences, but they have not produced what they are selling. The networks merely *sell* the time that has been produced for them by others (by the audience). It is only because they own the means of communication that they have title to the commodity which has been produced for them by others. The way they talk about producing what they only exchange recapitulates the opinions of Manchester manufacturers more than a century ago (see, for example, Engels's important 1891 preface to Marx 1952). Both suffer from the self-serving myth of the productivity of capital. Once we have sorted out these confusions we can see that the answer to this second question is that *both* audiences and the networks produce the commodity audiences' watching time.

*What is the source of value and surplus-value?* Through their own station licences and those of their affiliates, and through their ownership of the means of communication, the networks have control of the twenty-four hours a day of broadcasting time. How, then, is this time that the networks control made valuable—how is it *valorised?* The surface economics of commercial television seem quite simple. Network expenses can be defined as operating costs plus programme costs. Their revenues are advertising dollars from advertisers who buy the time of the audiences which the programming has captured. Networks hope that revenues are more than expenses. This is more than an empty hope, of course, for it is almost impossible to lose money if one owns a VHF station. The average cost of a thirty-second prime-time network commercial in 1985 was $119,000. Based just on prime-time sales (8–11pm) each network collects $60 million a week from advertisers.

We need, however, to dig beneath the seeming superficiality of commercial television economics and ask specifically how and by whom value and surplus-value (profit) is produced. Let us trace through the process in detail. The networks buy (or license) programmes from independent producers to entice the audience to watch. Networks then fill this empty time they control by buying the *watching-power* of the audience—the capacity or the power to watch. Having purchased this watching activity, this 'raw material', they then process it and sell it to advertisers for more than they paid for it. Let us take a concrete example. A network pays independent producers $400,000 a show for a half-hour situation comedy. The show is in fact twenty-four minutes long. The other six minutes is advertising time. Let us presume that this six minutes is divided into twelve thirty-second spots which sell for $100,000 each. Network costs are $400,000 and income is $1,200,000, leaving a surplus of $800,000 for thirty minutes of the broadcasting day.

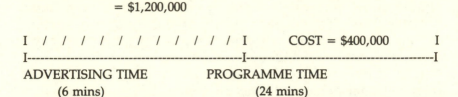

REVENUE    [ 12 × $100,000 ]
                 = $1,200,000

```
I  /  /  /  /  /  /  /  /  /  /  /  /  I        COST = $400,000        I
I--------------------------------------------I--------------------------------------------I
ADVERTISING TIME              PROGRAMME TIME
     (6 mins)                      (24 mins)
```

We have to remember that the vital element in this process is the watching activity of the audience. It is *their* time that is being bought and sold. Without the audience watching, advertising time would be valueless. With that in mind we can now see precisely where value and surplus-value are produced. For four of the twelve advertising spots the audience is watching to cover the cost of the programming (which the audience presumably wants to watch). It is *necessary* for the audience to watch for four spots to produce value equal to the cost of programming. For four spots the audience watches for *itself*. For the remaining eight spots the audience is watching *surplus-time* (over and above the cost of programming). Here the audience watches to produce surplus-value for the owners of the means of communication, the networks or the local broadcasters.

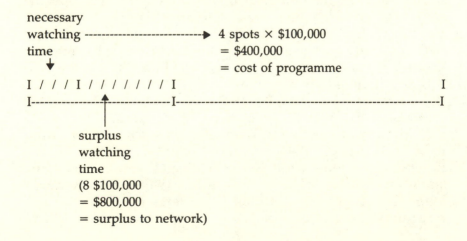

```
necessary
watching  ---------------------------▶  4 spots × $100,000
time                                    = $400,000
   ▼                                    = cost of programme

I / / / I / / / / / / / I                                                    I
I--------------▲--------------I-------------------------------------------------------I
               |
            surplus
            watching
            time
            (8 $100,000
            = $800,000
            = surplus to network)
```

Networks wish to make necessary watching time as short as possible and surplus watching time as long as possible. It is the *ratio* between necessary and surplus watching time that is vital to the networks. As Livant (1982, p. 213) writes:

The struggle to increase surplus time and decrease necessary time animates the mass media. On this proportion the rate of surplus value produced in the media depends. The trade literature is full of studies which strive, one and all, to convert necessary time into surplus time.

One way in which this ratio can be manipulated is to make the advertising time *longer*. Programme time is made into advertisement time so that in the example above two more thirty-second spots could be added by making the programming only twenty-three minutes long. In that case the ratio between necessary and surplus time (presuming programme costs remain the same) falls from 4:8 to 4:10. This indeed is what local stations do to syndicated shows. Portions of the programme are cut out to make space for more advertisements. This strategy, based upon extending advertising in real time, can be labelled the extraction of *absolute* surplus-value. In this scenario there is a continual attempt to expand advertising time in total.

However, at a certain point, there is a limit to the expansion of advertising time. Audiences will simply stop watching if there is too much advertising and not enough programming. The TV Code of the National Association of Broadcasters (NAB) limits non-programming time to 9.5 minutes per hour in prime-time—although most stations violate this limit (see Ray and Webb 1978). The networks in this situation must adopt new strategies to manipulate the necessary–surplus time ratio. While the networks can no longer make people watch advertising longer in absolute terms, they can make the time of watching advertising more *intense*—they can make the audience watch *harder*. This is accomplished by reorganising both the audience and the watching time. As Lawrence Bergreen (1980, p. 289) notes: 'While they cannot expand time either, they can divide it, a process which amounts to a form of expansion.' This process, based not on extending the time of watching, but on dividing a limited amount of time, may be labelled the extraction of *relative* surplus-value. The ratio between necessary and surplus time is accomplished by redividing within a set amount of time.

There are two major ways in which this can be accomplished. The first is by reorganising the watching audience in terms of *demographics*. Since the late 1950s, as market research grew in sophistication and advertisers were able to pinpoint quite precisely their target market, the media have found it profitable to deliver these segmented audiences to sponsors. Erik Barnouw (1978) has given a powerful account of how the obsession with producing the right demographics has come to dominate the everyday practices of broadcasters (see also Gitlin 1983). Advertisers judge the effectiveness of various media in terms of how much it costs to reach 1000 people (cost per thousand). However, the watching time of all types of audience is not the same—some market segments are more valuable because that is who advertisers wish to reach. For instance, in prime-time advertisers will pay much less to reach 1000 viewers than will advertisers who buy time during sporting events. This is because the audience for sports includes a large proportion of adult males whom advertisers of high-price consumer articles (such as motor cars) are anxious to reach. To reach 1000 males advertisers of these products will be willing to pay more than to reach 1000 female viewers through prime-time advertising. As John DeLorean says (Johnson 1971, p. 224):

The difference in paying $7 a thousand for sport and $4 a thousand for 'bananas' (prime-time) is well worth it. You know you're not getting Maudie Frickert. You're reaching men, the guys who make the decision to buy a car. There's almost no other way to be sure of getting your message out to them.

Now males certainly do watch prime-time as well but not in so concentrated a manner. In prime-time, motor-car advertisers are paying not only for the male audience but also for the rest of the audience, many of whom have no interest in purchasing cars. For every thousand people whose time is bought by advertisers on prime-time there is much 'wasted' watching by irrelevant viewers. Specification and fractionation of the audience leads to a form of 'concentrated viewing' by the audience in which there is (from the point of view of advertisers) little 'wasted' watching. Because that advertising time can be sold at a higher rate by the media we can say that the audience organised in this manner watches 'harder' and with more intensity and efficiency. In fact, because the value of the time goes up, necessary watching time decreases and surplus watching time increases, thus leading to greater surplus-value.

To illustrate this point, presume the following: on a Saturday afternoon a local station puts out programming that costs it $2,000 for a thirty-minute show. The audience for this is 100,000 and is comprised of a mixture of females, males and children. For this audience's time an advertiser is willing to pay $10 per thousand for a thirty-second advertisement. There are 10 advertisements during the thirty minutes and each costs $1,000 ($10 × 100). Advertising revenue is thus $10,000. Necessary watching time by the audience here consists of watching for two spots—sixty seconds. The remaining four minutes are surplus time for the broadcaster. The ratio between necessary and surplus time here is 2:8.

To increase the ratio between necessary and surplus here broadcasters could attempt to insert more advertising time. Let us presume that is not possible. Another strategy would be to schedule programming that will attract audiences who can be sold for a higher price to advertisers. The broadcaster now buys a sports event for $3,000 for that thirty minutes. The audience remains at 100,000 but now it is comprised mainly of adult males. Advertisers are willing to pay $20 per thousand to reach this audience. Now each thirty-second spot will cost $2,000 ($20 × 100) so that advertising revenue is now $20,000. Necessary watching time by the audience necessitates time that will produce value equivalent to the cost of programming ($3,000). The audience has to watch for one spot and half (forty-five seconds) to cover this. Thus the ratio of necessary to surplus is now 1.5:8.5—a decrease in the ratio. It is exactly this type of reasoning that has resulted in the huge expansion of televised sports in the last twenty years. It is also the economic reasoning behind the 'kid-vid Saturday morning ghetto'. For the networks Saturday morning was largely empty space. They filled it with a very fragmented child audience whom advertisers of toys, candies and drugs were anxious to reach in an efficient manner. This indeed is the economic logic behind the move to cable television and narrowcasting and is based upon the simple fact that specification produces more value than heterogeneity within an audience group. As John B. Vanderzee, advertising manager of the Ford Motor Company's Lincoln Mercury Division says:

As the price of a car goes up, clearly there are fewer and fewer people who can afford it or aspire to it . . . As the price of your product goes up, the attractiveness of network advertising goes down. Cable TV viewers are more likely to be able to purchase . . . This so called mass communications is very rapidly changing. Maybe there won't be such a thing as mass communications (in the future). It's going to be targeted communication (*Vancouver Sun*, 1983).

Now clearly, the networks are not going to be swallowed up by cable in the near future and the sheer numbers that they can deliver through prime-time will assure their dominance of the field. However, they are themselves moving to specification during certain time periods and they have lost some viewing and advertising dollars to the narrowcasting technologies of cable. I will return to the implications of narrowcasting later.

The other major way in which relative surplus-value operates in the media is through the division of time. Whereas the concern with demographics reorganises the watching population, the concern with time division is with the watching *process*. This involves a redivision of the limited time available to increase the necessary–surplus ratio. The major way to accomplish this is to move towards *shorter* commercials and indeed over the last twenty-five years, although the absolute amount of advertising time has only increased by 2.5 minutes an hour, the number of non-programme elements has risen dramatically. In 1965 the three networks showed an average of 1839 advertisements per week. In 1970 the figure was 2200, in 1975 it was 3487, in 1980 it was 4636 and in 1983 it was 4997. (*Television/Radio Age*, June 1985). Today the thirty-second commercial is the most predominant although there are also a great number of fifteen-second commercials.

In 1985 the latter comprised 6.5 per cent of all network advertisements and it is estimated that in 1986 this will climb to 18 per cent.

The basic economic logic works in the following manner. Presume there are five thirty-second commercials in a commercial break. They each sell for $100,000. Income to the network is $500,000. To increase the revenue derived from this time the network could make the following changes. Instead of five spots the time could be divided into ten fifteen-second slots that would be offered to advertisers for $60,000 each. If there were enough demand to sell these spots the income to the network would be $600,000 instead of the previous $500,000.

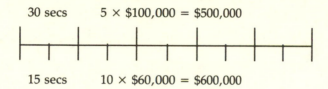

30 secs      5 × $100,000 = $500,000

15 secs      10 × $60,000 = $600,000

But why would advertisers agree to this price hiking? After all, they are now paying more per second, though less per spot. Advertisers, however, are not concerned about the value of time but about the *frequency* with which the market can be reached. This gives them twice the number of advertisements without raising the price by a proportionate amount. And indeed advertisers believe that a combination of thirty-second and fifteen-second versions of the same advertisement works well in conveying almost the same information. If the programme price remains the same then viewers will have to watch for less necessary time to cover its cost.

The other major way in which this can be accomplished is by the technique known as 'time-compression'. With this a thirty-six-second message can be squeezed into thirty-seconds without pitch distortion. Where there were previously five thirty-six-second spots, time compression of these messages produces six thirty-second spots. If the networks can charge $100,000 for the five longer spots (total

$500,000) and give a reduced rate of $90,000 for the six
compressed spots (total $540,000) they will decrease
necessary time and increase surplus time. Let us presume that
the cost of programming remains the same at $100,000.
Necessary time in the first case (thirty-six seconds) is thirty-six
seconds. With six thirty-second advertisements the necessary
time is thirty-three seconds. Surplus time is then correspond-
ingly longer.

36 secs      5 × $100,000 = $500000

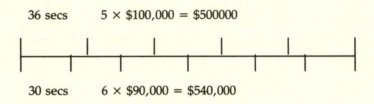

30 secs      6 × $90,000 = $540,000

Again, why would advertisers be interested in this? John
Andrew (1981) writes:

Common sense might say that advertisers and others could save
money by simply getting their actors to talk faster. Not so . . . People
tend to slur their words when they talk fast. Time-compressed
voices don't sound slurred. Another problem: People can only talk
as fast as they can think.'

Indeed, one study found that time-compressed commercials
actually attained higher recall scores in research (MacLachlan
and Siegel 1980).

   In this section I have been concerned with coming to a
proper understanding of the economic logic of commercial
broadcasting, and I have stressed that it is the way in which
the time that networks control is valorised that is the vital
factor. Before moving on to the next stage of the argument
I wish to stress that the time under consideration here is the
time of audiences. It is the particularity of this time based
around certain audiences that is the key to the demographic
component of this process. It is also the limits of human
perception (that is the limits to watching) that guides the
division of time. Advertisers may be able to construct beauti-
fully crafted ten-second commercials but if these do not work

on the audience in that short time then they are useless. It is human watching, listening, perceiving and learning activity that acts as a constraint to this system. As one advertising executive says: 'If we can demonstrate that the American consuming public can absorb and act on a 15-second unity, can the 7.5 second commercial be far behind' (*Fortune* 23 December 1985). I will come back to the issue of more and shorter advertisements in a later section on 'clutter' and advertising content.

## Watching as working: viewing and wage labour

In the last section I have, of course, used the familiar concepts of Marxian economic theory to analyse the valorisation of time by the networks. It was not a coincidental choice because central to the whole paradigm of Marxian economics is the notion that it is human *labour* that is the basis of the productivity of societies. It is not capital or technology that produces value in capitalist society, it is labour. Similarly, in the analysis of broadcasting economics, it is audience *watching* that is vital to the whole process. Without the activity of the working class capitalism would grind to a halt. Without the activity of the audience broadcasting, too, would collapse in its present form. In a very real sense we can see that there are many similarities between industrial labour and watching activity. In fact watching is a form of labour. I wish to argue in this section that in fact when the audience watches commercial television it is working for the media, producing both value and surplus-value. This is not meant as an analogy. Indeed, watching is an extension of factory labour, not a metaphor. Let us compare the basic concepts that explain the productivity of the working day in the factory and those that explain the productivity of the viewing day within broadcasting.

In Marx's analysis of the working day, the productivity of capitalism is based upon the purchase of one key commodity—labour power. This is the only element in the means of production that produces more value than it takes to reproduce itself. Like all commodities, it has a value, a cost—the cost of its production (or reproduction). The cost of labour power (the capacity to labour) is the cost of the socially determined level of the means of subsistence: that is, what it costs to ensure that the labourer can live and be fit for work the next day. The amount of labour time that it takes to produce value equivalent to this minimum cost is labelled by Marx socially necessary labour (necessary to reproduce labour power). Socially necessary labour time produces value equivalent, then, to wages. The remaining labour time is labelled surplus labour time and it is on this time that the profitability of capital rests. This is where surplus value is generated.

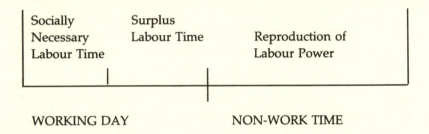

In the non-work part of the day workers spend wages (on shelter, food, children, and so on) that will ensure that they will be fit and healthy enough to go to work. During non-work time they *reproduce* their labour power. If they did not (if they did not eat, for example) then they would not be able to sell their labour power to capitalists because they would not be healthy enough to work. During the necessary labour time they make commodities that produce value equivalent to their wage. The remainder of the time they work for capital.

Notice how similar this model is to the previous analysis of the valorisation of viewing time. The production of audience time is like any other industrial production process. The capitalist (the network) owns the means of production (communication) which makes possible the production of commodities and which gives the capitalist (network) *ownership* of that product (see Jhally 1982). Also employed is the *value-creating* element of the means of production —human labour power. Just as workers sell labour power to capitalists, so audiences sell *watching power* to media owners; and just as the use-value of labour power is labour, so the use-value of watching-power is watching, the capacity to watch. In addition, as the value of labour power is fixed at the socially determined level of the means of subsistence (thus assuring that labour power will be reproduced) so the value of watching power is the cost of its reproduction—the cost of programming, which ensures that viewers will watch and be in a position to watch extra (the time of advertising). In this formulation it is only the time of *advertising* that comprises the 'working day' for the audience. The programming, the value of watching power, is the *wage* of the audience, the variable capital of the communications industry. It is also time for the reproduction of watching power, the time of *consumption*, the time of non-work. As the working day is split into two so the work part of the viewing day, advertising time, is split between socially necessary watching time and surplus watching time (see previous section).

Labour and watching share many other characteristics in addition to this formal analysis. Historically, they have evolved in similar ways. For instance, the early history of industrial capitalism is tied up with attempts by capital to extend the time of the working day, to manipulate the necessary–surplus ratio by extending in an absolute sense the time of work (the extraction of absolute surplus value). Within the development of the commercial media system, this phase is represented by broadcasting from the late 1920s to the early 1960s. In the first years of commercial broadcasting (extending into the 1930s) broadcasters struggled to persuade advertisers to sponsor shows. After Paley's dramatic shift in giving away all unsponsored programming (see p. 70–1) the networks could no longer generate revenue from selling messages but only from selling audience-time: the more shows that were sponsored, the more audiences that could be sold to advertisers. This was an extension in time that people watched or listened for capital. It also has to be remembered that until the introduction of spot-selling in the 1960s, programmes were advertising agency creations with the sponsor's name and product appearing everywhere—not only in advertisements (see Bergreen 1980).

However, Marx realised that this absolute extension of the working day cannot go on indefinitely. Working-class resistance through unions and collective bargaining limited the length of the working day. In such a situation, capital has to increase the *intensity* of labour. The concept of relative surplus value initially meant the cheapening of consumer goods that reproduce labour power so that the amount of necessary time would be decreased. In the era of monopoly capitalism two other major factors contribute to the extraction of *relative* surplus value—the reorganisation of the workplace and introduction of technologically efficient instruments of production (see Braverman 1974). As Marx (1976, p. 645) writes: 'The production of absolute surplus value turns exclusively upon the length of the working day: the production of relative surplus value revolutionises out and out the technical processes of labour and the composition of society.' I have already referred to the stress on demographics (reorganisation of the working population), the redivision of time (reorganisation of the work process) and time-compression (technological innovation). Thus watching and labour display many historical similarities in the movement between absolute and relative surplus value.

In a very important text, published in English for the first time in 1976, Marx talks about the transition from absolute to relative surplus value in a more concrete and detailed manner. In 'Results of the Immediate Process of Production' (Marx 1976, pp. 943–1085) a distinction is made between the *formal* and the *real* subsumption of labour. Marx here is writing about the expansion of capitalism and the relations that prevail between capitalism and other modes of production. Thus, as capitalist relations of production expand, they come into contact with other types of relations of production—for example, feudal relations in agriculture. The two different sets of relations cannot ignore each other for they have become interdependent. However, in the first instance capitalism does not effect a change in these other relations. It merely 'tacks on' these relations to its own operations. Marx writes that 'capital subsumes the labour process as it finds it, that is to say, it takes over an *existing labour process*, developed by different and more archaic modes of production'. Thus while capital subsumes it, it does not establish specifically capitalist relations of production in that sphere. It does not need to. The old relations are used in ways that benefit capital without being organised under its relations of production. Marx argues that the formal subsumption of labour is based upon increasing the length of the working day: that is, on absolute surplus value.

In broadcasting, the formal subsumption of watching activity is linked to the period when advertisers had direct control of programming (when they wrote and produced it). Broadcasting did not develop initially as an advertising medium. Its first purpose was to aid in the selling of radio sets. It was only later that time on the airwaves began to be sold by AT&T to bring in additional revenue. Even when advertising became prominent in the late 1920s and 1930s networks did little more than lease facilities and sell airtime to advertisers who had total control of broadcasting. In this way we can see how capital (advertisers) took over 'more archaic' modes of watching for their own ends. Advertisers were interested primarily in the activities of the audience as they related to the consumption of their products. Watching here was tacked on to specifically capitalist relations of production without being organised in the same manner.

However, Marx writes, the two different relations of production cannot exist side by side indefinitely. Indeed capitalism constantly works to make the other mode of production 'wither away' and to introduce capitalist relations of production into that previously independent (from capitalist relations) domain. This is labelled the *real* subsumption of labour. At this stage (which corresponds with the extraction of relative surplus value) 'the entire real form of production is altered and a *specifically capitalist form of production* comes into being (at the technological level too)' (Marx 1976, p. 1024). The old 'archaic' forms of production disappear to be replaced with capitalist relations of production. The old realm is no longer directly subordinate to other domains but itself becomes a proper capitalist enterprise. It is interested primarily in its own productivity rather than being a peripheral (yet vital) activity to something else.

In broadcasting the shift from the formal to the real subsumption of watching took place in the late 1950s. It was then that the networks started to move against advertisers' total control of programming by introducing the concept of 'magazine programming', whereby the network would control the programming and sell spots within it to different advertisers. It was proving inefficient (for the network) to have the audience watch exclusively for one advertiser for thirty to sixty minutes. The media could generate more revenue for themselves if they could *reorganise* the time of watching by rationalising their programme schedule. The move to spot-selling was an attempt to increase the ratio of necessary to surplus watching time. More value could be generated by networks producing programming that would attract audiences that could be sold to several advertisers than by selling watching time to one advertiser. There was a limit to how much one advertiser could pay for a thirty- or sixty-minute programme. If the networks could control the programming and the advertising time within it, then they could generate more revenue (by selling spots) from multiple advertisers, all of whom individually paid less. Initially advertisers resisted this rationalisation and the subsumption of their individual interests under the general interests of media capital. In the end, however, rising programme costs, legal objections to advertisers' control, and old-fashioned scandals drove the networks to move towards full control of their schedules (see Barnouw 1978). This resulted in the double reorganisation of the watching population and the watching process under specifically capitalist relations of production.

There is, in addition to these, another dimension along which watching-labour shares characteristics with labour in the economy in general—both are viewed as *unpleasant* by the people who have to perform either activity. The history of working-class resistance to the process of wage labour and various sociological studies illustrate that for many people in modern society, work is not an enjoyable activity. People, on the whole, work not because they like their jobs but because they have to, to get what they really need—wages to spend in consumption. Work has become a means to an end rather than an end in itself. Labour is a form of *alienated* activity. Similarly, consider the attitudes of the watching audience to the time of advertising. Despite the fact that huge amounts of money (much more than on programming) are spent on producing attractive commercials, people do all they can to avoid them. They leave the room, they talk with other people, or they simply switch channels in the hope that they can find

another programme to watch, rather than more advertisements. (Switching between the major networks is rather
unproductive on this score as they all tend to have their
commercial breaks at the same time.) Indeed a 1984 report by
the J. Walter Thompson advertising company estimated that
by 1989 only 55 to 60 per cent of television audiences will
remain tuned in during the commercial break. Commercial
viewing levels are decreasing. The remote channel changer
is a major factor in this 'zapping' of commercials. In addition
to this, American data indicate that almost 30 per cent of
viewers simply leave the room or get into alternative
technologies during the commercial breaks (Fiber 1984). The
spread of video cassette recorders (VCRs) is also a major
threat to the viewing levels of commercials. When programmes are recorded to be watched at a later time, one can
simply skip over the commercials by fast-forwarding through
them. The owners of the means of communication are faced
here with a curious problem—the audience could watch
programmes (get paid) without doing the work (watching)
that produces value and surplus-value. (I will return to the
reactions of advertisers to this problem later.)

All these findings have not been lost on the advertising or
the television industry and there has been an increasing
recognition in recent years that the traditional concept of a
'ratings point' may no longer be valid. Ratings measure
programme watching rather than commercial watching. Indeed it seems that there is much disparity between the two
and advertisers are starting to voice their discontent at having
to pay for viewers who may not be watching their advertisements at all. This has led the ratings companies to experiment
with new measures of the audience. The most intriguing
development has been the experiment with 'people meters'.
This involves a device on the TV that has a separate button
for each individual member of the household that is
participating in the measuring of watching. Individuals
would 'punch in' when they start watching and 'punch out'
when they cease watching. In this way advertisers and
broadcasters will have a more precise measure of the level of
commercial viewing. It seems there could be no clearer
indication of the similarities between watching and labour.
Just as workers in a factory punch in and punch out, so

viewers too will be evaluated along similar lines. It is constructive to note that no one would be worried if people were 'zapping' the *programmes* and watching advertisements in greater numbers. The industry would be undisturbed. But when the new technologies of cable and VCRs threaten the viewing patterns of commercial time then the very foundations of the broadcasting industry begin to shake in anticipation of the consequences.

## 'Blurring': broadcasting, narrowcasting and the two media revolutions

I argued before that a stress on demographics ('narrowcasting') was one of the strategies for the extraction of *relative* surplus-value. However, in a very major way, the move to narrowcasting simultaneously extends the total amount of time that the audience watches (and thus watches advertising time). Since the continued spread of cable in the 1970s and the 1980s there has been a very dramatic shift in viewing patterns in the United States. In 1975–6 the three major networks commanded between them 89 per cent of the watching audience during prime-time. By 1985 that figure was down to 73 per cent. This does not mean that people are watching less television. Indeed by 1984 the average family viewed an all-time high of almost fifty hours a week. People thus are watching more TV and less of the networks. The extra viewing has been diverted largely into offerings available on cable television. Figures published in 1985 show that those homes with access only to regular over-the-air broadcast television watched only 42 hours and 22 minutes a week while those with cable and subscription services watched almost 58 hours a week. Clearly cable television (based upon narrowcasting to specific audiences) increases the total amount of time that people watch television. While some of this extra watching goes to Pay-TV services (without advertising) much of it is still bound up with commercially sponsored programmes. Narrowcasting then also increases absolute surplus-value.

Up to the present, for analytic purposes, I have made a rather strict distinction between programming and advertising. In the historical development of the commercial media system, however, the boundaries between the two were very often 'blurred'. This is because the function of programming is much more than merely capturing the watching activity of a specific demographic group of the market. Programming also has to provide the right *environment* for the advertising that will be inserted within it. Advertisers seek compatible programming vehicles that stress the lifestyles of consumption. Thus in the 1950s the very popular and critically acclaimed 'anthology series' were dropped by the networks because they focused on working-class settings and complex psychological states. Neither of these things was conducive to the advertisers' needs of glamourous consumption lifestyles and the instant and simple 'fixes' offered by their commodities to the problems of modern living. The anthology series were replaced by programmes much more suited to the selling needs of advertisers. Further, actors and stars moved easily between programmes and commercials. At a more explicit level advertisers sought to have their products placed *within* the programme itself. In all these ways we can see a 'blurring' between the message content of the commercials and the message content of the programming.

Many writers (for example, Barnouw 1978) have commented on this phenomenon. However, they have not noticed how this 'blurring' is enormously *intensified* by the move to narrowcasting. In each portion of the fractionated audience, from the point of view of the message content, the difference between the programme content and the advertisement content constantly diminishes. Because of the specialised nature of the audience, the point of reference upon which both advertisements and programmes draw is very similar. Both draw upon the specific audience to construct their message 'code' (see Chapter 4). The drawback of the mass audience for broadcasting is usually thought to be that the programme may attract a mass audience without necessarily attracting a mass *market* for certain commodities. Hence the importance of demographics for advertisers. But the problem has not usually been perceived within the sphere of watching itself. Broadcasting produces only a loose compatibility between programmes and commercials. Broadcasting *limits* blurring while narrowcasting overcomes these limits.

What does 'blurring' mean in terms of message content? The phenomenon has two aspects: (a) part of the programme is really an advertisement: and (b) part of the advertisement is really a programme. Although there may appear to be a formal *symmetry* at work, within the socio-material conditions of the media (a) dominates (b). It is the commercial form that is the dynamic element in the process. If part of the programme is really an advertisement, then part of the programme time is not really consumption time: rather it is labour time, and the length of the working day has been extended. The programme as the extension of the advertisement shows us the increase in the magnitude of labour time of watching. It contributes to *absolute* surplus-value. Within narrowcasting, the progressive fractionation of the audience *intensifies* both absolute and relative surplus-value. From such a viewpoint there appear to be two 'media revolutions': the first (broadcasting) converts non-work leisure time into the sphere of watching time (both consumption watching time and labour watching time); and the second (narrowcasting) converts consumption watching time (programming) into labour watching time (advertisements). Because there is a limit to the time of advertising, media have to gain more surplus from the existing time. 'Blurring' accomplishes this by converting programme into advertisement; by converting consumption watching time into labour watching time. While the process is observable within broadcasting it is hugely intensified by narrowcasting (see next section on MTV).

Televised sports are one such example of blurring. Values of masculinity and fraternity are present in both advertisements and programme, and sports personalities flit between the two. The sponsorship of televised sporting events (such as the Volvo Grand Prix of Tennis or the AT & T Championships) are also attempts to convert programme into advertisement. Within the field of broadcasting itself segmented programming leads to blurring. For instance, in 1983 the consumer group ACT (Action for Children's Television) petitioned the Federal Communications Commission to recognise certain Saturday morning children's programmes (that used toys that had successfully sold in the stores as their primary characters) for what they really were—thirty-minute commercials rather than programmes.

One of the best examples of the blurring under consideration is that of the 'commercial on the commercial'. 'The Commercial Show' is a new programme on cable TV in Manhattan. It consists of old commercials; advertisers can buy time to put new commercials between the old ones' (*Wall Street Journal*, 4 February 1982). The blurring here is so complete that it shows dramatically the *difference* between consumption time and labour time. There is no better example of the fact that the same kind of message has two fundamentally different functions. One could hardly find a better reason to abandon a message-based definition of the messages themselves.

## Rock video, MTV and the 'commercialisation' of culture

The most important development in the realm of popular culture in the 1980s has undoubtedly been the emergence of the phenomenon termed 'rock video' or 'videomusic'. Rock videos are song-length clips of video that use a track from a musical album as soundtrack. Their prime function is to act as a commercial for the album, to help boost the sales of records. The most direct indication of their status is the fact that the money for the production of videos comes from the advertising budget of record companies. Indeed, the rock video has taken over in large part from the heavy costs incurred by record companies of financing a tour by a new band in conjunction with the release of an album. Like commercials in general, there are huge sums expended on these videos. It is not unusual today for videos of the more popular bands to cost a quarter of a million dollars and more. Indeed Michael Jackson's 'Thriller' video (directed by film director John Landis) cost over one million dollars to produce. The video, then, is primarily a *marketing* tool used in the sale of record albums. John Kalodner of Geffen Records says: 'Rock video is not the art form. Rock video markets the art form.' Similarly Simon Fields, the head of a major video production company notes: 'We have to remember that we are making a sales tool. These are little commercials. It is our job to make an artist look good.'

There are two principal places where these promotional pieces are seen: on broadcast television where the networks have their own video shows (such as 'Friday Night Videos'), and, more importantly, on cable television. For the latter, one cable network, Music Television (MTV) has dramatically changed the nature of the popular music industry in the United States. Formed in 1981, MTV is run much like a radio station. In its early years MTV got videos free from the record companies who hoped that exposure would increase record sales. Recently, however, MTV has started to negotiate with the major record labels for exclusive rights to the videos of some bands, for which it pays a considerable fee. Its revenue is derived from charging cable operators a fee for each subscriber to the service and, of course, by selling advertising time to the manufacturers of non-musical commodities. Although MTV lost money for the first few years of its existence, by 1984 it was being seen in 2,900 cable markets and had 24.2 million subscribers. For the first nine months of 1984 it had profits of $7.3 million on revenues of $46.9 million. Beyond its profitability, however, the importance of MTV for the analysis of popular culture rests in the unique position it holds now in the marketing of popular music. In a very short time MTV has become the vital factor in the marketing of rock groups.

The emergence of MTV is not a fluke of the marketplace —indeed, MTV was the most researched station ever to be formed. The basic premise of its foundation was that an important segment of the market, music enthusiasts aged between 14 and 34, were proving very difficult for advertisers to reach. As Ron Katz, director of media concepts for the J. Walter Thompson advertising agency noted: 'You can't put commercials on the records they buy, and they don't watch much regular TV' (*USA Today*, 27 December 1984). MTV's goal would be to capture this elusive market for advertisers. To this end there was wide and extensive research conducted at all levels of the market. Six hundred 14–34-year-olds were interviewed to establish if there would be interest in a channel that showed nothing but rock video. An astonishing 85 per cent responded positively. Research was also conducted on which artists should be shown and on the lifestyles and attitudes of the potential MTV audience so that the choice of settings, clothes and 'veejay' personalities could reflect this. On the business side, surveys of advertising agencies were conducted to see if they wanted to reach this audience and record companies were contacted to establish if they would supply MTV with videos. MTV's selling point to the record companies was simple—they were offering them free publicity for their commodities. As Bob Pittman, chief operating officer of MTV remarks: 'If you look at our advertising rate card, we're giving them a million dollars worth of exposure for a hit song.' Indeed it was very easy to show record companies how MTV increased record sales. Six weeks after MTV started, sales of certain artists who were being strongly featured started to rise in places that had MTV available on cable. Steven Levy (1983, p. 35) writes:

Like any good television commercial, the videos had their effect—MTV viewers went out and bought the records. You could almost make a tactical map of the country, darken the MTV areas and see the sales of certain records increasing in those areas.

The bands to benefit most from this new exposure were new English bands that were not getting airplay on the radio and who had sophisticated videos already available. (The rock video field was more developed in England than in the USA in the early 1980s.) Groups such as Duran Duran owe their enormous success to MTV. For instance, their album *Rio* was noted to be selling extremely well in Dallas, but it was selling well in only half of the record stores, not all of them uniformly. The areas where it was selling well coincided remarkably with areas of the city that were wired for cable and MTV. That MTV is now a vital factor in the success of an album was reinforced by an A. C. Nielsen poll that showed that MTV viewers averaged 9 album purchases a year and that 63 per cent of these viewers said that MTV influenced their purchasing decisions. A hit video now is an indispensable part of the process of producing a hit record. The music is no longer enough. Record albums owe their success or their failure to the production (or non-production) of the commercial video.

This, however, has deep implications for the type of music that people will be exposed to in this new media environment for, like any advertising-based service, MTV's programming will have to 'reflect' the desires of its demographic target audience. In this particular case, the targeted audience is largely *white suburban teenagers*. As Steven Levy (1983, p. 35) writes, MTV's purpose is

not to provide the best, most challenging music possible, but to ensnare the passions of Americans who fit certain demographic or, as Pittman puts it, 'psychographic' requirements—young people who have the money and the inclination to buy things like records, candy bars, videogames, beer and pimple cream.

Early in its history MTV was involved in a heated controversy over the failure to play the music of *black* bands and artists. The basic decisions were not based on musical considerations but on a 'fear of alienating the white kids in the suburbs, who according to research, didn't like black people or their music' (Levy 1983, p. 36). The huge success of Michael Jackson with both black and white audiences has temporarily alleviated this problematic area for MTV, although even now the best and most challenging black music is not featured. Just as in network television, it is the demographics (and psycho-graphics) that determine the 'programme' content. Black audiences (who tend to be largely poor with little money to spend on the kind of things that MTV advertisers want to sell) in this case are simply undesirable, as is their music.

On MTV the 'blurring' of the content between programmes and advertising is complete on both the objective and subjective levels. On the *objective* level we can see that, viewed from an economic perspective, on MTV everything is a commercial. Videos are promotional pieces for record albums while the commercials that appear between these are promotions for other commodities. Further indication that the videos are nothing more than advertisements is provided by the fact that when a particular video does not make it on to MTV's playlist, the record company can pay MTV to play it just like any other commercial. Thus at one level MTV is based upon the extraction of *absolute* surplus-value in that the entire twenty-four hours of the viewing day is commercial time. However, because MTV also sells the time of a particular segment of the audience (and not a heterogeneous mass) it also based upon the extraction of *relative* surplus-value.

This 'blurring' is also clearly observable at the *subjective* level. In the actual viewing of the messages transmitted by MTV it is sometimes impossible to distinguish between programming and non-programming, between video and advertisements. Style, pacing, visual techniques, fantasies and desires are all interchangeable in the MTV messages. Lionel Ritchie switches from a Pepsi rock video to one of his own that mimics the style of the commercial (or is it vice versa?). Similarly directors of commercials (such as Bob Giraldi and George Lois) become directors of videos, fusing the two together with their distinctive styles. Videos (like commercials and unlike other programmes) employ such things as storyboards to sketch the action prior to shooting. While on network television it is relatively easy to distinguish between programme and advertisement, narrowcasting such as MTV dramatically intensifies the 'blurring'. Indeed, advertisers are trying to place commodities *in* rock videos. Brian Harrod, Vice President of McCann Erickson in Toronto says: 'The rock video thing is very exciting. We start to advertise subtly (like public TV now). It is a tough audience to get hold of. They don't read too much, it's part of the TV generation. We've got to get ourselves into the rock video or we won't have a way to talk to them.'

MTV's most stunning achievement has been in domesticating the relatively media-primitive field of rock and in coaxing it into the ultracommercial video arena, where products lose identity as anything but products, where it is impossible to distinguish between entertainment and sales pitch.

MTV is perfect for a generation never weaned from television, because its videos contain few lines between fantasy and reality. Sexual fantasies blend with a toothless gossip about a rock community that does not exist, having dissipated maybe a decade ago. It doesn't matter. There are no dissenting opinions or alternative views telecast on MTV. Profit-making television creates an unreal environment to get the people into what is called a 'consumer mode': MTV as its executives boast is pure environment. It is a way of thought, a way of life. It is the ultimate junk-culture triumph. It is a sophisticated attempt to touch the post-Woodstock population's lurking G spot, which is unattainable to those advertisers sponsoring *We Got it Made* . . . After watching hours and days of MTV, it's tough to avoid the conclusion that rock and roll has been replaced by commercials (Levy 1983, p. 33).

Given this search for environment and the stress of demographics and psychographics, it should not be surprising that more and more advertisers are starting to produce commercials specifically for MTV.

There are four important effects that emerge from MTV's valorisation of audience time. First, signing and touring. The effect of the central place that rock videos now hold in the marketing of artists goes beyond whether a particular record will be successful. It also extends to who record companies will sign to contracts in the first place. Companies check out the 'video potential' of artists before committing to contracts, and artists, too, recognising the importance of video, ask for commitments about video promotion. In such a situation record companies are more likely to finance a group if they have the potential for successful exposure on MTV. Cindy Lauper was signed to CBS partly because of her video performance. Increasingly, new bands are going to have to come up with not only a demonstration record or tape but a demonstration video. As Keith Richard of The Rolling Stones says: 'If new bands have to worry about the cost of making a record and also about making a video, how is that going to weigh out?' In addition, concert promoters negotiate with bands on the basis of their MTV performance.

Second, composition. Given the central importance of video in the contemporary music scene, it should not be too surprising to hear that many writers of popular music are beginning to write with the video specifically in mind. In 1983 Rickie Lee Jones reported that she was writing the songs and the video simultaneously while Olivia Newton-John actually hired a video writer to develop a script that songwriters would later fill in with music. Billy Joel says: 'I've written songs sometimes just thinking about a visual.' Former Doobie Brother's member Patrick Simmons, when asked if he will write specifically with video in mind, replied: 'Definitely, I think that's just the natural progression for music to take at this time. It's really exciting. I want my MTV.' The point here is that the commercial for the music is actually affecting the music itself. As David Marshall (1984) notes:

With the move into the realm of the dominant visual image for success, the artist effectively abdicates much of his control of his message . . . If that abdication is true, then the introduction of video can be seen as the loss of *potential* free expression and opposition in favour of corporate commodification.

Third, consumption. Similarly, the way audiences consume the cultural products of the popular music industry is affected by the video technology of its marketing. For instance, we have a different experience of a song when we have only listened to it. We can give a personal interpretation to the song, link it up to particular times in our lives, specific places, ideas and moods. The conceptual circle of consumption is in some way left *open*. Listening to a song after we have viewed the visual images completely changes the nature of our consumption. The visual interpretation of the song tends to fix the *meaning* that it comes to have for the audience. 'MTV is a context that seems to abolish context, removing the freedom of the record listener to edit his or her experience, or the radio listener to imagine the music as playing some indirect part of his life' (Gehr 1983). Steven Levy (1983) writes: 'In the pre-MTV world we used to construct our own fantasies to music, provide our own images rich in personal meaning. Now mass images are provided for us.' David Byrne of the group Talking Heads, one of the few musicians who directs his own videos, says of this link between visuals and music: 'I tend to like to have relatively few visual links to the lyrics of the song. I feel that you pigeon-hole the song that way, that you detract from the lyrics by interpreting them.' Most bands, however, have not been this thoughtful about the style and content of their videos. Largely they have abdicated responsibility for this to video specialists. This may be the reason why, in many videos, the visuals seem not to be connected with the subject of the song. It is almost as if video directors are choosing images that are powerful for the audience but are divorced from the musical content. This should not be too surprising given that video directors know that they are not involved in making art, but in marketing the art form.

The primary criterion for choosing these images is not artistic validity or even what the songwriter had in mind, but what might sell the song. MTV and the advertisers who fund the service hope that the effect of these rock images will be to put us into the mood to buy anything that comes to our attention, from chewing gum to MTV satin jackets, yours for only a modest $49.95. MTV has turned rock & roll songs into advertising jingles (Levy 1983, p. 78).

Working within the conventions of the advertising industry, video writers, producers and directors have access to a limited pool of images that are known to work in the selling of commodities. 'It sometimes appears on MTV that each group is handed a menu of images and is then told to pick five to be used in their video. The list includes beautiful Caucasian women, cats, high-heeled shoes, hotel rooms, fog, leather, snow, detectives, and beautiful Oriental women—the comic-book fantasies of adolescent males and James Bond fans' (Gehr 1983, p. 40).

Fourth, videos and the consumer ethic. Although videos are primarily commercials for records, they are located within a curious context in the structure of narrowcasting for they are at the same time, of course, the programme material of MTV. Their function at one level is to reorganise the watching population along demographic and psychographic dimensions so that audience time can be sold to advertisers, and at another level it is to provide a suitable environment for the commercials of those advertisers. In this way MTV videos are the same as network programmes—they should reflect the ethics of consumption. Thus not any video by a popular rock band will make it onto MTV—Duran Duran, The Rolling Stones, and The Cars have all had their videos refused on the grounds of 'indecency'. Arlene Zeichner (1983, p. 39) writes:

The sex on MTV probably never will get really hot: Pittman runs a tightly censored ship. According to rock critic John Pareles,

Pittman rejected The Tubes 'White Punks on Dope' because it pictured scantily-clad women and a pro-drug message...The fevered spirit of teen rebellion against family, school, and state, which energised rock music from Buddy Holly to The Clash, is sorely lacking at MTV.

MTV sells advertisers not only audiences but pure environment, a form that is 'nonlinear, using mood and emotion to create an atmosphere' (Pittman, cited in Levy 1983). In its early history, MTV frightened off some mainstream advertisers because of its programming environment, but since then the advertising industry has learnt that, with compatible commercials, MTV offers a unique consumption environment. As it attracts more mainstream advertisers MTV videos will become even more middle-of-the-road while selling the illusion of 'sex and drugs and rock & roll' to the huge consumer teenage suburban market.

| ADVERTISERS FOR CANDY, BEER, ETC. RECORD companies | → | VIDEOS FOR MTV | → | SIGNING AND TOURS COMPOSITION CONSUMPTION OF MUSIC SELLING AUDIENCE TIME |
|---|---|---|---|---|

MTV stands at the centre of modern popular culture. Its use-value in the realm of meaning is immensely important. Yet what drives it is the valorisation of audience time. While the audience derives meaning from rock video (use-value), the context within which this takes place is dominated and structured by the system of exchange-value within which rock video is located.

Further, the influence of MTV is not limited to the messages emanating from its own channel. MTV Networks in 1984 launched another video service called VH-1 which would be targeted at an older audience (aged 25–54). The videos here featured older artists and musical styles (country, soft rock, ballads) not available on MTV. MTV has even made itself felt on network television with shows such as 'Miami Vice' where content is totally abandoned in the search for style and young affluent audiences. It may in fact be the only show on television where certain colours (red and brown) are not allowed to be shown. As Michael Mann of NBC notes of the show, 'the secret of its success? No earthtones. We want to feel electric.' Similarly, many motion pictures (for example, *Flashdance*) today are little more than glorified rock videos. MTV has tapped the heart of teenage America with a message format that is pure commercial and is derived from the accumulation dynamic of advanced capitalism. Not content to languish on the sidelines any more, the 1980s has seen the ultimate triumph of the 'commercialisation' of culture.

## Labour and consumption in watching: communication versus attention

In the last section I examined that domain of the media system that displays the most advanced manifestations of the inherent logic of the commercial communication system. MTV, however, is not typical of the relationship between programming and advertising in broadcasting, or even in other realms of narrowcasting. Narrowcasting is certainly part of the future of the development of the communications industry, although to what extent it will dominate the situation is unclear at the present. It will be the extent of the penetration that cable is able to achieve that will provide an answer to that question. For the present, however, it is still the three major broadcast networks that dominate the structures and relations of commercial television, even though their share of the prime-time audience has declined to 73 per cent. The remainder of this book will concentrate, then, on coming to terms with the subject of network advertising and programming.

I started off this chapter by arguing that to achieve a proper understanding of the commercial media system in the United States, we have to break with a message-based analysis and to focus instead on comprehending the system of exchange-value within which media messages are located. The argument advanced thus far in this chapter has established a study of the media based upon a study of the *value form of time* and the idea that audiences perform labour for the owners of the means of communication (broadcasters and networks). This does not mean that I am not interested in the use-values of messages (their meaning) but only that an analysis of messages must be based upon a proper materialist understanding of their concrete context. It is to the messages now that I wish to turn, and to pose the question of what the system of exchange-value does to the system of use-value (meaning). The present chapter will not examine in detail the manner in which people derive meaning from messages but will focus instead on understanding why media messages (both advertisements and programming) are shaped as they presently are, for it is with these messages that the audience interacts in the construction of meaning. Just as in the realm of commodities, meaning is not arbitrary but is based upon properties that both the audience and the message bring to bear on their interaction. The initial question that we must answer in our understanding of the system of messages is what function messages perform within the system of exchange-value. An answer to this requires us to differentiate within the message system. Looked at from a purely material viewpoint, the basic distinction seems to be between advertising messages and programming messages. In terms of production costs twenty-four minutes of network programming requires approximately $300,000 (roughly $12,500 per minute). In 1984 the average thirty-second commercial shown on network television cost approximately $50,000—twenty-four minutes of commercials would add up to $2,400,000 ($100,000 per minute). Why such a disparity? What are the different functions that advertising and programming perform within the system of exchange-value?

Within cultural analysis in general, there is a widespread disillusionment with network programming and no hope in sight that it will be able to raise itself from the depths of the deep mediocrity to which it has sunk. The general explanatory feature of this has been laid at the search for large audiences and the need to appeal to some (lowest) common denominator in the watching population. While this is undoubtedly a valid observation, I wish here to focus on another dimension of the situation—this concerns the function of programming. What are network executives interested in when they are trying to decide their programme schedules? What they sell as a commodity to advertisers is of course audience time and thus the imperative for them is to get as many people as possible of the right demographic make-up to watch their show, to look at the set and to pay *attention* to what is on. The cheaper they can do this (reproduce watching power) the less necessary time the audience will have to watch and the more surplus time for the network. The creators of programmes (and the networks as the buyers of shows from independent producers) have no real interest in *communicating* a particular message to the audience, in making the audience think and react in some manner to the message. They just want to get the audience to watch so that their time can be sold to advertisers.

The reason we have shows of such poor quality then is that the networks do not have to have high-quality programming to challenge and excite the audience. There is no economic need for 'quality' programming. Simple attention-getting, as opposed to communicating interesting and thought-provoking material, is enough. The former is far easier to accomplish than the latter. Indeed there is a set network formula whose component parts are occasionally adjusted for particular programmes: sex, adventure and violence. As Erik Barnouw (1978, p. 109) comments about the latter: 'On television it has proved supremely effective as ratings builder, seizing and holding the dial-turner—as an accident or murder stops a crowd'. There is also, however, a more precise formula that is employed in the construction of various scenes within a show. Gary David Goldberg, the producer of the successful NBC show 'Family Ties', says (in a CBS documentary, 'Don't Touch That Dial', 1982):

Network has little terms for what we do as writers—to describe little hooks to use one of their terms. For instance, topspin—a great network word. There's not enough topspin. *Topspin* in network terms is something that happens to propel you into the next scene. Usually someone loses a briefcase or something really exciting, and that's topspin into the next scene. *Heat* is tension, it's argument, usually someone calling someone a fat mother or some great thing. *Pipe*—they say we've got to lay pipe here guys, we're not dealing with college people, lots of pipe. Pipe is the history of every character from the moment of their birth until the moment they stepped into that room. God forbid that anyone watching could give any closure to a character on their own. Then you have a blow, a hook, a button. For some reason in network TV no-one can leave a room without a joke. I don't know how it is in your home but in my house a lot of time people will just go out, but here you cannot, you must deliver a joke and leave the room. That's a *blow* or a *button*. We don't like the button, change the button, get a better blow. And the *hook* would be something like a man just landed, he's from another planet, that's the hook. Then the audience is going to watch it—we have an alien in our living room, the audience is hooked.

You never hear discussion any deeper than that about the writing, about character development and motivation and reality and the truth of the moment. But you'll always see a show that'll have heat, topspin, pipe, hopefully a good button and a hook and a great blow.


It is little wonder that Todd Gitlin (1983) has labelled commercial television as a form of 'recombinant culture' in which the same elements are constantly rejuggled and arranged. The language of network programme producers is the language of formula and predictability, not that of originality and creativity.

One of the reasons that programming on network television does not have to be really good and of high (or even) moderate artistic quality, is that programmes do not have to persuade viewers that they should watch television as opposed to doing something else. The networks know that people do not turn on the television set to watch particular shows: they turn it on to watch television. It is a habitual activity; regardless of what is being broadcast, the total television audience is remarkably stable. In such a situation, the networks do not have to provide quality programming to draw people to the set. They know they can do little to effect the overall size of the total television audience. The challenge, then, is only in making sure that the people who are watching watch your show and not somebody else's. The overriding aim is to draw people away from rival networks and to accomplish this as cheaply as possible so that necessary watching time will be as short as possible.

In opposition to programmes, what function are commercials supposed to perform and why does this cost eight times as much as the functions of programming? In contrast to programmes, commercials are constructed with lavish care and no expense is spared. What we see on the screen is the best possible performance and execution of the communications strategy. 'Wretched excess' is the way one producer of commercials describes the process. Michael Arlen's *Thirty Seconds* (1981) documents the enormous effort, time and expense that went into the making of a single thirty-second AT&T advertisement. Editing work, co-ordinating visuals, voice and music, have to be meticulously done to split-second timing, and the cinematography is state-of-the-art. Paul Goodman has remarked that 'the commercial is the only part of television that has fulfilled its potential', while Erik Barnouw has described commercials as an 'American art form'. There is little doubt then that commercials, rather than programming, have become the focal point of creative effort within the media system.

The basic explanatory feature of this artistic and creative concentration in one realm of the media system is that the function of the commercial is to *communicate* something rather than just to attract audience attention. Its aim is to affect behaviour after the time of viewing. Advertisements have to move us in some way, make us think or react; they have to pull at our emotions, desires and dreams; they have to engage the audience actively in some thought process that will, advertisers hope, lead to the purchase of their product in the marketplace. As one advertising creator put it: 'The function of advertising is to communicate what you want to communicate. I can get your attention by showing a nude shot of a man on TV but it might not communicate what I want to communicate.' Communication is much harder to achieve than attention-getting and thus requires that the resources be concentrated there rather than in the creation of programmes.

Further, as has already been shown in the analysis of relative surplus-value and the redivision of time, in recent years a severe time limitation has been introduced into the media system as regards advertising. Most commercials today last thirty seconds and the move is towards even greater numbers of shorter commercials. Commercials have to do their job quickly, being able to count on not much more than a quick glance from many in the audience. Advertisers want to utilise every split second of the time for which they must pay so dearly. Commercial film editor Howie Lazurus comments on the changes he has observed in the last twenty years (Arlen 1981, pp. 180–2).

When I first started editing, most commercial work was done the way you do a soap opera; in other words, all the scenes matched and balanced . . . What you definitely didn't do was jump from one scene to another. When you had a cut you made sure the music carried the cut—signalled that a cut was coming, signalled that a cut was taking place, and signalled that now a new scene was starting. Also you had lots of dialogue. In even the most sophisticated commercials, people were talking all the time. After the technique of balance, in my opinion, came a lengthy period in the 1960s when many directors were just experimenting with visual technique for its own sake . . . I think the most popular technique was shooting into the sun . . . Nowadays, the basic new technique is your vignette commercial. In my opinion it's a classic film approach—meaning that there's often no dialogue and the style emphasis is on the visual, but not on gimmicky visual. The key thing to remember about the vignette commercials is that you can get so much more information into them. In fact, *the vignettes more or less originated in response to the switch from 60 second spots to 30 second spots.* They're a wonderful way to pack in information: all those scenes and emotions—cut, cut, cut. Also they permit you a very freestyle approach—meaning that as long as you stay true to your basic vignette theme you can usually just drop one and shove in another. They're a dream to work with because the parts are sort of interchangeable.

Much of the style and content of advertisements then is structured and conditioned by how much time is available to work with. The shorter length of advertisements has led to a preponderance in the modern era of the vignette and lifestyle advertisement. Erik Barnouw (1978, p. 83) writes:

As a dramatic medium that can draw on the resources of every art, and has as its stage the privacy of the home, television has unparalleled opportunities for this psychic pressure. It has intensified as the 30 second commercial has become the dominant vehicle, favoured over the roomier 60 second form. There is scarcely time now for technical persuasion, documentation, 'reason-why' advertising. Everyone knows what the job is: instant drama, posing threat and promise'.

Closely connected to the issue of time is the problem of 'clutter'. This refers to the contemporary media situation in which, as I have noted before, there has been a huge increase in the number of different advertising messages. The concern among advertisers is the effect that this 'environmental noise' will have on the effectiveness of their message—that is, how can a particular advertisement stand out from the crowd? Will the sheer number of advertisements lead to less effective advertising because of an information overload from commercials on the part of the audience? Because of the demand for commercial time, it is in the interest of the broadcaster to have more time-spots for sale at a higher per-second cost (the per-spot price for advertisers is lower). The advertiser has to determine at what point it is more cost-effective to run thirty-second instead of fifteen-second advertisements, or vice versa. It is noteworthy that, in researching the problem of 'clutter', advertisers are interested in the reactions of the *audience* to their message, of how it is perceived and how meaning is constructed by viewers. It is audience watching activity that is the key component in resolving the problem of clutter. Advertisers, it seems, are very well aware of the nature in which the use-value of their messages is constrained by the system of exchange-value within which those messages are located. To stand out from the crowd, commercials thus are going to have to be better and more entertaining than the ones that surround them to make an impression on the audience. This might account also for why European advertising has generally been regarded as artistically superior to North American advertising. An art director explains:

The Europeans had no advertising for years. But when they did it was in the 'magazine format'—that is they would group all the commercials together. Each one would do something charming and then say the name of the product at the end. At that time the English agencies would get kids from North America to come over and teach them how to sell Tide—how to hit hard in selling. But as products reached the parity point there was the same need for charm here. While the Europeans had gone from the emotional thing into a use of the hard sell (but still with charm), so very recently things have changed. We took some lessons from them. We in North America used to be conceited and think we knew it all, but we learnt from

them. TV was the reason, because they had been doing the magazine format with all the 20 commercials altogether, so the question
was how do you get them to remember you if you are number
1094? How do you stand out and be memorable? If you adopt the
hard sell approach the consumer might say, 'oh who needs this, I'll
go get a beer'. In England and in Japan they learnt to be subtle,
entertaining, amusing. So more emotion came to this country. We
learnt that. So you get attention and interest and people remember
the product. There's a great creative drive. (SCA p. 141-2)

All of these problems will be compounded by the spread of
the video recorder and the remote channel changer (see
p. 89.) Commercials will have to be even better to make sure
that they do not get 'zapped' by the audience. 'For advertisers, the solution may be in commercials that are more entertaining and visually attractive, and so less likely to be turned
off or skipped over' (*New York Times*, 20 October 1985). In the
new media environment the commercials will not merely
have to sell but to entertain, even more so than they do now.
It should not be surprising, then, that the advertising industry
has sought to employ the 'brightest and the best' of the
society's artistic and creative talent. (See *SCA*, Chapter 7)

The constraints imposed by the system of exchange-value
in the media then impinge upon the styles and content of
commercials. Exchange-value structures one side of the
message–audience relation. In thirty seconds there is no time
for reasoned rational arguments for the superiority of a
particular brand. The time-constraints force, as it were, the
move towards lifestyle-image-based advertising. The problem of clutter and the remote channel changer force the move
to fast-paced and visually appealing commercials that focus
on people and not on products. Undoubtedly there are other
factors (such as marketing theory, psychological and
sociological thinking) that have moved advertising along in
this direction, but the system of exchange-value as presently
constituted provides the framework within which the
creators of advertising have to think about their activity.
Much agency–client interaction at the present time is based
upon the advertiser wanting to provide as much information
as possible about the product in thirty seconds and the
creative personnel in agencies trying to convince them that
the audience will not comprehend more than one point per

thirty second advertisement. If the discourse about goods is indeed carried on at a superficial level, we must look to the surrounding material context as one possible explanation, rather than merely at the intentions of the actors involved. For instance, the move to more fifteen-second spots may well alter the stress on the vignette commercial as the solution to the problem of time constraints. Some advertising practitioners believe that fifteen seconds is not long enough for image-building advertisements (soft-sell spots that use mood and hazy camera focus rather than facts) and that fifteen-second spots will have to bang out their message abruptly and quickly (much like billboards). 'Jack Smith, vice chairman and creative director at the Leo Burnett agency, says 15 second spots should communicate a single message, such as "cures headaches faster", while leaving additional claims about not upsetting stomachs to 30 second spots. "It's important not to try to do too much", he says' (*Fortune*, 23 December 1985, p. 75).

Surprisingly, not much attention has been paid as to the effect the shortened messages will have on consumers and the way the person–object relationship is conceptualised. However, many commentators have noted the negative impacts thirty-second commercials for presidential candidates can have on the quality of political debate. Charles Guggenheim argues (*New York Times*, 15 November 1985) that a political system based upon short political advertisements is

eroding the dignity of the election process...Ask any media advisor and he will tell you what he can do best given 30 seconds. Create doubt. Build fear. Exploit anxiety. Hit and run. The 30- and 60-second commercials are ready-made for the innuendo and half-truth. Because of their brevity, the audience forgives their failure to qualify, to explain, to defend.

In addition, accountability disappears from the discourse as the political messages are crafted by hidden and faceless producers. Guggenheim suggests that a mere insistence that commercials be at least two minutes long would alter the tone of the political discourse and lead back to a focus on real content rather than superficial visual imagery. If such is true for politics, might it not also be true for the discourse surrounding the person–object relationship in product advertising?

Based upon this understanding of the functions of messages we are now in a position to be able to see the basic divisions in the message system of the commercial communications industry. The reason why advertisements are so good and programmes generally so poor is that they have a different status within the communications commodity system. Programmes are messages that have to be 'sold' to consumers—they are in fact *consumer goods*. Like most consumer items found in the modern marketplace they are products of a mass production system based upon uniformity and are generally of a poor quality. Programme messages like consumer goods in general are for instant, superficial gratification and long-term disappointment that ensures a return trip to the marketplace. They are produced as cheaply as possible for a mass audience. On the other hand, we can regard commercials as *capital goods*—they are used by the owners of the means of production to try and stimulate demand for particular branded commodities. Like machines in a factory (and unlike consumer goods) they are not meant to break down after a certain period of time. Although the objects of their attempted persuasion are consumers, they are not 'sold' to consumers and consumers do not buy them (as far as we know people do not tune in television to watch commercials as a first priority). Commercials can indeed be considered as capital goods that are used in the sphere of the circulation and distribution of commodities. Like other objects used by capital, no expense is spared in producing the best possible goods for that particular function. Also like capital goods, they are tax-deductible. During programming time (consumption watching time) audiences create meaning *for themselves*. During commercial time (labour watching time) audiences create meaning *for capital*. It is little wonder that commercials whose function is to communicate and not just get attention should literally be the 'best things on television' and the only part of television to have realised the potentials of the medium.

**Alternative explanations I: ratings as commodities**

Broadcasters are the owners of audience time and advertisers are the purchasers of this commodity. However, these two actors do not relate to each other directly in negotiating the transaction—their relationship is mediated by a couple of other industries. First the advertising industry acts as a *bridge* between the two realms (see *SCA*, Chapter 6 and 7). However, the agencies themselves use the services of the *ratings industry* to help secure the best possible audience buys for their clients. The buying and selling of audience time is not based, of course, on the direct and observed behaviour of the entire watching population, but on the measured behaviour of a small sample of it that 'represents' the entire audience. In the realm of national television ratings one company dominates the industry and relations between broadcasters and advertisers—A. C. Nielsen. It is this company that provides 'the numbers' by which audience time is bought and traded.

While the ratings industry has traditionally portrayed itself as a purely objective research institution that measures the watching and listening activities of the audience (and then sells this information to interested parties), some recent commentators have stressed instead that what appear as seemingly objective data about the audience are in fact a *social* creation—the result of political and economic factors. Donald Hurwitz (1984, p. 207) suggests that our view of the audience depends largely on what the research shows us and 'this in turn depends upon who is asking and for what purpose'. The need for broadcast ratings arose because both the broadcasting industry and advertisers required some trusted objective measure of the audience that they could both use in their negotiations with each other. In such a situation it was obviously in the interests of broadcasters to have the ratings as high as possible (leading to higher advertising rates) while advertisers would benefit from low measures of audience watching. Depending on what perspective is taken, commentators on the history of the ratings industry have seen them as 'slaves' either to the broadcasting industry (Shanks 1977) or to the advertising industry (Barnouw 1978). Others such as Smythe (1977) see them as serving both equally.

Eileen Meehan (1983; 1984) believes that all these perspectives are incorrect and that 'ratings per se must no longer be treated as reports of human behaviour, but rather as products—as commodities shaped by business exigencies and corporate strategies' (Meehan 1984, p. 221). The ratings companies do not measure the real viewing audience in some neutral objective way—they produce a commodity (information about viewing) that is shaped less by scientific procedure and more by the divergent demand they satisfy and the imperative to produce and sell this commodity at a substantial profit.

The most obvious point at which economic factors impinge upon the objective measure of the audience concerns the size of the sample that A. C. Nielsen uses to generalise to the whole of the viewing public. The Nielsen sample for many years was set at 1200 households (although recent pressure from competitors has forced Nielsen to expand this to 2000 by 1990). This means that each house in the sample 'represents' approximately 70,000 homes. Thus the viewing habits of any one of these homes have a tremendous overall impact in the measures of the audience. For instance, ten homes represents a ratings point (worth millions to producers of programmes and networks). (Consequently, when the stakes are so high, the potential for corruption is enormous—see Reel 1979). The sample is so small because it fits within a reasonable allowance of statistical error and because it would cost the Nielsen company much more money to expand the number of households without any corresponding rise in the price they could charge for that information.

While the size of the sample is one problem, a much more serious concern that has been raised by a number of critics is the *representativeness* of the sample in terms of the total viewing population. For instance, not everyone chosen by Nielsen to be in the sample agrees to participate and various studies have shown that indeed the non-participants watch less television on the whole than people who agree to take part. Also co-operators tend to be younger, better educated and live in larger families. Added to this is the concern that the Nielsen sample is based upon houses and apartments, while almost 3 per cent of the population live in institutions, military barracks, dormitories, boarding houses, hotels and motels.

The most serious way in which the Nielsen sample could be distorted in its representativeness of the total watching population is along the dimension of race. Todd Gitlin (1983, p. 52) writes on this point:

Are the preferences of blacks, Hispanics, older people and the poor being systematically undercounted? Advertisers might not mind if this were the case; these people are not big buyers anyway . . . Blacks and Hispanics might be underincluded in the Nielsen household survey, for two reasons. The first is that Nielsen draws its samples from census data. If the Census Bureau still undercounts the housing units of the poor, as minority groups have charged in the past, then the Nielsen sample, too, would be, as former NBC executive Paul Klein says, 'upslanted'. The second reason is that, in most surveys, the less educated are less likely to cooperate even if asked and the less educated are still disproportionately black and Hispanic.

Additionally, once a household is in the sample it is likely to stay a part of it for some time because it simply costs Nielsen too much money to install the audimeters in different households for short periods of time. There is thus a very slow turnover of the sample, meaning that certain viewing habits become a 'permanent' feature of the watching measure.

There are many ways, then, in which what the ratings measure is different to what the total viewing population watches. This has important implications for debates about cultural policy, for the networks often point to the seemingly impressive viewing figures to legitimate their own actions. However, if the ratings are indeed skewed away from the poor and from minorities, then the ratings are not measures of watching, but statistics produced for certain ends within prescribed economic limits. From this perspective, Eileen Meehan (1984, p. 223) argues,

neither messages nor audiences are exchanged: only ratings. And those ratings are produced at a particular juncture by a single company that—like any other company in any industry at any point in time—seeks to maximize its profit and minimize its cost, to safeguard its market position and expand its sphere of independence, to manipulate discontinuities in demand and satisfy continuities.

Meehan's point is well taken. However, it does not challenge the framework that I have outlined in this chapter concerning the production and selling of the commodity of audience time. The focus on ratings adds depth and texture to understanding the relations between broadcasters and advertisers. Ultimately though, however flawed the ratings might be, they are still accepted as the negotiating language of the commercial communications industry by its chief economic actors and they measure, in whatever unscientific way, the audience time that is the focus of the buying and selling.

## Alternative explanations II: differential rent

I realise that the framework that I have outlined in this chapter is controversial and unusual as an explanation of the dynamics of commercial television. This argument has been elaborated in outline in other papers (Jhally 1984) and at various conference sessions and has drawn substantial criticism from a number of sources (Truchill 1984; Lebowitz 1984). The most fundamental objection to the theory of watching as labour is that while workers in the economy in general are *compelled* to labour for capital in order to survive, no such imperative drives the activities of the audience. The audience is free simply to stop watching and thus producing surplus-value for the media. I will deal with this objection in Chapter 6.

Surprisingly, the negative response to the watching-as-working theory has not come from commentators who might be described as outside of the critical tradition, but has instead been focused on theorists firmly within the school of Marxian social thought—the most serious objections have come from *within* the 'paradigm', from 'orthodox' Marxists. More importantly, the criticism has not been just a negative one in terms of debunking the perspective I have outlined, but has offered an alternative view of the place of the commercial media within the commodity system of advanced capitalism.

I wish in this section to outline this alternative view and to offer comments on it from the perspective of audience watching as valorisable activity. In what follows I draw on the explicit criticism offered by Mike Lebowitz (1984) and the implicit criticism present in the work of Patricia Arriaga (1983; 1984).

Lebowitz's central point of critique is that the watching-as-labour perspective is unscientific and un-Marxist in its very starting point. Marx believed that the task of science was to reduce the visible and merely apparent movement (appearance) to the actual, inner movement (essence). He approached this task by considering capital as a whole, capital in the abstract as it moved through its necessary circuits—before exploring the real forms of existence of capital as subdivided, as existing in competition. The starting point, then, has to be capital in general, capital which has commodities which contain surplus–value latently. This surplus-value is the result of the exploitation of workers within production but which can only be made real (realised) through the sale of those commodities. Every moment those commodities remain unsold is a cost to capital: a lengthy time of circulation ties up capital in the sphere of circulation and requires the expenditure of additional capital if production is to be continuous; similarly, a lengthy period of circulation reduces cash flows, reduces the turnover of capital, and thus reduces the annual surplus-value.

It is then in the interests of capital to undertake expenditures which will reduce the time of circulation and thus the total costs of circulation. Such expenditures are logical so long as their cost is less than what is saved through more rapid sales, through a reduced time of circulation. Capital will thus distribute its circulation expenditures among a variety of avenues (including media advertising) in order to secure the maximum reduction in its total circulation costs. Media costs here are credited to selling expenses. In this 'fundamentalist' account consumers enter into the calculation only as buyers of commodities. What Lebowitz has described here is the inner movements of capital, its deep essence.

However, this deeper logic is not reflected in the surface appearance of capital. Here we have differing competing media capitalists competing for the expenditures of competing industrial capitalists. The form of this competition is to attempt to demonstrate that a particular media capitalist will be able to increase the commodity sales of industrial capitalists most rapidly (permitting the greatest possible reduction in circulation time) by offering access to the most attractive audience. On the surface, nothing in essence is altered. Industrial capital seeks a means of reducing its circulation costs. Media capitalists offer access to audiences to accomplish this, thus sharing in the surplus-value of industrial capital. Consumers participate in the process by buying. However, viewed from the self-conception of the media capitalist (broadcasters) it seems as if it produces audiences for sale to advertisers. It *appears* that broadcasters sell consumers to industrial capitalists rather than seeing their activities as part of the process of selling commodities of industrial capitalists to consumers. Lebowitz (1984, p. 8) writes:

Now, as Marx noted on many occasions—in competition, every-thing is inverted. The ideas and conceptions of the actual agents of capitalist production on the surface are 'necessarily quite upside down'. These are the illusions created by competition... And it is precisely because of this necessary inversion of the underlying relations and movements that Marx insisted on the necessity to begin by considering capital-as-a-whole abstractly rather than relying upon the way things appear to the real actors. That is what Marx meant by science. That is why science was necessary. In the paradigm in question, however, the starting point *is* the self-conception of the media capitalists. The starting point—buttressed by quoted evidence of these self-conceptions—is the inverted concept of the sale of audiences and audience time to industrial capitalists.

In short, the starting point reveals a complete rejection of Marx's methodological premise. And, however much Marxian verbiage may *subsequently* enter into the discussion—value, surplus-value, valorisation, absolute and relative surplus-value, surplus watching time, etc.—it cannot alter the fact that what is produced is an entirely un-Marxian argument with un-Marxian conclusions that follow from the initial premise. It is not accidental that this premise leads us to the conclusion that audiences work, are exploited in this work and are a source of surplus-value.

According to Lebowitz, then, I (with Livant) have mystified the source of media profit through a rampant idealist expansion of the category of labour. Indeed, there is no mystery to explain. All value is produced in the productive industrial sphere of the capitalist economy. The media have merely become essential to the realisation of this value; they mediate selling of the products produced elsewhere. The media, in fact, receive a portion of industrial surplus-value as *rent*. Marx has thoroughly analysed the division of the surplus-value into profit, interest and rent. The activity of audiences in their activity of *watching*, the generic characteristic of audiences, generates no value. There is therefore nothing to explain.

Lebowitz in his critique only hints at the concept of rent as an alternative to the valorisation of time and does not develop it in any concrete way. However, Patricia Arriaga (1983) has gone some way to expand this notion. Her starting point is Marx's theory of rural rent: specifically the theory of *differential rent*. Rent is what the owners of land can charge for the right to use that land. It is paid by capitalists to landlords, or is simply part of the fixed costs of operation. Marx was concerned with how different lots of land commanded a different rent. He develops two concepts to explain this: Differential Rent I (DF-I), which is based upon different land having different levels of fertility; and Differential Rent II (DF-II), which is built upon the first but is based upon differential applications of capital. The combination of these factors produces Differential Rent. Based upon this understanding, Arriaga (1983, pp. 43–4) writes:

The Marxian theory of differential rent is not limited to capitalist agriculture but can be applied whenever a greater productivity of capital is related to a natural or external condition not reproducible by capital . . . I therefore propose that the broadcasting media can be analyzed within a rent framework . . . the determining factor in the case of the broadcasting media is the location of the station in terms of the concentration of consumers in the area in which a station operates. What is more, given the advertising orientation of the media, the importance of the number of consumers reached lies in the amount of consumer income they represent. Locational advantages are as important to certain branches of industry as they are to agriculture and they are usually outside the control of individuals. And it is because of differences of location, that equal investments in broadcasting stations yield different outputs, that is, different sizes of audiences reached by a given broadcaster . . . But these differences in productivity are not related to reproducible factors but to a specific external condition, i.e., a socio-economic and demographic condition which characterizes each market in which stations operate and which is not reproducible by capital.

Arriaga then goes on to explain pricing mechanisms for rent of the audience based upon the 'natural fertility' of certain markets.

In the comments that follow, I do not wish systematically to construct an argument against Lebowitz and Arriaga, but more generally to use their critique positively, so to speak, to bring out some of the features of my own approach. There are two basic points I wish to make. First, Arriaga's position seems to be built really upon DF-I—the natural 'fertility' of the audience in any broadcasting market. Thus equal investments of capital (in the means of communication and in programming) will yield differential productivity in markets of different sizes. A station in a larger market will be able to generate more advertising revenue than a station in a smaller market. More 'fertile' conditions are not reproducible by the capital of the station in the smaller market. However, in earlier sections of this chapter, I have argued that broadcasters in fact can do a great deal to affect the productivity of the time they control by reorganising the watching population and/or the watching process in terms of the division of time. Indeed, it seems to me that Arriaga and Lebowitz's critiques are rooted in what Marx calls the 'formal subsumption of human labour' rather than the 'real subsumption'. They are stuck, in fact, in older agricultural modes of thinking about capital and its effects on social organisation. Also, with the new national cable networks (such as MTV, ESPN, and so on) capital *is* able to reproduce the productivity and fertility of old broadcast markets.

The second point builds upon the first because it seems that the critiques are based upon a particular conception of rent— that of *rural* rent. The classical theories of rent are based on the use of *land* in production, and it was the *natural qualities* of the land that explained differential returns to the owners of that land. More recently, critical geographers such as David

Harvey (1982) have begun to rethink the whole idea of rent and productivity in terms of urbanisation and the city. Bill Livant (1985) comments on the relationship between rural and urban land:

The classical theories of rent, drawn from rural production, are useless in explaining returns to the owners of *urban* land. And the reason is simple. In the process of social production, urban *land* becomes *urban space*. In this transformation of land into space, *all the natural qualities of the land*, so central to the determination of rural rent, *drop out*. The rent to the owners of urban land is determined entirely by the differential valorisability of human activities, of human labours which 'occur' on that land. It is human activity alone which transforms this land into 'space' itself. Under capitalism, therefore, urban 'land' is the spatial form of valorisable human labour . . . Geographers have always dealt with 'natural qualities' of land, in themselves and as they enter human affairs. It is the *indifference* of the city to these natural qualities, which sets the terms of the modern problem of rent, and indeed of the modern form of all human labour in space, *human labour as spatial*. To clarify the nature of urban rent is therefore to *constitute the meaning of 'urban space' itself*.

In urban contexts, it is *location* rather than *fertility* which becomes vital in confronting the problem of rent. Location is a relative concept and hugely dependent upon its relationship with valorisable human activity. In the theory of 'broadcasting rent', however, human activity (watching) as a power simply disappears. Instead we have the audience as a raw material, being worked upon and processed by the agents of capital (both capitalists and workers in the broadcasting industries).

## Conclusion

The main thrust of this chapter has been the contention that watching activity through the commercial media system is subject to the same process of valorisation as labour time in the economy in general. This is not to suggest that they can be identified as exactly the same type of activity for clearly they produce different types of commodities. Factory labour produces a *material* object whereas watching activity does not. In earlier papers (Jhally 1982; 1984) I suggested that there was an objective, although intangible, commodity being produced and exchanged. But I was uncomfortable with this, for it seemed that I was attempting to force-fit categories from one sphere (factory labour) into another (watching). I can now see that my error consisted in using industrial labour as the model when in fact I was dealing with a different phenomenon.

The modern evolution of the mass media under capitalism is governed by the appropriation of surplus human *objective* activity. The *subjectivity* of watching achieves objectivity under the appropriate development of material conditions. The development of this appropriation is a *higher* stage in the development of the value-form of capital. Its logic reproduces the *logic* described by Marx for the earlier form, but its concrete form is in fact a new stage: the value-form of human activity itself. The empirical reflection of this is that the process of consciousness becomes valorised. There is thus a partial truth in the label which writers such as Smythe affix to the modern mass media—'consciousness industry' —except that they have so far conceptualised it 'upside-down'. It is not characterised primarily by what it puts into you (messages), but by what it *takes out* (value).

We can now come back to the starting point of this chapter—the traditional conception of messages and their use-value (meanings). But now we can approach the study of advertising messages from a proper materialist perspective: we can see how *the constitution of meaning takes place under conditions of the valorisation of time*. What we have here, in the realm of meaning (just as in the realm of the economy) is the subjugation of use-value by exchange-value. Any attempt at understanding the content of commercials must start with a recognition of the conditions within which this content is created and within which the constitution of meaning (for capital) takes place. The following chapter picks up the implications of this starting point for an understanding of television commercials.

# 4 The codes of the audience

In the previous two chapters I have examined the broader frameworks within which commercials are located. This involved an examination of the dynamics of the economy in general through a study of the Marxian concept of the fetishism of commodities. The use of fetishism in the anthropological and psychoanalytic traditions in addition proved useful as a way to fill out the concept as regards the relationship between people and things. Chapter 3 involved a very detailed analysis of the specific political economy of the commercial media. This examined the way that during the time of advertising on television, not only is meaning being generated in the relation between people and commercial messages, but that this is framed by the valorisation of that watching activity (the relationship between use-value and exchange-value of audience time). It is from an understanding of these two broad frameworks that we can now attempt a proper understanding of commercial messages themselves.

I am not suggesting here that this is all we need to understand commercial messages. In *SCA* we examined many other elements that came to structure the form and content of advertisements: these included broad movements of the capitalist economy itself that destroyed traditional modes of living; the reactions of the advertising industry to the opportunities opened by the development of new media forms through the twentieth century; the changing assumptions within the advertising industry itself as to what would be effective appeal strategies; and the broad changes underway in popular culture that the agencies had to mediate and internalise within the industry. In this work, however, I am concerned with exploring what *SCA* did not.

In this chapter I will start to lay out a more concrete and more specific conceptual framework for an understanding of commercial messages that emerges from the issues examined in the last chapter. At the end of this chapter I will develop some hypotheses concerning advertising's form and content which Chapter 5 will seek to test through an empirical project.

## The move to specification: market segmentation

Although the last chapter stressed the need to focus on the specificity of commercial mass media, this does not imply that communications systems are in any way *autonomous* institutions, divorced from wider material and social processes. Indeed, Smythe's (1980) emphasis on the manner in which viewers participate in the realisation of surplus-value of commodities in general is absolutely vital for understanding the dynamics behind the internal movements of the broadcasting industry. Without the production of commodities in general there would be no opportunity for audiences to work for anybody, either advertisers or media. Without the need to market goods, there would be no buyers for audience time and thus no reason for its creation as a commodity. (See especially the section on differential rent in Chapter 3.)

The move to the extraction of relative surplus-value (through narrowcasting, fragmentation and specification) is based upon movements taking place within the broader economy and especially the changing strategies of manufacturers. The most important of these strategies is what has been termed *market segmentation,* which Wendell Smith (1972) defines as consisting of 'viewing a heterogeneous market (one characterised by divergent demand) as a number of smaller homogeneous markets in response to differing product preferences among important market segments'. Instead of trying to differentiate a brand from its competitors for the entire market, segmentation concentrates on trying to reach a specific market within the mass market. It is recognised within business as one of the most important and influential marketing concepts of the twentieth century (Frank 1972). Daniel Pope (1982, p. 265) writes:

In fact, the advent and ascendancy of market segmentation as a principle of national advertisers may well be the most far reaching development in national advertising in recent decades. In the last generation it has affected the structure and conduct of the advertising agency business, the standards and principles of advertising professionals and the form and content of advertisements themselves.

The basis of the new market segmentation is the development in the last twenty-five years of statistical data capable of measuring and segmenting the audience along demographic and psychological characteristics. This segmentation can be achieved in many ways, although by far the most important dimension is *economic*—the income of the target audience. Further descriptive definitions can be introduced by adding categories concerning geographical location, socio-economic status, personality, usage patterns and brand loyalty. However, according to marketer Michael Ray (1982), of all these factors the ones that would prove to be the most useful (for the primary objective of creating brand purchasing loyalty) are also the most difficult and unreliable to obtain. One solution to the segmentation descriptor problem has been the development and use of *psychographics*, which essentially combine different types of descriptive categories. This type of research is also referred to as identifying 'lifestyle patterns'. According to advertising executive Joseph Plummer (1979, pp. 125–6) this research combines hard demographic data with the 'richness and dimensionality of psychological characteristics and depth research'.

Life-style deals with behaviorally-oriented facets of people as well as feelings, attitudes, and opinions. Life-style also resembles tougher-minded approaches in that it is amenable to quantification and large samples. Life-style also is designed to answer questions about people in terms of their activities, interests and opinions. It measures their activities in terms of how they spend their time in work and leisure; their interests in terms of what they place importance on in their immediate surroundings; their opinions in terms of their stance on social issues, institutions and themselves; and finally, basic facts such as their age, income and where they live.

By tabulating the results with cluster and factor analysis, this procedure identifies the basic lifestyle segments in the audience, such as 'the active achiever' or 'the blue-collar outdoorsman'. Psychographic research can also be used to identify the attitudes and living styles of consumers of particular types of product; for example, in 1970 General Foods used psychographic research about the buyers of dog food to break into the canned dog-food market (Bernstein 1979).

One of the most prominent of these types of study is that reported by Arnold Mitchell in *The Nine American Lifestyles* (1983) which uses the term 'lifestyle' to describe 'a unique way of life defined by its distinctive array of values, drives, beliefs, needs, dreams, and special points of view'. Mitchell and his research colleagues where looking for a scheme that would encompass individual, social, and marketplace dimensions of life and that would be successful in predicting how a change in one dimension would affect the others, and also how the size and compositions of social groups would change over time. To do this they devised what they called the 'VALS' (values and lifestyles) typology and arrived at a scheme made up of nine identifiable lifestyles.

> Need-driven groups—11%
>> Survivor lifestyle—4%
>> Sustainer lifestyle—7%
> Outer-directed groups—67%
>> Belonger lifestyle—35%
>> Emulator lifestyle—10%
>> Achiever lifestyle—22%
> Inner-directed groups—20%
>> I-am-me lifestyle—5%
>> Experimental lifestyle—7%
>> Societally conscious lifestyle—8%
> Combined outer- and inner-directed group—2%
>> Integrated lifestyle—2%

The figures give the proportion of the adult population in the United States which, it is claimed, fall into each of these categories on the basis of responses to the survey questionnaire completed by respondents in 1980. A rudimentary application of the typology was also made for

France, Italy, Sweden, the United Kingdom and West Germany. As Mitchell indicates, the scheme combines elements from familiar conceptions of need- or drive-hierarchies, the most famous of which is Abraham Maslow and David Riesman's inner-outer-directed distinction. Its most challenging feature is that it attempts to describe both actual social groupings and a hierarchy of stages in personal self-development that culminates in psychological maturity. Mitchell notes: 'Perhaps the most fundamental business use of research lies in market segmentation.' The typology can, it is claimed, assist business in the great task of 'matching product to consumer' through precise design and targeting in advertising. Lifestyle advertising can help to produce commercials that communicate with segmented audiences in terms of their 'predispositions', of making sure that advertisements 'get to the right people with the right message at the right time' (Ray 1982, p. 482).

In broadcasting in particular (and in the new cable technologies) this concern with segments of the audience led in the direction of narrowcasting and specification, in which the commercial media tried to match the *market* segment of the manufacturers with the *audience* segment that they could deliver. As we saw in Chapter 3, it is not abstract time that is sold to advertisers, or even the time of any general audience. It is the production and sale of the time of particular audiences that is the driving element behind the material processes of commercial broadcasting. As Erik Barnouw (1978, p. 71) writes of the 1970s:

Network executives now tended to survey their schedules in terms of demographic product demands. Negotiations resembled transactions to deliver blocks of people. An advertising agency would be telling a network, in effect: 'For Shampoo Y, our client is ready to invest $1,800,000 in women 18–49. Other viewers are of no interest in this case; the client doesn't care to pay for irrelevant viewers. But for women 18–49 he is willing to pay Z dollars per thousand. What spots can you offer.

Barnouw commented that in the 1970s the dramaturgy of television reflected the demographics of the supermarket. Perhaps we can say that the new narrowcasting of the 1980s (such as MTV) reflects the psychographics of the segmented marketplace. MTV offers not only demographics but a whole consciousness of living. Although the effect of market segmentation on television programming is an extremely important and interesting topic, I will not pursue it further at this point. Instead I wish to focus on the effect of the new market segmentation and the medium of television on the form and content of advertising.

## Advertising and the domain of meaning

Daniel Pope (1982) argues that market segmentation has been at the root of three important interrelated trends: the growth of user-centred advertising; the rise of dramatic or narrative forms; and the subordination of specific product claims. First, comparing segmentation strategies of marketing (which seek to pinpoint a certain target audience) with those that seek merely to *differentiate* a brand from its competitors, Pope notes that the former tend to be *user-centred* and the latter *product-focused.* Product-focused advertising dominated the industry from approximately 1900 to 1950 and was based on the strategy of showing (through the device known as the Unique Selling Proposition, or USP), that one brand was *superior* to another. As the leading proponent of USP, Rosser Reeves, put it (Pope 1982, p. 287): 'Our problem is—a client comes into my office and throws down two newly minted half-dollars onto my desk and says, "Mine is the one on the left. You prove it's better".' In contrast to this, segmentation strategies are user-focused and stress the benefits to the consumer rather than the superiority of the brand to other brands along certain dimensions. Commenting on the application of traditional standards of truth and deception to the new 'lifestyle' advertising, Pope (1982, p. 280) writes:

Segmentation and the rise of service marketing have apparently increased the proportion of user-centered campaigns. An ethical evaluation that looks only at the veracity of product claims will miss much of the persuasive action of these advertisements. Where ads appeal to the consumer to enter a 'consumption community', they stress the attractiveness of the community, not just the desirability of the product. It comes as no surprise that ads show products in pleasant surroundings and that models and actors are generally attractive. But when the context, rather than the product becomes, in a sense, the object of the consumer's desires, judging an ad by its product claims is insufficient.

In *SCA* we were able to show this shift to user-centred (or situation-centred) advertising in our historical study of magazine advertising. This latest stage (beginning in the mid-1960s) emphasises the relation between persons and settings, fused not through use and its consequences, but in a 'situation' emblematic of a particular way of life.

Second, and closely related to the growth of user-centred advertising, there is the increase in narrative and dramatic forms that stress benefits to the consumer, rather than product characteristics. While this type of stylistic device has always played a role in advertising, there has been a notable shift, accompanying segmentation strategies, from an emphasis on social conformity and acceptance to 'self-fulfilment, escape and private fantasy'. The introduction of television into the marketing framework obviously has had an effect on this development because it 'permits effective demonstration of the product in use and its benefits for consumers, and dramatic commercial vignettes are often effective ways of staging these demonstrations' (Pope 1982, p. 291). In *SCA* the period after 1945 is described as the era of 'personification' where the product performs in fetishistic ways (magically) to transform the self and to allure other people.

Third, market segmentation has been accompanied by a decline in the amount of hard or explicit information presented about a product. User-centred advertising is able to draw on the shared experiences, perceptions and attitudes of the segmented audience, rather than relying on product claims to appeal to a mass market. This new direction of advertising was undoubtedly hastened by the application of research from the late 1960s into the nature of brain activity involved with television viewing. Herbert Krugman, now manager of public-opinion research at General Electric, found that, typically, the left hemisphere of the brain which processes input in a logical, rational and analytical manner was much less active than the right side of the brain, which processes information emotionally and holistically. While in 'normal' situations the right and left hemisphere process information in combination, the television experience shatters this bond, leaving the viewer vulnerable to non-rational emotional appeals.

Tony Schwartz (1974) has given the most eloquent expression of this discovery in his 'resonance' theory of communication, whereby 'the critical task is to design our package of stimuli (ads) so that it resonates with information already stored within an individual and thereby induces the desired learning or behavioral effect'. Schwartz's concern is not with the message itself as a communicator of meaning, but rather with the use-value of the message for the audience.

The meaning of our communication is what a listener or viewer gets out of his experience with the communicator's stimuli. The listener's or viewer's brain is an indispensable component of the total communication system. His life experiences, as well as his expectations of the stimuli he is receiving, interact with the communicator's output in determining the meaning of the communication (Schwartz 1974, p. 25).

The job of the advertiser is to understand the world of the segmented audience, so that the stimuli that are created can evoke the stored information: it has to *resonate* with information that the listener possesses. However, we should not confuse this resonance with *reflection*. As adman Jerry Goodis says (Nelson 1983): 'Advertising doesn't always mirror how people are acting, but how they're dreaming...In a sense, what we're doing is wrapping up your emotions and selling them back to you.' Thus advertising draws its materials from the experiences of the audience, but it reformulates them in a *unique* way. It does not reflect meaning but rather *constitutes* it. Advertisers, according to Schwartz, should be in the business of 'structured recall'. The purpose is to design commercials that create pleasurable emotions that will be triggered when the product is viewed in the marketplace. As Schwartz (1974, p. 69) says: 'I do not care what number of people *remember* or *get* the message. I am concerned with how people are affected by the stimuli.'

The approach derived from the discipline of semiology has proved to be very useful in examining the process by which people derive this meaning from advertisements (see *SCA*, Chapter 8, for a much fuller discussion). Semiology is the study of signs, or more specifically the *system of signs*. A sign is something that has significance within a system of meaning and is constituted of two key elements: the *signifier* (the material vehicle) and the *signified* (the mental construct, the idea). The two elements are equally necessary and can be separated only analytically. For instance, in our culture diamonds signify never-ending love ('A diamond is forever'). Although in reality we have only 'love-enduring diamonds', in analytical terms we have three elements: the signifier— diamonds; the signified—never-ending love; the sign, the unity of signifier and signified—love-enduring diamonds. In another meaning system, or another culture, diamonds could mean something entirely different, for there is nothing inherent in them as objects to signify only unending, deep love. This is the difference between the signifier and the sign. The diamond as signifier is *empty* of meaning. The diamond as sign is *full* of meaning. In terms of my earlier discussion in Chapter 2, regarding the manner in which capitalism has initially to empty commodities of meaning, we can say that production produces commodities as signifiers while advertising produces them as signs. In relation to diamonds, for example, Edward Epstein in *The Rise and Fall of Diamonds* (1982) has described the way in which an advertising campaign (conducted by the N.W. Ayers advertising agency on behalf of DeBeers) turned a stone whose value lay primarily in its scarcity, into the most important symbol in our culture for deep and committed love.

Judith Williamson, in her book *Decoding Advertisements* (1978), has attempted the most detailed analysis of the manner in which the audience derives meaning from commercial messages. Her central point is that meaning is created *through* the audience, rather than meaning being directed *at* audiences. Typically, there are three stages to the constitution of this meaning. The first is that of *transferring* the meaning of one sign to another (that is, transferring the meaning of a person, a social situation, something in nature, another object, or an emotional feeling *to a commodity*). An example would be a bottle of sherry on a table where a couple was enjoying a romantic candlelight dinner without any text or commentary linking the sherry and the situation. The transference is accomplished by the juxtaposition within the formal internal structure of the advertisement.

This transference of meaning from one sign to another is very rarely made explicit in modern advertising by the content of the advertisement itself. For instance in advertisements for Dingo boots featuring the ex-football star, O.J. Simpson, nowhere is it stated that the boots are like the person. *We* transfer the meaning of O.J. Simpson to Dingo boots. However, a sign only replaces something for someone else if it has *someone to mean to*. The transference requires the active participation of the viewer of the advertisement.

Advertising seems to have a life of its own; it exists in and out of other media, and speaks to us in a language we can recognise but a voice we can never identify. This is because advertising has no 'subject'. Obviously people invent and produce adverts, but apart from the fact that they are unknown and faceless, the ad in any case does not claim to speak from them, it is not their speech. Thus there is a space, a gap left where the speaker should be; and one of the peculiar features of advertising is that we are drawn in to fill that gap, so that we become both listener and speaker, subject and object (Williamson 1978, p. 13–14).

We do not *receive* meaning from above, we constantly re-create it. It works through us, not at us. We have to do the work that is not done by the advertisement, 'but which is only made possible by its form'. We are drawn 'into the transformational space between the units of the ad. Its meaning only exists in this space; the field of transaction; and it is here that we operate—*we are this space*' (Williamson 1978, p. 44). This crucial mediation by the audience is the basis of what Schwartz calls 'partipulation' whereby the advertisement does not manipulate the audience but invites their participation in the construction of meaning. It is also behind Marshall McLuhan's notion that the audience 'works' in the consumption of the television image. This transference is based on the fact that the first object, the first sign (O.J. Simpson) has a significance to be transferred. The advertisement invites us to make that transfer of meaning to the commodity, to make the signifier a sign. We must already know what O.J. Simpson stands for, what he means within the world of popular culture and sports. These systems of meaning from which we draw the tools to complete the transfer are referred to by Williamson as *referent systems*. They constitute the body of knowledge from which *both* advertisers and audiences draw their materials. As such, mass media advertising literally plays the role of a mediator. For the audience properly to 'decode' the message (transfer meaning), advertisers have to draw their materials from the social knowledge of the audience, then transform this material into messages ('encode'), developing appropriate formats and shaping the content in order that the process of communication from audience to audience be completed (Hall 1980).

## Gender and the allure of advertising

The recognition that the activity of the audience itself plays a vital role in the use-value of messages takes us away from the ultimately fruitless notion of manipulation and conspiratorial control by advertisers. It forces us instead to understand the context within which this watching activity takes place. In the last chapter I examined this from the viewpoint of valorisation. Here I am concerned with understanding the context of meaning within which advertising itself fits as meaning. Particularly, I wish to understand what lies behind the considerable power that advertising seems to have over its audience without reverting back to crass explanations of manipulation and technique.

Erving Goffman in his book *Gender Advertisements* (1979) was concerned with similar types of questions although he did not phrase them in the same way. He instead asked another question: why do most advertisements not look *strange* to us? Goffman believes that when we look at them carefully, they are in fact very strange creations, particularly as regards their portrayals of gender relations. Through his extremely perceptive comments and examples he shows us that in advertising the best way to understand the male–female relation is to compare it to the parent–child relation in which men take on the roles of parents while women behave as children normally would be expected to. In advertising women are treated largely as children. (See *SCA* for a much fuller discussion of Goffman's work, especially Chapter 8.)

Goffman supports his argument by pointing to a number of aspects of gender relations in advertising. For instance, in examining the portrayal of hands, he finds that women's hands usually are shown just caressing an object, or just barely touching it, as though they were not in full control of it, whereas men's hands are shown strongly grasping and manipulating objects. Goffman is concerned with what such social portrayals say about the relative social positions of men and women. Beds and floors, for example, are associated with the less clean parts of a room; also, persons using them will be positioned lower than anyone who is sitting or standing. A recumbent position also leaves people in a poor position to defend themselves and thus puts them at the mercy of others. These positions are, of course, also a 'conventionalised expression of sexual availability'. Goffman's sample of advertisements shows that women and children are pictured on beds and floors much more than are men. In addition, women are constantly shown 'drifting away' mentally while under the physical 'protection' of a male, as if his strength and alertness were enough. Women are also shown in the finger-to-mouth pose, directly reminiscent of children's behaviour. Further, when men and women are shown in physical contact, invariably the woman is 'snuggling' into the man in the same way that children solicit protection and comfort from their mother. The difference between male and female behaviour is highlighted by Goffman's suggestion that we try to imagine a reversal in the positions of the male and female models.

If grown women are largely treated as children in advertisements, why does this not look strange to us? Goffman comments that indeed the most negative statement we could make of advertisements is that as pictures of reality, they do not look strange to us. To answer this question, he reverts back to the vocabulary of social anthropology, particularly the concepts of ceremony, display and ritual (which are used interchangeably). These are actions, or events, that seek to give structure and stability to a shared social life, to communicate the system of meaning within which individuals are located and within which they must be viewed. Goffman is particularly interested in how gender is communicated socially. While 'sex' refers to the biological distinction between males and females, 'gender' is the culture-specific arrangement of this universal relationship. Relations between men and women are very different the world over and can be given many different definitions depending upon the specific cultural pattern that exists in any society. As such there is nothing *natural* about gender relations—they are socially defined and constructed. As such, any culture must constantly work to maintain existing gender relations. This is achieved during the course of social life by 'gender displays'—these are conventionalised portrayals of the 'culturally established correlates of sex'. In our daily interactions we are constantly defining for ourselves and other people what it means to be male and female in this society. From the way we dress, the way we behave, and the structure of our interactions, to things such as body posture and ceremonial activities (opening doors, giving up seats, and so on) we are communicating ideas about gender using culturally conventionalised routines of behaviour. These displays, or *rituals of gender behaviour*, help the interpretation of social reality, they are guides to perception. It is from these conventionalised portrayals of · gender that advertising borrows so heavily, and that is the reason why, according to Goffman, most advertisements do not look strange to us, for they are an extremely concentrated reflection of one aspect of our social lives—they are a reflection of the realm of gender displays. Advertisers largely do not *create* the images they depict out of nothing. Advertisers draw upon the same corpus of displays that we all use to make sense of social life. 'If anything, advertisers conventionalise our conventions, stylise what is already a stylisation, make frivolous use of what is already something considerably cut off from contextual controls. Their hype is hyper-ritualisation' (Goffman 1979, p. 84).

I wish to stress again, however, that this is not merely a simple reflection—advertisements are neither false nor are they true. As *representations* they are necessarily abstractions from what they 'reflect'. Indeed, all communication is an abstraction at some level. For too long the debate on gender has been focused on the extent to which advertising images are true or false (see *SCA*, Chapter 12, for further discussion). Advertisement images are neither false nor true reflections of social reality because they are in fact *a part* of social reality. Just as gender displays are not true or false representations of real gender relations, neither are advertisements true or false representation of real gender relations or of ritualised gender displays—they are *hyper-ritualisations* that emphasise some aspects of gender displays and de-emphasise others. As such, advertisements are part of the whole context within which we attempt to understand and define our own gender relations. They are part of the process by which we learn about gender.

In so far as our society defines sex as gender through culture (and not through biology or nature), we are not fundamentally different to any other past or present society. All cultures have to define gender for their own purposes and they all have conventionalised forms to accomplish this socialisation. Gender relations are social and not natural creations in any setting.

However, I believe that our culture is different in one very important sense. Gender is only one aspect of human individuality; the political, occupational, educational, creative, artistic, religious and spiritual, and so on, are also very important elements of individuals' lives. Human existence is potentially very wide and very varied in the experiences it offers. In our culture, though, advertising makes the balance between these things very different—indeed, everything else becomes defined through gender. In modern advertising, gender is probably the social resource that is used most by advertisers. Thousands of images surround us every day of our lives that address us along gender lines. Advertising seems to be obsessed with gender and sexuality.

There are two reasons for this obsession. First, gender is one of our deepest and most important traits as human beings. Our understanding of ourselves as either male or female is the most important aspect of our definition of ourselves as individuals. It reaches deep into the innermost recesses of individual identity. Second, gender can be communicated at a glance (almost instantly) because of our intimate knowledge and use of the conventionalised codes of gender display. Advertisers are trying to present the world in ways that could be real (Goffman calls advertisements 'commercial realism') and so they are forced to draw upon the repertoires of everyday life and experience. What better place to draw upon than an area of social behaviour that can be communicated almost instantly and which reaches into the very core of our definition as human beings? As Goffman (1979, p. 7) writes,

one of the most deeply seated traits of man, it is felt, is gender; femininity and masculinity are in a sense the prototypes of essential expression—something that can be conveyed fleetingly in any social situation and yet something that strikes at the most basic characteristics of the individual.

While every culture has to work to define for its members what gender relations should be, no other culture in history, I believe, has been this obsessed with explicit portrayals of gender relations. Gender and sex have never been as important as they are in our culture. Never in history has the iconography of a culture been so obsessed or possessed by questions of sexuality and gender. For the reasons stated above, through advertising, in our cultural discourse, questions of sex and gender have been elevated to a privileged position.

This may also offer an answer as to where the power of advertising derives from. The representations of advertising are part of the context within which we define or understand gender. Advertising draws us into *our* reality. As hyper-ritualistic images, commercials offer an extremely concentrated form of communication about sex and gender. The essence of gender is represented in advertisements. That is the reason why advertising is relatively immune from criticism about its portrayals of gender. The feminist critique (both the content-analysis critique and the objectification critique) is pitched at an intellectual level that does not recognise the emotional attraction of the images. We cannot deny the messages of advertising; we cannot say they are false because they bear some resemblance to ritualised gender relations. Further we cannot deny them because we define ourselves at our deepest level through the reality of advertising. We *have* to reach a socially accepted understanding of gender identity in some way. If we do not cope at this level then the evidence suggests that it is very difficult to cope at any level. Gender confusions cloud the entire domain of social identity for individuals. To deny completely the messages of advertising is to deny our definition of ourselves in gender and sexual terms—it is to deny ourselves as socially recognisable individuals in this culture. If the dominant definitions of gender are not accepted, 'deviant' individuals are relegated to the 'perverted' section of our culture (as with transsexuals and transvestites). I believe that is the reason why the feminist critiques concerning regressive representations in advertising have not been very successful; they have not recognised the basis of its *attraction*. If the critique does not recognise this attraction then the attack on advertising becomes an attack on *people*. People thus feel guilty about being attracted to the images of advertising while being told that they should not find it attractive. Annette Kuhn (1985, p. 8) writes of this:

Politics is often thought of as one of life's more serious undertakings, allowing little room for pleasure. At the same time, feminists may feel secretly guilty about their enjoyment of images they are convinced ought to be rejected as politically unsound. In analysing such images, though, it is possible, indeed necessary, to acknowledge their pleasurable qualities, precisely because pleasure is an area of analysis in its own right. 'Naive' pleasure, then, becomes admissible. And the acts of analysis, of deconstruction and of reading 'against the grain' offer an additional pleasure—the pleasure of resistance, of saying 'no': not to 'unsophisticated' enjoyment by ourselves and others, of culturally dominant images, but to the structures of power which ask us to consume them uncritically and in highly circumscribed ways.

A critique of advertising has to start by giving people permission to recognise the strength of the images of advertising, of where that power rests. From that we can start to unfold the exact role that advertising plays in our culture from a critical perspective.

The definition of gender and sexual identity is a difficult activity at the best of times; in modern society this difficulty is compounded by individuals being 'bombarded' by extremely concentrated images of what gender is actually about. Advertising, it seems, has a privileged place in the discourse on gender in consumer societies due to its prominence in our daily lives. As a result *what* advertising says about gender is a very important issue to understand. Gender could be defined in many ways (achievement, control of our lives, independence, family, creativity, and so on ). It is a multi-dimensional aspect of human individuality. In advertising, however, gender is equated almost exclusively with sex. Women especially are defined primarily in sexual terms. What is important about women is their sexual behaviour. As the debate on pornography has indicated, viewing women from this narrow and restricted perspective can result in treating women as less than truly human. The concentration on one aspect of behaviour detracts from seeing people as people rather than as standing for something or being associated with one thing. As Judith Williamson (1978, p. 169) notes on this point:

If meaning is abstracted from something, from what 'means' it, this is nearly always a danger signal because it is only in material circumstances that it is possible to 'know' anything, and looking away from people or social phenomenon to their supposed abstract 'significance' can be at worst an excuse for human and social atrocities, at best, a turning of reality into apparent unreality, almost unlivable while social dreams and myths seem so real . . . Advertising may appropriate, not only real areas of time and space, and give them a false content, but real needs and desires in people, which are given a false fulfilment. We need a way of looking at ourselves: which ads give us falsely . . . we need to make sense of the world: which ads make us feel we are doing in making sense of *them*.

Advertisements, then, give us a false way to look at ourselves. I wish to clarify this point, to establish where precisely the falsity lies. It does *not* lie in the individual advertisement. There is nothing 'false' about the consumption of individual messages. That is what draws us in. Individually each message communicates a certain meaning. Each individual advertisement is produced for a certain strategic purpose in terms of communication. Conventionalised sexual imagery (such as high heels, slit skirts, nudity) draws us in and makes an advertisement attractive for us. It is very difficult to criticise a single advertisement in isolation (even the ones that objectify women—we all objectify men and women in some way at some time—it can fulfil a socially positive function). Parts of daily life do have to do with sexuality and thus there is nothing wrong with individual messages that focus on sex and gender. (That is, unless one took a moralistic stance on advertising in which some messages are *inherently* unacceptable for public, or private, viewing—groups on the political right criticise advertising from this perspective). The falsity arises from the *system of images*, from the advertisements as a totality and from their cumulative effect. All (or at least many) messages are about gender and sexuality. It seems that for women it is the *only* thing that is important about them. The falsity then arises from the message *system*, rather than individual advertisements. It arises from the institutional context within which advertisements are produced and suggests that attempts to modify its regressive features should be concentrated at this level.

## The codes of the marketplace

Advertisements, then, draw us in in two ways. First, we depend upon the meaning that they provide for the definition of our own social lives. Second, they depend upon our knowledge of referent systems for the operation of meaning. I will explore this second point in more detail in this section. The meaning of advertising is not there on its surface, waiting to be appropriated by just anyone in the same way. Meaning is dependent upon the manner in which signs are organised internally to the commercial and on the relationship of the commercial to external belief systems. The construction of signs does not take place at a *denotative* level alone but includes also a *connotative* level. The first level is the literal meaning of the advertisement. Thus on the denotative level 'sweater' means 'a piece of warm clothing'. However, by a further extension into the connotative level we could also say that it means 'keeping warm', 'the coming of winter' or 'a cold day'. Within particular systems of fashion, 'sweater' may connote a 'fashionable style of *haute couture*', a certain 'informal' style of dress, and so on. Similarly within a romantic sub-code and against the right background, 'sweater' may connote 'long walks in the woods'. Stuart Hall (1973, p. 176) refers to these codes of connotation as

the configurations of meaning which permit a sign to signify, in addition to its denotative reference, *other implied meanings*. These configurations of meaning are forms of social knowledge, derived from social practices, the knowledge of institutions, the beliefs and legitimations which exist in a diffused form within a society, and which order that society's apprehension of the world in terms of dominant meaning patterns.

For Roland Barthes in *Mythologies* (1973), the denotative level is the level of *language* while the connotative is the level of *myth*. The concept that unifies the different elements of the process of meaning construction ('referent systems', 'ceremony/display', 'connotation') is that of *code*. A code is the store of experience upon which both the advertiser and audience draw in their participation in the construction of 'commodity meaning'. This is similar to Gillian Dyer's (1982, p. 131) definition of code as 'a set of rules or an interpretive device known to both transmitter and receiver, which assigns a certain meaning or content to a certain sign'. Stuart Hall (1980) describes a process whereby media have to produce 'meaningful' discourses by encoding messages that are shaped by factors including the framework of knowledge, relations of production, and technical infrastructure. It is this message that is decoded by audiences, who are constrained in turn by similar factors (Hall 1980, pp. 130–1):

Production and reception of the television messages are not, therefore, identical, but they are related: they are differentiated moments within the totality formed by the social relations of the communication process as a whole . . . In a 'determinate' moment the structure employs a code and yields a 'message'. At another determinate moment the 'message', via its decodings, issues into the structure of social practices . . . The codes of encoding and decoding may not be perfectly symmetrical . . . [but] there is no intelligible discourse without the operation of a code.

In the semiotic tradition this is referred to as the utilisation of *paradigmatic* structures of interpretation (which make use of resources outside of the text) rather than strictly *syntagmatic* structures (based on a purely internal reading of the text) (see Kress 1976).

This focus on code as the key to studying advertising is not anything new of course. However, while the notion of code is insightful and imaginative in its conceptual outline, the specific applications of it to advertising content too often lapse into vague generalities. For instance Williamson (1978) starts promisingly by dissecting the codes of fashion that embrace both Catherine Deneuve and Margaux Hemingway as models yet which differentiate each from the other. Later on though, where the content of these 'referent systems' is presented, the discussion abandons the sensual codes of the fashion world for the more abstract and 'deeper' codes of ancient cultural traditions.

These deeper codes are explained in terms of complex anthropological notions, fashioned from the realm of magic and alchemy and from broad sweeps of time, narrative and history. Doubtless the purpose here is to show how advertisements divorce these deeper sources of life and culture from the material and historical context that makes them truly meaningful, so that we are left with a hollow notion of things such as 'nature' and 'history'. However, *all* of modern culture crawls with references to archaic impulses concerning the animals we love or fear, the idiosyncrasies of dining and dressing, sex roles, puberty and adolescence, marriage and courtship, power and domination. And most of modern culture remains rooted in the old oppositions: good and evil, sacred and profane, life and death. Certainly one finds all this ancient baggage dumped helter-skelter into advertisements, but one finds it just about everywhere else, too. Although it is fascinating to unpack it, doing so does not tell one all that much about advertising.

Varda Leymore's *Hidden Myth* (1975) also seeks to transpose the notion of code into culture. Leymore tries to study modern advertising using the same type of structural analysis that anthropologists use to study the systems of myth in primitive societies. The codes of advertising are the same as the codes of myth and reveal the 'essential underlying unity of the symbolic function of the mind'. In advertising are found the universal problems of life (good and evil, life and death, happiness and misery), as well as their promised resolution. Advertising is an anxiety-reducing institution, serving a function assigned to other institutions in premodern societies. In these approaches the 'rangefinder' in the analytical lens is set to infinity, yielding a lack of resolution in the images.

This generality of referent systems is reflected also in the more theoretical discussions concerning the general role of the media in the social construction of reality and the audience's role therein. Much of the European semiotic tradition has drawn on psychoanalytic theory to explain the external referents to which the audience has access in the construction of meaning (for example, Lacan). Although there has been a healthy reaction against this direction, especially in England, that stresses the *historical and social subject* rather than the psychoanalytic one, even this has remained at the general level of cultural and symbolic systems, particular 'conjunctures' or particular 'institutional' spaces. For instance, David Morely (1980, p. 172) writes: 'While any posited relationship between discursive formations and class formations is too "reductivist", we must recognise that audiences are determined economically, politically and ideologically.'

Advertising absorbs and fuses a variety of symbolic practices and discourses. The substance and images woven into advertising messages are appropriated and distilled from an unbounded range of cultural references. Advertising borrows its ideas, its language, and its visual representations from literature and design, from other media content and forms, from history and the future, from its own experience, and also from the specific experiences and discourses of its particular targeted market; then it artfully recombines them around the theme of consumption. Through advertising, goods are knitted into the fabric of social life and cultural significance. The borrowed references are fused with products and returned to cultural discourse. Mass media advertising in the modern age presents us with a good opportunity to pinpoint in a concrete manner the relationship between the constructs of advertisers and the referent systems of the audience: that is the *codes of advertising*. As one advertising expert explains the situation:

First, you work out who you are talking to—say men ages $x$ to $y$, macho in attitude—demographic and psychographic information. We get this from research people and from the marketing people just digging around in the market. Then you know you are talking to these psychographics, attitudes about themselves—anything. I'll take anything I can get on that. The ideal target market is one person—tell me everything about them, their dreams, how they feel about the meals they eat, how they save, where they went to school. Tell me everything about them and I can sell them Hitler. So could you. But if we sold to one person it wouldn't be worthwhile so you have to find something that has a collective set of appeals (*SCA*, 156).

The marketing concept of segmentation, the 'resonance' theory of communication, the appeal to referent systems, the fragmentation and specification of media audiences, the redivision of time and the ever-shortening length of commercial messages suggest that different audiences will be appealed to by reference to different *codes of understanding* for completing the meaning of the advertisements. This hypothesis is tested in an empirical study in Chapter 5.

In a more general way the thesis being tested is the degree to which the use-value of commercial messages (their meanings for their audiences) is constrained by the conditions created by the system of exchange-value within which they are located. Specifically, I am interested in how fragmentation of the audience and the redivision of time (relative surplus-value) affect the form and content of different parts of the commercial message system. However, although I am interested in subjugation of use by exchange in this process, I intend to make no claims about audiences' interpretation of the message. That is a separate project. I am interested at this stage only in how the material that the audience works with in the construction of meaning is shaped by wider material conditions. Specifically, then, I am interested in how advertisers perceive the codes of the audience. To measure this in a systematic manner I focus on the *texts* of advertising, looking for what they can show us about the perceptions that the creators of the messages have about their intended audiences.

# 5 Advertising codes and fetishism: an empirical study

In the preceding four chapters I identified two key concepts as being crucial for a critical study of advertising: the fetishism of commodities; and the valorisation of time and 'codes' of audience comprehension. In this chapter I wish to examine these abstract notions from an empirical perspective through a study of broadcast television. Specifically I wish to ascertain to what degree the concepts of code and fetish are useful tools in the understanding of modern advertising.

In approaching an empirical study of advertising content, I attempted to construct a combined semiological and content-analysis methodology that would allow me to utilise the positive features of the two major ways that advertising has thus far been analysed: the systematic and 'objective' features' of content analysis with the interpretive sensitivity of semiology (see *SCA*, Chapters 8 and 9, for a much fuller discussion of this strategy). My starting point for this was the coding protocol that had been developed by Stephen Kline and William Leiss for the study of magazine advertising. Although this protocol was indispensable to my own study, the adaptation of it to handle audio and visual material that changed during a thirty-second commercial format and that utilised a totally different medium meant that the long process (eighteen months) of developing a coding protocol more suited to my specific needs produced a much different result (see Jhally 1984 for full discussion of the methodological issues and the full results of the study).

The final protocol that I developed was applied by myself alone to 1000 American network commercials. As such, although the protocol was tested (successfully) for intercoder reliability, I make no claims that the results which I report here 'prove' or 'disprove' any of my theoretical hypotheses. For that to occur, other coders would have to have been involved. As such I regard this as a preliminary study that will either point to the need to take another direction in research or indicate whether further resources need to be channelled in the present direction. Taking into account the huge number of hours demanded by the empirical study alone, I make this disclaimer with much hesitation and regret.

The commercials that I studied were collected by a random stratified (by product type) sample of 500 from each of two time periods: network prime-time and network sports-time. (Only product advertisements were included in the sample.) These time periods were chosen so that I would be able to say something about the advertising that the most number of people watch (prime-time) as well as to look at the messages that are directed by advertisers to two different audiences: although prime-time is watched in large numbers by many different kinds of audience, for advertisers it is the most efficient way to reach a *female* audience; similarly, while the sports audience is not homogeneous (although more so than prime-time) it is the most efficient way for advertisers to reach *adult males*. Within my 1000 advertisements I have, then, two subsamples of males and females. The commercials were collected over a one-year period (September 1980 to August 1981) from all three networks and, for sports, from all three major team sports (basketball, football and baseball). My sampling procedures enable me to claim 99 per cent precision. Once I had developed the protocol (operationalised the concepts) and had collected my sample, I applied the categories to each single advertisement. The advertisements were collected on ¾ in. colour video tape and I could replay and view them as many times as necessary to complete the coding adequately.

Before proceeding with the data analysis, there needs to be a justification of the specific descriptive statistics employed. The vast majority of the operationalised variables are *nominal-level* variables, i.e. they deal with discreet non-ranking categories rather than ordinal, interval, or ratio-level ranked and numerical categories. Statistical Package for the Social Sciences (SPSS) offers six statistics for strictly nominal-level data: chi-square, phi, Cramer's *V*, contingency coefficient, lambda, and uncertainty coefficient. In choosing the correct measure of association I was concerned that it should satisfy five criteria: (a) that it should range from 0 to 1; (b) that a value of 0 should indicate no association; (c) that the value of 1 should indicate perfect association between two variables; (d) that it should be applicable to all sizes of tables, both square and rectangular; (e) that it should be appropriate to the level of measurement.

Chi-square has no upper limit, phi can only be used for 2 × 2 tables, and the maximum value of the contingency coefficient depends on the size of the table. Of the rest, lambda and the uncertainty coefficient are based on the concept of proportional reduction in error (PRE) which is concerned with how accurately one can predict values of the dependent variable from the value of the independent variable. While advertisers have to draw upon the experiences or aspirations of their segmented audiences, the fact that brands must differentiate themselves ensures that there will be no narrow range of encoding/decoding elements in each time period. There is no notion of predictability in the traditional sense; and there is no one-to-one fixing of code and time period, but rather a range of possible alternatives. The concept of code as I use it here implies an interrelationship and coexistence of categories of one variable, as opposed to a narrow notion of code as a single predictable element (given a certain explanatory variable). While useful for other kinds of problem, PRE measures are not that applicable to my present concerns. The measure of association that I used is Cramer's *V*, which is a modified version of phi for larger tables. It ranges from 0 to 1 (indicating respectively no association and perfect association), and is applicable to all sizes of tables and to the nominal level of measurement. However, while it does measure the strength of the relationship between two variables, it does not measure the direction of the relationship—only its existence and strength. For present purposes that is sufficient. Following my comments above regarding the range of alternatives that a commercial code implies, I will treat as significant any *V* over 0.3.

## Code and audience

In this section I am concerned with establishing patterns in the data that can be broken down in terms of the messages directed at different audiences. A number of variables will be correlated with time period (either prime-time (PT) or sports-time (ST)).

### Use-type

Table 1 shows the different types of product advertised and their breakdown by time period.

**Table 1.** Use-type by period (per cent)

| Use-Type | Total (n = 1000) | PT (n = 500) | ST (n = 500) |
|---|---|---|---|
| Alcohol | 13.8 | 3.2 | 24.4 |
| Food | 13.1 | 23.2 | 3.0 |
| Clothing | 3.4 | 5.2 | 1.6 |
| Transportation | 20.7 | 10.0 | 31.4 |
| Personal care | 23.3 | 26.4 | 20.2 |
| Household | 9.2 | 11.6 | 6.8 |
| Drugs | 6.9 | 12.0 | 1.8 |
| Pets | 1.4 | 2.8 | 0.0 |
| Leisure technology | 6.1 | 3.8 | 8.4 |
| Other | 2.1 | 1.8 | 2.4 |
| Total | 100.0 | 100.0 | 100.0 |

The differences between the two periods is quite significant. The correlation of period with use-type produces a *V* of 0.54—very high for an empirical project of this type. The product types advertised in ST are much more concentrated, as would be expected with a narrowly cast audience: three use-types (transportation, alcohol and personal care products) make up over 76 per cent of the products advertised. By contrast the top three use-types in PT (personal care, food and drugs) make up 61.2 per cent. Also the types of product are very different in the two time periods: transportation and alcohol dominate in ST, and personal care and food predominate in PT. This finding indicates that even if one finds significant differences between the time periods, one must check for use-type as a significant factor and control for it.

## Person code

In *SCA* we identified advertising as being composed of the relationships between three elemental codes: the product code, the setting code and the person code. Here I am concerned with identifying the nature of the appeal made through people in television advertising.

**Table 2.**  Person code by period (per cent)

| Person | Total (n = 1000) | PT (n = 500) | ST (n = 500) |
|---|---|---|---|
| None | 6.4 | 3.8 | 9.0 |
| Company employee | 5.8 | 4.6 | 7.0 |
| Expert | 6.2 | 5.2 | 7.2 |
| Ordinary person | 36.1 | 42.6 | 29.6 |
| Ideal person | 26.1 | 29.0 | 23.2 |
| Child | 1.2 | 2.4 | 0.0 |
| Fictional mythical | 3.0 | 2.8 | 3.2 |
| Famous person | 15.2 | 9.6 | 20.8 |
| Total | 100.0 | 100.0 | 100.0 |

The three types of person most often used as the medium for the person code were ordinary people, idealised persons and famous persons. However, correlation with time period (audience) highlights some interesting distinctions. Although the *V* is only 0.25 and the three modal categories are the same, we find that for PT ordinary person appeal is used in 42.6 per cent of the advertisements as opposed to 29.6 per cent in ST, and that famous person appeal is used in 9.6 per cent of PT advertisements compared with 20.8 per cent in ST. The sports world seems to be more glamour-orientated than the 'ordinary' world of PT.

## Dominant Social Grouping

This variable measures the predominant social grouping that is present in any commercial.

**Table 3**. Dominant social grouping by period (per cent)

| Social Grouping | Total (n = 1000) | PT (n = 500) | ST (n = 500) |
|---|---|---|---|
| No persons | 8.1 | 5.4 | 10.8 |
| Single | 39.4 | 39.8 | 39.0 |
| Singles/potential couple | 1.8 | 1.8 | 1.8 |
| Coupled collective | 2.1 | 1.6 | 2.6 |
| Couple | 14.1 | 17.8 | 10.4 |
| Family/nuclear | 10.9 | 15.8 | 6.0 |
| Family/extended | 2.2 | 3.4 | 1.0 |
| Female collective | 2.3 | 4.4 | 0.2 |
| Male collective | 9.7 | 2.0 | 17.4 |
| Collective not coupled | 3.2 | 3.0 | 3.4 |
| Mixed | 0.8 | 0.2 | 1.4 |
| Grouped not collective | 4.9 | 3.8 | 6.0 |
| Grouped children | 0.5 | 1.0 | 0.0 |
| Total | 100.0 | 100.0 | 100.0 |

For the data set as whole a single person is by far the most numerous (39.4 per cent), followed distantly by couples, the nuclear family, and the male collectivity. The cross-tabulation with time period produces a significant $V$ of 0.37. The major differences appear in the family and collectivity categories. The nuclear family appeared in 15.8 per cent of PT advertisements as compared to 6 per cent of ST advertisements; the extended family appeared in 3.4 per cent of PT and only 1 per cent of ST; female collective scored 4.4 per cent in PT and 0.2

per cent in ST; and male collective 2 per cent in PT and 17.4 per cent in ST. A minor difference is found in the category of couple, which appears in 17.8 per cent of PT and 10.4 per cent of ST advertisements.

The appearance of single persons is equally important in both PT and ST, and there is a slight difference in the importance of the male–female sexual relation. But when family and collectivity are examined more closely, some interesting distinctions emerge. Aggregating the nuclear and extended family categories, one sees their appearance in 19.2 per cent of PT and only 7 per cent of ST advertisements. Similarly, aggregating the categories that stress group membership (coupled collective, female collective, male collective, and uncoupled but mixed collective) one sees their appearance in 11 per cent of PT advertisements compared with 23.6 per cent of ST. Family is more important in PT and collectivity in ST.

*Interpersonal relations*

This variable is closely related to the last and seeks to break down the social groupings in more interpersonal terms.

**Table 4**.    Interpersonal relations by period (per cent)

| Inter-personal Relations | Total (*n* = 1000) | PT (*n* = 500) | ST (*n* = 500) |
|---|---|---|---|
| Independence | 2.0 | 2.2 | 1.8 |
| Romantic love | 17.2 | 20.4 | 14.0 |
| Family togetherness | 8.0 | 10.8 | 5.2 |
| Parental | 3.5 | 6.6 | 0.4 |
| Friendship | 15.7 | 10.8 | 20.6 |
| Confidence in authority | 3.6 | 4.8 | 2.4 |
| Worker–client | 2.0 | 1.8 | 2.2 |
| Competition/teasing | 6.0 | 3.6 | 8.4 |
| Absent | 42.0 | 39.0 | 45.0 |
| Total | 100.0 | 100.0 | 100.0 |

In general terms the two most important categories to emerge are those of romantic love and friendship, followed by family togetherness and competition/teasing. Cross-tabulation with time period (excluding zero data) produces a significant *V* of 0.35. Romantic love is more important in PT than ST (20.4 per cent against 14 per cent), as is the parental relationship (6.6 per cent against 0.4 per cent). On the other hand, friendship is more important in ST than PT (20.6 per cent against 10.8 per cent), as is competition/teasing (8.4 per cent against 3.6 per cent).

## Activities

This variable sought to identify the activities that people in advertisements are engaged in. However, because the television commercial is a 'dynamic' message rather than a static one, there are often more than one set of activities shown. As such, there were two codings for this variable to capture this element. The total category in Table 5 is the aggregate of these two codings. The other two columns are the way that the first coding only was divided between PT and ST. It is not possible to subdivide the aggregated categories. The most frequent coded activity is the explicit production of the commercial (14.6 per cent). In this category were included all those advertisements where there is no attempt at explicit fictionalisation, story-telling or other types of commercial stylisation. This is followed by personal maintenance (of the body), social activities with friends, recreational activities, and ordinary (as opposed to glamorous) work situations. The cross-tabulation with period produces a significant *V* of 0.40. The major differences occur with respect to housework (8.6 per cent in PT and 0.6 per cent in ST), social activities with friends (3.2 per cent in PT, 9.6 per cent in ST), the maintenance of possessions (1.6 per cent in PT, 6 per cent in ST), travelling (2.4 per cent in PT, 9.4 per cent in ST), eating (4.6 per cent in PT, 0.8 per cent in ST), and sporting activities (participating or spectating) (3.2 per cent in PT, 10.4 per cent in ST).

**Table 5**.   Activities by period (per cent).

| Activities | Total (n = 1000) | PT (n = 500) | ST (n = 500) |
|---|---|---|---|
| None | 7.7 | 8.3 | 8.4 |
| Rest/relax | 5.7 | 6.2 | 3.6 |
| Recreation activity | 9.0 | 8.6 | 8.0 |
| Work—ordinary | 9.4 | 7.1 | 9.2 |
| Work—glamorous | 3.2 | 2.0 | 4.0 |
| Housework | 6.8 | 8.6 | 0.6 |
| Social—friends | 12.8 | 3.2 | 9.6 |
| Social—romance | 6.5 | 3.6 | 3.0 |
| Personal maintenance | 10.4 | 12.0 | 8.8 |
| Maintain possessions | 4.2 | 1.6 | 6.0 |
| Purchasing | 3.1 | 3.8 | 1.6 |
| Educational | 0.7 | 0.8 | 0.2 |
| Religion | 0.6 | 0.6 | 0.0 |
| Sports spectating | 0.4 | 0.6 | 0.0 |
| Travelling | 5.9 | 2.4 | 9.4 |
| Eating | 3.6 | 4.6 | 0.8 |
| Sleeping | 1.4 | 1.6 | 1.0 |
| Sport | 7.6. | 3.2 | 10.4 |
| Child care | 0.7 | 1.2 | 0.0 |
| Making advertisement | 14.6 | 15.2 | 12.0 |
| Mixed | 4.2 | 4.8 | 3.4 |
| Total | N/A | 100.0 | 100.0 |

*Lifestyle*

The two most popular lifestyles depicted in advertisements are healthy/athletic and ordinary/middle class (see Table 6). These are followed by sophisticated/chic, fun-loving young adults, and glamorous. Cross-tabulation with period produces a *V* of 0.39. There are highly significant differences for some of the categories; healthy/athletic (7 per cent in PT, 18 per cent in ST), fun-loving young adults (10.6 per cent in PT, 5.2 per cent in ST), middle class (19.4 per cent in PT, 4.8 per cent in ST), traditional/rural (3 per cent in PT, 8 per cent in ST), and busy professional (4.4 per cent in PT, 1.8 per cent in ST).

**Table 6.** Lifestyle by period (per cent).

| Lifestyle | Total ($n$ = 1000) | PT ($n$ = 500) | ST ($n$ = 500) |
|---|---|---|---|
| None | 27.7 | 20.8 | 34.6 |
| Healthy/athletic | 12.5 | 7.0 | 18.0 |
| Back to nature | 1.4 | 1.8 | 1.0 |
| Family togetherness | 3.9 | 4.8 | 3.0 |
| Fun-loving young adults | 7.9 | 10.6 | 5.2 |
| Fun-loving teens | 0.7 | 1.0 | 0.4 |
| Sophisticated/elite | 8.6 | 9.0 | 8.2 |
| Glamorous | 6.7 | 7.8 | 5.6 |
| Middle class/suburban | 12.1 | 19.4 | 4.8 |
| Old-fashioned | 2.2 | 2.6 | 1.8 |
| Traditional/rural | 5.5 | 3.0 | 8.0 |
| Working class/urban | 5.2 | 5.6 | 4.8 |
| Busy professional | 3.1 | 4.4 | 1.8 |
| Exotic | 1.7 | 0.6 | 2.8 |
| playful/children | 0.8 | 1.6 | 0.0 |
| Total | 100.0 | 100.0 | 100.0 |

## Rhetorical form

This variable, and the next, measure not so much the depiction of content but the presentational form of the commercial. Here I am concerned with identifying what kinds of rhetorical structure are used to sell the product. There were two ranked codings for this variable (Table 7). Although there is widespread distribution along the categories of this variable, one can still detect some dominant categories. The argument based on the *effects* of product use is the most popular in both the first and second codings. This is followed by the association of the product with statused or popular reference groups and popular activities appeal. This latter feature is perhaps a little misleading, for it was difficult to separate the two from each other in many advertisements. If they were treated as a single category, it would account for 21.2 per cent of advertisements. The other important categories are: comparison with other products; famous star appeal; sports star appeal; sensual appeal (appeal to the

**Table 7**.   Rhetorical form by period (per cent).

| Rhetorical Form | 1st (n = 1000) | 2nd | PT (n = 500) | ST (n = 500) |
|---|---|---|---|---|
| None | 0.0 | 17.0 | — | — |
| Rational appeal: reasoned arguments based on product qualities | 3.9 | 3.8 | 2.8 | 5.0 |
| Economy/price appeal | 5.4 | 2.6 | 3.8 | 7.0 |
| Effects appeal: results of use are spectacular | 15.9 | 15.4 | 17.6 | 14.2 |
| Comparison appeal: comparison with other products, other effects | 8.0 | 4.8 | 10.2 | 5.8 |
| Worry appeal: if you don't use, something will happen | 1.9 | 1.5 | 1.2 | 2.6 |
| Expert appeal | 4.7 | 3.5 | 4.0 | 5.4 |
| Typical person appeal | 5.5 | 13.1 | 4.8 | 6.2 |
| Statused/popular reference group appeal: association with popular set | 12.9 | 7.8 | 14.0 | 11.8 |
| Popular activities appeal: exciting setting, special occasion | 8.3 | 9.7 | 5.0 | 11.6 |
| Famous star appeal | 6.8 | 1.2 | 7.0 | 6.6 |
| Sports star appeal | 7.0 | 0.7 | 1.4 | 12.6 |
| Peer appeal: product depicted as popular with everyone | 0.6 | 2.0 | 1.2 | 0.0 |
| Relief appeal: reduction of anxiety | 6.2 | 3.1 | 9.2 | 3.2 |
| Nostalgia appeal: recaptures old values | 1.3 | 2.1 | 2.0 | 0.6 |
| Sensual appeal: feels, looks good, delights senses | 6.6 | 9.4 | 11.4 | 1.8 |
| Exotic appeal: foreign, exotic, surreal | 1.4 | 1.4 | 1.8 | 1.0 |
| Offer appeal: special, limited time offer | 3.6 | 0.9 | 2.6 | 4.6 |
| Total | 100.0 | 100.0 | 100.0 | 100.0 |

senses, not sexual); and relief appeal. The cross-tabulation of the first ranked coding with period produces a significant $V$ of 0.38. The major differences occur with respect to economy/price appeal (3.8 per cent in PT, 7 per cent in ST), popular activities appeal (5 per cent in PT, 11.6 per cent in ST), sports star appeal (1.4 per cent in PT, 12.6 per cent in ST), relief appeal (9.2 per cent in PT, 3.2 per cent in ST), and sensual appeal (11.4 per cent in PT and 1.8 per cent in ST).

*Style*

Again, there could be two ranked codings for this variable.

**Table 8.** Style by period (per cent).

|                                              | 1st<br>(n = 1000) | 2nd | PT<br>(n = 500) | ST<br>(n = 500) |
|----------------------------------------------|------|------|------|------|
| None                                         | 0.0  | 22.2 | 0.0  | 0.0  |
| Excitement/movement                          | 2.7  | 6.0  | 1.8  | 3.6  |
| Song and dance                               | 1.7  | 0.5  | 2.8  | 0.6  |
| Interview                                    | 3.7  | 0.5  | 5.2  | 2.2  |
| Presenter speech/testimonial                 | 21.9 | 6.7  | 24.2 | 19.6 |
| Studio setting for product                   | 2.4  | 3.0  | 1.6  | 3.2  |
| Tells story/fictionalised                    | 24.8 | 7.3  | 30.6 | 19.0 |
| Generalised depiction of lifestyle           | 11.7 | 6.0  | 7.4  | 16.0 |
| Pleasing imagery/product shown in setting    | 4.4  | 6.4  | 1.6  | 7.2  |
| Before and after use of product              | 3.6  | 3.6  | 3.6  | 3.6  |
| Cartoons/graphics                            | 2.7  | 0.6  | 1.6  | 3.8  |
| Demonstration of product use                 | 8.2  | 9.8  | 5.6  | 10.8 |
| Escape/fantasy                               | 0.7  | 0.9  | 0.8  | 0.6  |
| Humour                                       | 5.4  | 14.0 | 3.4  | 7.4  |
| Sentimental                                  | 0.7  | 1.2  | 1.4  | 0.0  |
| Sensuous images: sexy, lusty, teasing        | 2.7  | 6.9  | 4.0  | 1.4  |
| Cute: babies, animals                        | 1.8  | 3.7  | 3.4  | 0.2  |
| Surreal: mysterious                          | 0.9  | 0.7  | 1.0  | 0.8  |
| Total                                        | 100.0| 100.0| 100.0| 100.0|

For the first choice, it can be seen that there is not such a wide distribution among the categories as there is for rhetorical form. The top four categories here make up 66.6 per cent of the cases. The most popular is the fictionalised story (the 'slice of life' advertisement) (24.8 per cent), direct speech to the camera by a presenter (21.9 per cent), the depiction of a lifestyle (11.7 per cent), and the demonstration of the product in use (8.2 per cent). The codings for the second ranking are much more evenly distributed and two additional categories stand out. These were demonstrations of the product in use (9.8 per cent) and humour (14 per cent). The latter finding especially suggests that humour is an important part of much advertising, although it is not the main stylistic device used in the construction of advertisements. Cross-tabulating the first ranked coding with period produces a significant $V$ of 0.34. The major differences occur with respect to song and dance (2.8 per cent in PT, 0.6 per cent in ST), the use of fictionalised narrative (30.6 per cent in PT, 19 per cent in ST), lifestyle presentation (7.4 per cent in PT, 16 per cent in ST), the use of pleasing imagery (1.6 per cent in PT, 7.2 per cent in ST), demonstration of the product in use (5.6 per cent in PT, 10.4 per cent in ST), the use of humour (3.4 per cent in PT, 7.4 per cent in ST), the use of sensuous/sexually titillating images (4 per cent in PT, 1.4 per cent in ST), and the utilisation of 'cute' techniques (such as babies or animals) (3.4 per cent in PT, 0.2 per cent in ST).

## Values

The measurement of the predominant values in advertising is the most interpretative and least straightforward of all the variables under consideration. To ease the coding, the values variable was divided into four sections: values connected to activities, personal themes, general dimensions, and product values (Table 9).

For activity values, the most frequent activity in the data is leisure activities that stress relaxation and sociability—rest and companionship. This is in contrast to the category leisure 2 which stresses active leisure pursuits. Cross-tabulation with period produces a $V$ of 0.24. The most significant difference is in the housework category (18.6 per cent in PT, 6.8 per cent in ST).

For personal values, there are four categories important in the overall data set: beauty, ruggedness, family and romance. Cross-tabulation with period (with zero data excluded) produces a very significant $V$ of 0.52. There are divergences in many of the categories: beauty (17.8 per cent in PT, 5.2 per cent in ST), individuality (3.4 per cent in PT, 1.8 per cent in ST), ruggedness (4.4 per cent in PT, 18.8 per cent in ST), family (18 per cent in PT, 5.2 per cent in ST), sexual/romantic love (11.6 per cent in PT, 6.4 per cent in ST), and fraternity (1.2 per cent in PT, 12.6 per cent in ST).

**Table 9.** Values by period (per cent)

| Activity | Total (n = 1000) | PT (n = 500) | ST (n = 500) |
|---|---|---|---|
| Leisure 1: social, relaxation | 30.4 | 26.0 | 34.8 |
| Leisure 2: active adventure, recreation, sport | 14.4 | 13.0 | 15.8 |
| Work waged | 4.4 | 5.2 | 3.6 |
| Housework/domestic maintenance | 12.7 | 18.6 | 6.8 |
| Absent | 38.1 | 37.2 | 39.0 |
| **Personal** | | | |
| Beauty: sophistication, grace, elegance | 11.5 | 17.8 | 5.2 |
| Individuality | 2.6 | 3.4 | 1.8 |
| Rugged: macho, masculine, tough | 11.6 | 4.4 | 18.8 |
| Family: family love, motherhood, tradition | 11.6 | 18.0 | 5.2 |
| Sexual/romantic love: male/female attraction | 9.0 | 11.6 | 6.4 |
| Sorority | 1.5 | 2.6 | 0.4 |
| Fraternity | 6.9 | 1.2 | 12.6 |
| Friendship: males/females, mixed, non-sexual | 6.2 | 5.4 | 7.0 |
| Sexuality: product will make you attractive | 5.1 | 5.8 | 4.4 |
| Absent | 34.0 | 29.8 | 38.2 |
| **General** | | | |
| Patriotism | 2.9 | 1.6 | 4.2 |
| Traditional values: nostalgia, historical | 3.5 | 3.8 | 3.2 |
| Toughness/ruggedness | 7.9 | 4.4 | 11.4 |
| Peace/security: reliable, tranquil, gentle | 15.7 | 16.4 | 15.0 |
| Unknown: mystical, elusive, surreal, mythical | 1.8 | 3.0 | 0.6 |
| Freedom/independence | 10.2 | 13.2 | 7.2 |
| Eccentricity: unconventional, unique, exotic | 7.5 | 6.2 | 8.8 |
| Happiness/fun | 12.2 | 14.4 | 10.0 |
| Excitement | 5.4 | 2.8 | 8.0 |
| Satisfaction | 16.3 | 19.4 | 13.2 |
| Status: desirable, classy, enviable | 3.7 | 3.6 | 3.8 |
| Achievement | 3.8 | 2.0 | 5.6 |
| Absent | 9.1 | 9.2 | 9.0 |
| **Product** | | | |
| Best: general, claim | 35.3 | 34.0 | 36.6 |
| Craft quality: workmanship | 8.0 | 7.6 | 8.4 |
| Improved | 4.1 | 5.2 | 3.0 |
| Healthy/natural | 14.4 | 19.2 | 9.6 |
| Utilitarian/convenient: practical, easy, fast | 8.7 | 8.4 | 9.0 |
| Normal/popular: everyone uses | 6.9 | 7.4 | 6.4 |
| Thrifty/value for money/offer | 12.2 | 8.4 | 16.0 |
| Faith in technology/medicine | 5.8 | 6.0 | 5.6 |
| Absent | 4.6 | 3.8 | 5.4 |

For general values, there are again four important categories: satisfaction, peace/security, happiness/fun, and freedom and independence. Cross-tabulation with period (excluding zero data) achieves a $V$ of 0.28, although there appear to be significant differences in many of the categories: patriotism, toughness, unknown/mystical/surreal, freedom/independence, excitement, satisfaction, and achievement.

For product values, one category is by far the most frequent—that the product is the best available (35.3 per cent). Cross-tabulation with period produces a $V$ of only 0.18. The only noteworthy differences are in the categories of healthy/natural and thrift/economy.

The values variable also involved a second round of coding in which each of the categories of the four sections were treated as a separate variable that could be marked either present or absent. This was undertaken because in many advertisements there are clearly multiple values being appealed to and used by the creators of advertisers. Table 10 shows those values that appeared in at least 20 per cent of the advertisements for each time period. The asterisk marks those that appeared on only one list and suggests that, viewed from this perspective, there are substantial differences in the values that are stressed in the advertisements to the different audiences.

**Table 10.** Values most prevalent in each period (per cent).

| PT | | ST | |
|---|---|---|---|
| Best | 42.4 | Best | 48.5 |
| Satisfaction | 33.2 | Leisure 1 | 38.5 |
| Leisure 1 | 30.0 | *Rugged | 28.5 |
| *Happiness/Fun | 25.0 | Peace/Security | 26.7 |
| *Beauty | 24.0 | *Leisure 2 | 22.4 |
| Peace/Security | 22.6 | *Toughness | 21.8 |
| *Family | 21.8 | *Male Fraternity | 21.2 |
| *Healthy | 21.0 | Satisfaction | 20.2 |
| *Housework | 20.6 | | |

*Audience code?*

The data examined in this section suggests that there are substantial differences in the message systems of prime-time and sports-time advertising. Before examining this a little more closely, this correlation needs to be firmly established for it is possible that, given the differences in the product types advertised in the two periods, all that is being picked up is divergences along product type and not audience (food and personal care are very important in PT while alcohol, transportation and personal care are important in ST). Indeed when the variables are cross-tabulated with product type (use-type) then some significant $V$s emerge: person appeal (0.23), dominant social groupings (0.29), interpersonal relations (0.30), activities (0.40), lifestyle (0.28), rhetorical form (0.34), style (0.30), activity values (0.48), personal values (0.32), general values (0.29), and product values (0.32). There are two standard ways in which to control for the influence of use-type on the cross-audience figures. First, the use-type can be held constant (comparing only one use-type in the two periods along the defined variables). This was done for all the use-types along the important variables and time period still appeared as an important explanatory dimension. Second, a subset of the total data set can be examined. The subset would include those use-types that are prevalent in both time periods (such as transportation (50 advertisements in PT, 158 in ST), personal care (132 in PT, 101 in ST), household (58 in PT, 34 in ST), and leisure technology (19 in PT, 42 in ST)). This totalled 593 advertisements (259 in PT and 334 in ST). Again the correlation figures for the subset of the data remained quite constant along the dimension of period (audience). I can say now, with some considerable confidence, that the differences that can be seen between periods do actually measure period differences and not some other dimension that has crept into the correlation.

## Advertising and the fetishism of commodities

In Chapter 2 I explored at length the various uses to which the concept of 'fetishism' has been put. In this section I will apply the theoretical framework developed there in an empirical study of television and magazine advertising.

## Advertising and product information

The argument in Chapter 2 started off with the notion of 'information'. Here I wish to measure what precise information is communicated about product *characteristics*. Table 11 is my operationalisation and coding of themes in advertising connected to product characteristics. Each of the categories was treated as a separate variable and could be marked either absent or present.

**Table 11.**   Product information and characteristics (per cent)

| | |
|---|---|
| Shows/describes use-value: what it does | 43.1 |
| Shows how to use | 19.7 |
| Shows/describes objective product characteristics: sketchy, incomplete | 31.7 |
| Shows/describes objective product characteristics: detailed, complete | 6.2 |
| Scientific tests and proof of product performance | 9.4 |
| Subjective evaluation: great, good, best | 71.7 |
| Confidence in product: trust, reliable, long-lasting | 17.9 |
| Shows/describes production/history of product | 5.3 |
| Comparison with other products: general, no brands named | 22.9 |
| Comparison with other products: specific, brands named | 6.9 |
| Comparison: claimed to be better | 19.3 |
| Comparison: shown/demonstrated to be better | 10.0 |
| Personalisation: made just for you | 8.3 |
| Value for money/price | 12.3 |
| Reference to consumer, public or industry, joint interest and responsibility | 1.0 |
| Disclaimers/warnings | 13.6 |
| Where available/details of sale offer | 9.0 |

If this is the 'hard' information by which we are supposed to judge products prior to purchase, then one must conclude that the North American public is extremely ill-informed. The two categories that measure this hard information are those for 'objective-sketchy' and 'objective-detailed'. In 31.7 per cent of advertisements the 'objective-sketchy' category was marked as present. A defender of advertising might claim from these figures that almost one-third of the sample gives objective product information. However, this category was marked as present if *any* objective information was given at all (for example, the mention of a car being four-wheel drive, or a toothpaste containing fluoride). Any more precise information was recorded in the 'objective-detailed' category (6.2 per cent). If information about products is transmitted, it is not of the detailed variety. What are communicated are a great deal (71.7 per cent) of subjective claims (great, best, reliable, and so on) based largely on claimed but un-demonstrated superiority over rival, unnamed brands.

Also in Chapter 2, I examined Marx's notion of the 'fetishism of commodities', which in part consisted of the odd propensity among social commentators of his day to regard the domain of material production as somehow being detached from direct human control, subsisting autonom-ously as it were, almost as if the economy possessed a 'life of its own'. In this process, the real meaning of products (their history and production as social objects) is emptied out of them. As such I was interested in seeing to what extent advertising attempted to give back some of this history which is stripped from commodities. Does advertising give not only 'objective' information about product characteristics, but also the history of the social relations of their production? Judging from the data (Table 11) it seems not to be the case. One category was constructed to measure the history/production of products. The coding here was extremely generous and even the skimpiest information (for example, 'America's king of beers since 1883') justified its inclusion within this category. Only 5.3 per cent of the total sample mentioned anything at all about the production or history of the product. Those few advertisements that did gave only the most superficial and ideological of such information. TV advertising tells us very little about how products are produced. Commodities appear 'as autonomous figures endowed with a life of their own'.

## Fetishism, magic and advertising

A major element of the coding protocol was to operationalise the concept of fetishism as it had been used in the traditions of Marxism, early anthropological theory and Freudian psychoanalysis. As we have seen, for Marx fetishism consisted in commodities appearing autonomous and interacting with humans and other commodities as if they possessed life. Nineteenth-century anthropological literature described the religious practices of early societies (primarily in Africa) in these terms. Here material objects could capture natural forces, heal and cure sickness, bring happiness to their possessor, be used for defensive purposes to ward off evil consequences, induce romantic/erotic affection; and in addition they could be viewed as possessing animate life in and of themselves. Then in the twentieth century Freudian psychoanalytic theory used fetishism as a clinical term to describe those situations where the sexual act is impossible to complete except in the presence of a particular, non-sexual object. Here the function of the fetish is the capacity to change social relations, to make social relations possible, or to create the conditions for the possible consummation of social (sexual) relations.

In the last-mentioned function the object is transposed from being merely an adjunct of social relations to playing a central role, so that it defines the essence of the social relations of which it is a part. In the psychoanalytic model the fetish does not take the place of the love object; rather, it is a substitute for the mother's lost phallus, which eases the castration anxiety of the male and makes it possible for him to accept the (non-phallic) reality of the female sex partner. The object itself does not *do* anything. Its vital function is constituted solely by its *meaning*.

In operationalising the concept of fetishism I have created analytical categories that portray *all* the different relationships of people and things presented in advertising, including the connotations to be found in the various fetishism literatures.

1.  Personification of product: human qualities attributed to product (Marxism/anthropology).
2.  Describes finished state/job done efficiently: the object performs a task without effect on human emotions or relations (no fetishism).
3.  Emotional response based on product *directly*: emotional reaction is the effect of mere possession or sighting of

the object, irrespective of its use (anthropology/psychoanalytic).

4. Emotional response based on product *use*: use of the product elicits emotional reaction (anthropology).

5. Self-transformation: the product changes the physical constitution of people, for example either making them more attractive or curing them of sickness (anthropology).

6. Black magic I: consequences not of use/consequences of use—changes relations: use of the product changes social relations, such that before its use relations were incomplete and with its use they are complete. The before and after advertisement (anthropology/psychoanalytic).

7. Job done efficiently: consequences not of use/consequences of use—difference between products where social relations are *not* involved: the product performs better than another without effect on social relations (no fetishism).

8. Black magic II: effects of product *use* mediate relations; while the product may not be present in the social scene depicted directly, it is only its use that makes the scene possible. If the product had not been used, the relations depicted would not be possible or would be incomplete (anthropology/psychoanalytic).

9. Product *mediates* relations with others: the product does not *do* anything—its mere presence defines the scene as such. Without it the scene would still be possible, but it would be incomplete, less satisfying, and less meaningful. The lifestyle advertisement (psychoanalytic).

10. White magic: Product captures natural forces (anthropology).

Each of these is treated as a separate variable and is either present or absent. Table 12 presents the results of the coding.

Taking the data set as a composite, the most frequent categories are emotional response based on product use (32.4 per cent) and product mediating relations with others (21 per cent). The next two most important categories are the product producing physical changes in persons (16.8 per cent) and

**Table 12.**   Fetishism by period (per cent)

|  | Total (*n* = 1000) | PT (*n* = 500) | ST (*n* = 500) |
|---|---|---|---|
| Personification | 5.7 | 6.0 | 5.4 |
| Job done efficiently | 15.0 | 8.9 | 21.2 |
| Emotional response/direct | 6.9 | 8.3 | 5.6 |
| Emotional response/use | 32.4 | 39.3 | 25.9 |
| Self-transformation | 16.8 | 24.8 | 9.0 |
| Black magic I: consequences of use/not of use | 4.6 | 4.0 | 5.2 |
| Job done efficiently: consequences of use/not of use | 7.3 | 10.7 | 4.0 |
| Black magic II: effects of products use mediate relations | 8.4 | 10.3 | 6.4 |
| Product mediates relations with others | 21.0 | 13.3 | 28.9 |
| White magic | 7.4 | 9.3 | 5.6 |

showing a job efficiently accomplished (15 per cent). All other categories appear in under 10 per cent of advertisements.

Once period (audience) is introduced, significant differences emerge between the two groups. For a female audience the two most important categories are the elicitation of an emotional response based upon product use (39 per cent) and product as producing physical changes in persons (24 per cent). For a male audience the three most important categories are product mediating relations with others (28.9 per cent), emotional response to product use (25.9 per cent) and job being efficiently performed (21.2 per cent).

The study being reported here did not have an historical dimension to it. However, a study conducted by Steve Kline and Bill Leiss (reported in *SCA*) using magazine advertisements did include an historical perspective, and included categories that were very close to the ones that I used for fetishism. Figures 1 and 2 divide the fetish categories into two groups to clarify the presentation of historical developments. These groups correspond *roughly* to a 'magical/rational' distinction. Four of the eight variables developed for the magazine study are grouped under the designation 'magical fetishism': personification, black magic, white magic, self-transformation. Advertising content was coded in these categories for those instances where the product itself is

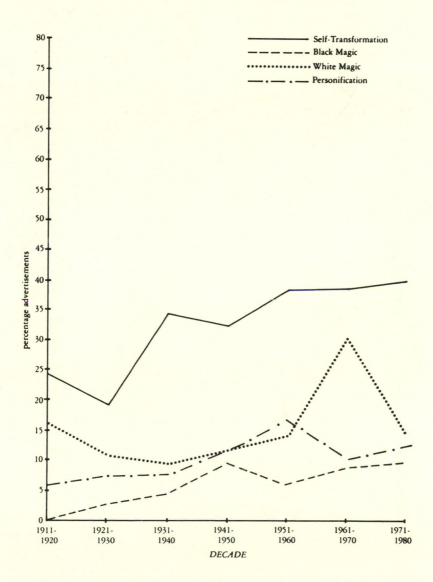

**Figure 1**.   'Magical' fetishism by decade
*Source*: Jhally *et al.* (1985)

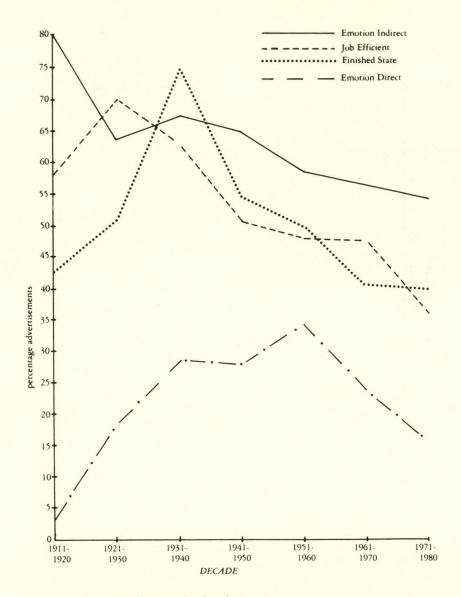

**Figure 2**.   'Rational fetishism by decade
         *Source*: as Figure 1

shown as exerting or representing some kind of autonomous power *vis-à-vis* human agents, or as embodying such powers. In most instances of this type the nature and origins of these powers are mysterious. The remaining four variables are together called 'rational fetishism', for although the advertisement content also shows here the effects of owning or using the product on human actions and emotions, these effects either are explained in the text, show familiar events or are otherwise unambiguous so far as their source is concerned. Figure 1 includes the 'magical' categories while Figure 2 deals with the 'rational' categories. The data shows that there has been much change during this century in how the relations of persons and things have been portrayed by advertising.

At a general level the data shows that there has been an overall decline in the rational categories and an increase in the magical categories. The movement of the two groups is in opposite directions. The most significant rise has been for the category of self-transformation.

Figure 3 presents the historical magazine data from the perspective of audience segmentation. The Kline and Leiss study was composed of advertisements from *McLean's* (male audience) and from *Chatelaine* (female audience). Three categories of 'magical' fetishism (black magic, white magic, self-transformation) are traced for the two magazines. There is a fascinating divergence for all three categories. The messages aimed at the female audience (*Chatelaine*) stress the three themes much more than those directed at the male audience (*McLean's*), although there is an increasing convergence in recent years.

Table 13 shows the cross-tabulation (for the TV data) of fetishism with product-type. This indicates that for contemporary TV advertising, alcohol is primarily associated with the product-mediating relations (lifestyle advertising). Food, clothing, pets and leisure technology bring emotional gratification. Household goods are concerned with utility, while personal care products and drugs deal with physical changes as a result of use.

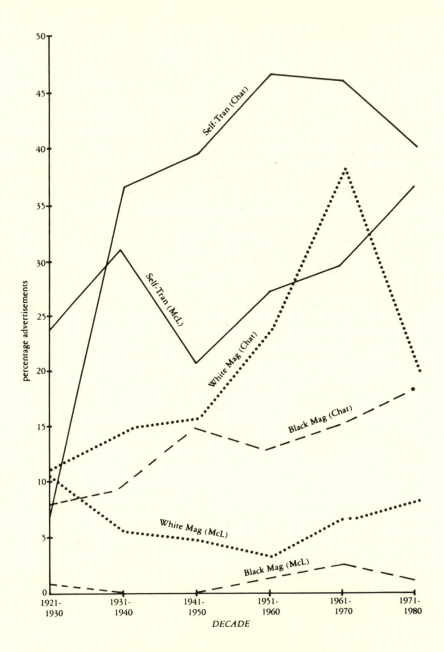

**Figure 3**.    'Magical' fetishism by magazine by decade.

**Table 13.** Fetishism by use-type.

| | Alcohol | Clothing | Food | Transport | Personal Care | House | Drugs | Pets | Leisure Tech | Other |
|---|---|---|---|---|---|---|---|---|---|---|
| Personification | 1 | 7 | 3 | 19 | 15 | 6 | 1 | 0 | 0 | 0 |
| Job efficient | 0 | 1 | 1 | 50 | 29 | 40 | 3 | 0 | 21 | 5 |
| Emotion/direct | 5 | 7 | 4 | 23 | 14 | 4 | 8 | 2 | 1 | 1 |
| Emotion/use | 35 | 79 | 17 | 37 | 61 | 35 | 6 | 8 | 30 | 16 |
| Self-transformation | 0 | 8 | 1 | 0 | 102 | 1 | 46 | 0 | 0 | 0 |
| Black magic I | 11 | 8 | 2 | 1 | 19 | 3 | 0 | 0 | 1 | 1 |
| Job efficient | 2 | 10 | 5 | 11 | 22 | 23 | 0 | 0 | 0 | 0 |
| Black magic II | 1 | 4 | 4 | 2 | 60 | 2 | 6 | 0 | 4 | 1 |
| Mediates relations | 111 | 48 | 6 | 13 | 7 | 7 | 4 | 1 | 12 | 1 |
| White magic | 9 | 12 | 2 | 8 | 18 | 9 | 0 | 2 | 11 | 3 |

## Conclusion: fetish and code

The data reported in this chapter indicate that there is no one relation of people to things in advertising or one message that is communicated through advertising. Different products and different audiences reveal divergent structures in the message systems of which they are a part. Psychological, physical, and social dimensions are all present and vary in importance between audiences and use-types. Indeed there are often multiple relations of people and products in a single advertisement: for instance, 392 of the advertisements in my television sample had more than one coding for the fetish categories. The historical analysis shows that particular forms of fetishism that arise at a particular time do not disappear, but rather are segregated as a mode of representation for particular products or audience segments: the self-transformation advertisement is used primarily in cosmetic commercials aimed at a female audience, while the lifestyle advertisements are particularly noticeable in alcohol and cigarette advertising. The point here is that it is difficult to speak of a single relationship to objects, at least as depicted in advertising. In the contemporary marketplace the person–object relation is articulated psychologically, physically, and socially. Some goods seem to serve primarily for display and social judgement, some for personal enhancement, some for locating us in the nexus of group relations, and some just for simple utility in everyday routines.

I do not want to give the impression though that there is no coherence to the world of advertising. Whilst not constructed simply, it is structured along some very definite lines, particularly audience codes. The first section of this chapter looked at the detailed separation of audiences from one another along the dimension of advertising message. I will give here a brief synopsis of what the *differences* between the prime-time code and the sports-time code consist of. Prime-time advertising focuses more on ordinary persons as the prototypical consumers, with family and parental relations playing an important part. Also romantic love and affection is more important. In prime-time the dominant groupings that are shown focus around young people (adults) engaged in 'fun' activities and orientated towards a middle-class lifestyle. The dominant values stressed are those concerned with individual physical beauty, the family and romantic love. In terms of rhetorical form and style prime-time advertising uses more arguments to do with the economy of products, their ability to provide relief and their ability to provide sensual pleasure. Stylistically, there is more reliance on fictionalised narrative and sensuous or sexually titillating images to communicate information about products and people.

Sports-time advertising relies heavily on the appearances of famous people associated with products and on notions of collectivity and friendship rather than family and romance. It is group activities around which images of products cohere. Especially visible in opposition to prime-time advertisements is the portrayal of competitive/teasing relations within the group and the stress on healthy/athletic types of activity. Male-orientated advertising, it seems, draws more on the past and idealised images of a traditional/rural lifestyle. The important values are those of ruggedness and fraternity. In terms of rhetorical form and style, sports-time advertising uses many more arguments based upon the association of products with popular group activities and with famous sports stars. Pleasing physical settings and the presentation of a product as part of a lifestyle are used more than in prime-time.

In terms of the precise measurement of fetishism, there are significant differences between the two audience codes. In prime-time advertising the commodity is used in a more 'magical' way to affect humans directly, while in sports-time advertising it plays a role which is more rational, magical and indicative of images of desired lifestyles.

If, following Marx, we say that commodity fetishism is present when goods are seen as autonomous, as entering into relations with each other, and as appearing in 'fantastic forms' in their relations with humans, then we can conclude from the data analysis that fetishism is an aspect of *both* production and consumption. Commodities appear in the marketplace as miraculous products of an invisible process of production and then enter into unique and changing relations with each other, jostling for position to satisfy the unique and changing needs of the consumer. In some instances, products explicitly take on animate features. In addition, the object world interacts with the human world at the most fundamental of levels: it performs magical feats of transformation and bewitchment, brings instant happiness and gratification, captures the forces of nature, and holds within itself the essence of important social relationships (in fact, it substitutes for those relations). In the interaction of humans and products as portrayed in advertising we can identify not only the fetishism described by Marx, but also the fetishism described in anthropology and psychoanalysis.

# 6 Conclusion: advertising, religion and the mediation of meaning

Let us summarise the argument thus far. Chapter 1 attempted to lay the groundwork for a proper materialist understanding of advertising by reviewing the major perspectives advanced concerning its social role and impact. Critics of advertising, while asking all the pertinent questions, were unable to formulate an adequate position on the issue of symbolism. In contrast, the defenders of advertising recognised the centrality of symbolism for human needing, but were unable to comprehend both its wider context and advertising's social effects. Other writers such as Hirsch, Scitovsky and Leiss broadened the framework of debate by not looking directly at advertising but rather by placing the relation of use and symbol at the centre of the relation between people and things and the process of satisfaction, while at the same time examining the effect that the wider (market) context has on that mediation. I ended with the conclusion that to understand the object world (and thus advertising) we need properly to conceptualise the relationship between the single object and its uses and the system of objects and exchange of which it is a part. An adequate understanding of this relation between use-value and exchange-value is necessary for grasping both the relation between people and things and the place of advertising within this complex. Chapter 2 provided the basis for this type of analysis by defending Marx's concept of the 'fetishism of commodities' and especially his notion of use-value against the critiques of writers such as Sahlins and Baudrillard. I concluded by arguing that the system of capitalist production empties commodities of their real meaning and the role of advertising is to insert meaning into this hollow shell. In this way use-value is subsumed by exchange-value. The concept of fetishism was further developed by tracing its genealogy in the anthropological and psychological literature, especially in terms of identifying the problematic relations between persons and things. Chapter 3 focused on the political economy of commercial broadcasting and the manner in which the form and content of the advertisements is constrained by this material context such that the derivation of meaning by the audience from the advertisement message is dominated by the exchange-value of that time of watching. Chapter 4 developed the notion of codes as flowing from the valorisation of time and Chapter 5 reported the results of an empirical project that measured the concepts of code and fetishism and concluded that both can be identified in television advertising.


## Watching and compulsion

To complete the logic of the argument developed thus far in this book I need to pick up the discussion at the point reached at the end of Chapter 3 where I claimed that television watching was a form of labour, an extension of the logic of industrial production relations. This was not offered as an analogy or a metaphor to describe watching activity. What I contend is that the valorisation of watching activity is a *real* extension of the domain of capital. The *logic* of the production of surplus value is the same as in the factory. When the watching activity of audience is valorised, watchers labour for capital to the same extent as do wage labourers in a factory. This issue is the key to the whole critical argument, and indeed the most serious objections to it have come from those who regard themselves as critical thinkers. The most fundamental objection to this view has focused on a key point to do with the basic characteristics of labour in a capitalist economy. Both Michael Lebowitz (1984) and Barry Truchill (1984) focus on the issue of the *compulsive* character of watching activity. While the exploitation of wage labour is based on the fact that the working class is compelled to sell its labour-power to capital in order to survive materially (because it is 'free' to do nothing else), it seems that the audience is under no such compulsion to watch or to sell its watching-power. Consumers as watchers are free simply to stop watching, to turn off the set and so cease the valorisation of their time. In essence, watching or not watching appears as a *free* activity. For example, Barry Truchill (1984, p. 60) writes along these lines:

Can we really regard the 'viewing day' as analogous to the working day? Workers *must* enter into a wage relation with capitalists in order to maintain subsistence. Are audiences obligated to view programming in the same way, or is viewing a form of compulsion that viewers are free to modify to a certain degree as they see fit?

While in labouring for capital in the factory the working class reproduces *itself* as well as capital, in its watching-activity the audience seems only to reproduce *capital*. Without the notion of compulsion the valorisation of the watching time seems not to be based on exploitation but on exchange (unequal, to be sure). The issue to be addressed is the extent to which this watching is compelled, or in other words, the extent to which this is *alienated* activity.

### Initial evidence

A number of observers have noted that there is something 'peculiar' about television viewing. American communication theorist George Gerbner comments that whereas consumers carefully choose what book or magazine they read or which movie they go to, viewers of TV rarely tune in for a particular programme. Instead they watch the *medium*, almost ritualistically, exposing themselves to messages they do not specifically select:

The total viewing audience is fairly stable regardless of what is on. Individual tastes and program preferences are less important in determining viewing patterns than is the time a program is on. The nearly universal, non-selective and habitual use of television fits the ritualistic pattern of its programming. You watch television as you might attend a church service, except that most people watch television more religiously (in Reel 1978, p. 14).

Indeed, a long-term review of viewing habits reveals that in the period 1953–72, for any one month in any year, the percentage of sets that were in use during prime-time remained almost constant, 'regardless of week or year or whatever was on the air' (Reel 1978, p. 14). Whether it was new shows or repeats, viewers watched in the same numbers. Further the A.C. Nielsen Television Index reports extremely stable patterns of viewing. The significant variables do not seem to be programme quality and content but the time of the day and the time of the year. For example, the most viewing takes place during prime-time in the winter months (Nielsen 1983, p. 5).

While theorists of television have been slow to recognise the importance of this stability, its significance has not been lost on those who shape the television schedule—the network executives. Their programming strategy is based on two loosely connected 'theories' of viewing behaviour. The first is that of *audience flow*, which holds that once an audience starts to watch a particular channel they will continue to watch past the initial programme unless there is some special reason to switch to another. A network vice-president responsible for audience studies says:

I wish that everyone watched the program that most appealed to them from among the competing programs; it would make my job much easier. Unfortunately that is not the way it works; the viewing habits of a large portion of the audience—at least the audience that Nielsen measures—*is governed more by the laws of inertia than by free choice*. Unless they have a very definite reason to switch, like a ball game, they continue to watch the programs on the channel they are tuned in to (Epstein 1979, p. 93, emphasis added).

Once the network has an audience, they can be fairly confident of hanging on to it. This audience flow theory also accounts for why it is the positioning of the programme with regard to other programmes that plays a large part in determining its audience size and why network executives are constantly talking in terms of programming schedules rather than individual programmes.

The second related theory of watching behaviour on which scheduling is based has been termed by ex-network programmer Paul Klein the 'Theory of the Least Objectionable Programme' (LOP). Noting the amazingly constant size of the viewing audience regardless of programme quality, he suggests that people watch TV 'because it's there'. The audience watches one show rather than another because it

can be endured with the least amount of pain and suffering. You view television irrespective of the content of the program watched. And because the programs are designed to appeal to the greatest number of people—rich and poor, smart and stupid, tall and short, wild and tame—you're probably watching something that is not your taste. *Nevertheless, you take what is fed to you because you are compelled to exercise the medium* . . . The best network programmers understand this. They are not stupid. They like most of the stuff they put on about as much as you do. But they also know that a program doesn't have to be 'good'. It only has to be less objectionable than whatever the hell the other guys throw against it (Reel 1979, p. 15, emphasis added).

Note the terms the executives use to describe this watching: 'inertia rather than free choice'; 'compelled to exercise the medium'; 'least amount of pain and suffering'. This seems to be not the language associated with free choice and democracy, but rather that of habituation and addiction.

### Addiction and alienation

The most popular way of describing the immense amount of television watching is to refer to it as an 'addiction', wherein the viewer is 'hooked' on watching; but the full (and serious) implications of this characterisation are rarely drawn out. Marie Winn, in her book *The Plug-In Drug* (1977), is an exception. She notes that the discussion of television watching usually concentrates on the content of the medium rather than the experience of the medium itself. She says: 'It is easy to overlook a deceptively simple fact; one is always *watching television* when one is watching television rather than having any other experience' (Winn 1979, p. 3). She provides much evidence for the view that the problem needs to be posed in terms of the medium itself.

In what follows I give full illustrations of this addiction, because it is important to establish watching as something other than a totally free activity—in fact as an activity that could be *alienated* from the agent. The following accounts point to the addictive nature of TV watching.

College English professor:

I find television almost irresistable. When the set is on, I cannot ignore it. I can't turn it off. I feel sapped, will-less, enervated. As I reach out to turn off the set, the strength goes out of my arms. So I sit there for hours and hours (Winn 1977, p. 21).

Handbag repair shop owner:

I'd get on the subway from work with the newspaper and immediately turn to the TV page to plan out my evening's watching. I'd come home, wash, change my clothes, and tell my wife to start the machine so it would be warmed up. And then we'd watch TV for the rest of the evening. We'd eat our dinner in the living room while watching, and we'd only talk once in a while, during the ads, if at all. I'd watch anything, good, bad or indifferent . . . All the while we were watching I'd feel terribly angry at myself for wasting all that time watching junk. I could never go to sleep until at least the eleven o'clock news, and then sometimes I'd still stay up for the late-night talk show. I had a feeling that I HAD to watch the news programs, that I HAD to know what was happening . . . I only had time for television. We'd take the telephone off the hook while watching so we wouldn't be interrupted. We like classical music but we never listened to any, never (Winn 1977, p. 23).

Lawyer:

I watch TV the way an alcoholic drinks. If I come home and sit in front of the TV, I'll watch any program at all, even if there's nothing on that appeals to me. Then the next thing I know is that it's eleven o'clock and I'm watching the Johnny Carson show, and I'll realize I've spent the whole evening watching TV. What's more, I can't stand Johnny Carson. But I'll sit there watching him. I'm addicted to TV, when it's there, and I'm not happy about the addiction. I'll sit there getting madder and madder at myself for watching, but still I'll sit there. I can't turn it off (Winn 1977, p. 24).

Housewife:

Sometimes a friend will come over while I'm watching TV. I'll say, 'wait a second, just let me finish watching this', and then I'll feel bad about that, letting the machine take precedence over people. And I'll do that for the stupidest programs, just because I *have* to watch somehow.

The following are excerpts from interviews conducted by Jerry Mander (1978): 'I feel hypnotised when I watch television'; 'Television is an addiction and I'm an addict'; 'If a television is on I just can't keep my eyes off it'; 'I feel mesmerised by it'. In a 1972 article, psychologist Donald Kaplan describes several cases of what he calls 'symptomatic television watching' where the patient, usually alone, watches TV (though no particular programmes) for hours on end, against their conscious will:

His watching overrides his intention to perform even ordinary actions such as answering mail and returning phone calls. It can override his intention to go to sleep at a particular hour. There is no internal motive strong enough to interrupt the behaviour. Only external circumstances may interrupt it—a standing appointment, an incoming phone call, etc. Otherwise the behaviour terminates in sleep.

While the issue of 'addiction' in adults is usually treated in a jocular fashion, as if there were no *real* problem, the matter appears more serious when the subjects of the addiction are children.

My ten-year-old is as hooked on TV as an alcoholic is hooked on drink. He tries to strike desperate bargains: 'If you let me watch just ten more minutes, I won't watch at all tomorrow', he says. It's pathetic. It scares me.

We were in Israel last summer where the TV stations sign off for the night at about ten. Well my son would turn on the set and watch the Arabic stations that were still on, even though he couldn't understand a word, just because he had to watch something.

We used to have very bad reception before we got on Cable TV. I'd come into the room and see my eight-year-old watching this terrible, blurry picture and I'd say, 'Heavens, how can you see? Let me try to fix it,' and he'd get frantic and scream, 'Don't touch it!' It really worried me, that he wanted to watch so badly that he was even willing to watch a completely blurred image (Winn 1977, p. 23).

Perhaps the most significant observation is that attributed to Kai, Jerry Mander's nine-year-old son: 'I don't want to watch television as much as I do, but I can't help it. *It makes me watch it.*'

There is, then, significant evidence that this watching activity is less than free, that it is somehow out of our control. Further, it is not as if there were no recognition of the harmful effects of this watching—people *know* what is happening to them.

Film-maker:

I remember when we first got the set I'd watch for hours and hours, whenever I could, and I remember that feeling of tiredness and anxiety that always followed those orgies, a sense of time terribly wasted. It was like eating cotton candy; television promised so much richness, I couldn't wait for it, and then it just evaporated into air. I remember feeling terribly drained after watching for a long time (Winn 1977, p. 22).

Nursery School Teacher:

I remember bingeing on television when I was a child and having that vapid feeling after watching hours of TV. I'd look forward to watching whenever I could, but it didn't give back a real feeling of pleasure. It was like no orgasm, no catharsis, very frustrating. Television just wasn't giving me the promised satisfaction, and yet I kept on watching. It filled some sort of need, or had to do with an inability to get something started (Winn 1977, p. 22).

Eighteen-year-old Yale student

If I had spent at the piano the hours I have on television, on all those afternoons I came home from school, I would be an accomplished pianist now. Or if I'd danced, or read, or painted . . . *But I turned on the set instead*, every day, almost every year, and sank into an old green easy chair, smothered in quilts, with a bag of Fritos beside me and a glass of milk to wash them down, facing life and death with Dr Kildare . . . Looking back over all those afternoons, I try to convince myself that they weren't wasted . . . Five thousand hours of my life have gone into this box (Kaplan 1972, p. 27).

Both Kaplan and Winn remark that people talk about their television 'habits' almost apologetically. They feel guilty because they know it to be an unproductive activity which they should not engage in and yet they are irresistibly drawn towards it. Sahin and Robinson (1981) report that television watching does not rate very high as an enjoyable way of spending time and that it is the daily activity most likely to be given up if something important comes up. Further, the results from the experiments that ask families to give up television indicate that subjects report many beneficial effects of the absence of television—although invariably families wind up going back to it once the experiments are concluded (Winn 1977, pp. 189–202).

Certainly, I would not want to claim that the anecdotal evidence presented in this section amounts to a proof of the addictive nature of television; but in the absence of other more reliable and systematic data it points to an important aspect of watching-activity. I think that many readers would recognise *themselves* in some of these statements. Further confirmation can be gained from looking at the viewing habits of the total population of watchers. Nielsen (1983) estimates that the average *household* viewing figure is six hours four minutes per day, while the average viewing of individuals has been estimated to be about four hours per day. Just the sheer amount of time spent watching by the population as a whole perhaps explains why people regard themselves as addicted and provides some warrant for generalising on the basis of the above statements.

What emerges from these anecdotal reports is a picture of an activity in which people overindulge, which they sense is beyond their control and which affords them no real sense of satisfaction. The activity seems almost to stand in a hostile relationship to the individual's self-perceived preferences. The activity seems to be *alienated* from the watchers themselves.

Those who regard this activity as a form of addiction and alienation (Mander, Winn, Kaplan and many viewers themselves) are largely in agreement as to its source—the *technology* of television. For Mander the problems are inherent in television, and—seeing no way to reform it—he advocates *elimination* of the technology altogether. Marie Winn argues that the nature of the television image eliminates peripheral viewing and removes distractions to 'abnormally heighten our attention to the televisual image'. In addition, because the television image is an electronic image it is constantly moving, even as it depicts stationary objects; the human eye is drawn to fixate more strongly on moving than on stationary objects. Another feature of the electronic image is that it is difficult for the eye to focus properly on it. The sensory confusion this defocusing causes is similar to that which accompanies various fantasy and day dreaming states and 'may well be a reason for the trancelike nature of so many viewers' television experience, and may help to explain why the television image has so strong and hypnotic a fascination... All these perceptual anomalies may conspire to fascinate the viewer and glue him to the television set' (Winn 1978, p. 55). The explanations posited by Mander and Winn point to the source of the addiction in the technology itself and tend to make a 'fetish' of it: 'It makes me watch it.' While there is a hint of truth in this idea, I think that we have to search much deeper for the source of the compulsion.

## The colonisation of time

It has long been recognised that much of what passes for free time in capitalist societies is not in fact free at all. Henri Lefebvre (1971) notes that within the realm of non-work time there are certain activities that must be performed and which fall under the heading of *compulsive time* (such as transportation to work, sleeping, formal occasions). Similarly, Staffan Linder (1975) refers to non-work time as 'harried'. Marxists, too, recognise that the reproduction of labour-power is carried on during non-work time and occupies significant amounts of that time (see, for example, Smythe 1977). The contrast between work-time and non-work time does not necessarily involve an oppositional (compelled versus free) component.

The analysis of how this non-work time is utilised is now being undertaken by social scientists. The multinational study edited by Szalai (1972) entitled *The Use of Time* is a good and comprehensive example of the work carried out in this field.

For the United States in particular, John Robinson has been at the leading edge of the research concerning time allocation. In his 1977 study *How Americans Use Time* he, too, divides up non-work time into its obligatory and free-time spheres. Obligatory activities include (in addition to work) the categories of housework, child care, personal needs and travel. All these represent activities that 'have to be done'. Contrasted to these are activities classified as 'free time', including discretionary activities (adult education, religion, boy scouts, union activity); mass media usage (broadcasting, movies, newspapers and magazines); and socialisation and recreation (visiting and conversations, sports and hobbies, relaxation, organised forms of entertainment). What is interesting here for my purposes is the manner in which the introduction of television after 1945 significantly affected the allocation of this free time.

Noting that the time freed from direct waged work has generally increased since the turn of the century, Robinson is concerned with how that free time was used, because 'the observed regularities of time use not only make up the structure of daily life, but often become the very contents of it by setting priorities, imposing constraints, and establishing guiding patterns in the use of the precious personal and social resources of free time' (Sahin and Robinson 1981, p. 87). By far the major 'coloniser' of free time has been television, which has usurped time spent previously on other forms of mass media, as well as free time and obligatory activities. In the decade 1965–75 the amount of 'free time' (as opposed to work time and obligatory time), increased for all sections of the population by approximately thirty-seven minutes per day. Practically the entire increase in free time was devoted to television viewing. Because there is a finite amount of time in any period, time is a 'zero-sum' phenomenon—the more time spent on one activity, the less can be spent on others. While TV is negatively correlated with work, it is negatively correlated in a much stronger sense with other free-time activities, especially socialising, going to bars and parties, free-time travel and religion (activities that occur away from the house). As reported previously, people on the whole do not find TV viewing to be immensely satisfying and it is the first activity to be given up if anything else should appear:

What emerges is a picture of an activity that is not seen as particularly enjoyable or necessary to one's daily life. If more important activities arise, it is easily the first activity to be sacrificed. *Once people are in their homes however, the set appears to have an irresistable hold on their time* . . . By people's own definition, television time is not an activity which brings particular satisfactions or significance, especially in contrast to most person-to-person encounters that occur in free time. Yet it is this very social life that people may increasingly be sacrificing for their increased time spent viewing (Sahin and Robinson 1981, p. 93).

Programming policy is based upon optimising the time spent viewing by each individual and has led to the concern with programme flow on the part of broadcasters (as outlined above). The basis of this action is of course the sale of audience time to advertisers:

In essence then, the colonisation of free time by television in the United States can be seen as another manifestation of the historical process in which free time has been turned into a commodity and re-expropriated by the forces in control of the realm of necessity (Sahin and Robinson 1980, p. 94).

While Sahin and Robinson are extremely useful in showing the expansion of watching activity within the context of total time use, they do not address the question of *why* the pattern of TV viewing should have gone in this direction—although Robinson (1977) provides a clue to this by reporting that income is negatively correlated with watching (those who earn less watch more). This is reflected also in the Nielsen data for 1982 which shows that while higher-income households do not view much less than lower income (those on $10,000–$15,000 watch 50–58 hours per week, while those with earnings greater than $30,000 watch 47–50 hours per week), much of this higher-income viewing is directed towards Pay-TV rather than the basic cable subscription or over-the-air broadcasting. Without Pay-TV the higher-income viewing figures would be much lower. There is thus a *class* dimension to watching, to the cultural consumption of meaning.

Nicolas Garnham (1983, p. 17) argues that there is a material basis to this 'class determination of cultural consumption' in terms of unequal access to time and money:

Members of lower socio-economic groups generally work longer hours in more tiring conditions than those higher on the social scale. In addition, consumption of cultural goods and participation in cultural practices increases in range and amount over virtually the whole spectrum of activities, except TV viewing, as income rises . . . The higher level of TV consumption among the poorer sections of the community is attributable to the higher proportion of their total discretionary expenditure tied up in the relatively fixed investment in the TV set and license. Once this investment is made, subsequent consumption is virtually free, making them a captive audience.

Lower income audiences thus do not have the same opportunities for cultural consumption as do those with higher incomes. Television offers them the most efficient investment over a long period of time for cultural consumption.

Introducing this class and material determination into the discussion also allows us to integrate recent developments in the 'economy of meaning' of advanced capitalism within the theme of valorisation and compulsion: for example, the movement in media usage from the consumption of 'free' (advertising-supported) television to the consumption of information *commodities* themselves (VCRs, home movies, Pay-TV, and so on). It seems that there is a movement here whereby the constitution of meaning for *self* will subsume the constitution of meaning for *capital*. How can this development be integrated into my analysis of the history of absolute and relative surplus-value in watching?

It is true that purchasing information commodities provides partial freedom from working at watching, partial freedom from the watching time in which we are producing exchange-value for capital embodied in the media. However, note that in order to purchase information commodities, we have to work for capital *outside* the media, in the rest of the economy at large. In order to obtain partial freedom from the *compulsion* to watch, we have to enter the compulsion to work in the economy. But it is the media, and media-related industries, which produce most of the information commodities. Hence we have to *realise* surplus-value for these industries in our purchase of information commodities. This in fact is the cycle by which working for the media is articulated with the media in the economy at large. Thus the movement of value is from absolute surplus-value in watching to relative surplus-value in watching to realisation of surplus-value in the economy. Now we can see the proper significance of Garnham's analysis. The middle and upper classes can purchase these information commodities and hence purchase freedom from working through the media. But for the mass of the population TV watching (for capital) does not diminish. Once they have purchased a TV, they watch. Reflected in the sphere of watching, then, is the increasing class separation of the population. One portion does not have to produce value for the media, whereas the larger part is compelled to do so. Hence with respect to the media we have again the familiar class separation around the fundamental point for capital—the necessity to labour.

But this *enforced participation*, this formally free time that is not totally free, is uneasily recognised by those who have examined it. Notice the phrases used to describe it: 'harried' (Linder), 'colonised' (Sahin and Robinson), held by the 'plug-in drug' (Winn), 'addictive' (Mander), 'captive audience' (Garnham). What is the unity among these explanations, what ties them together? What ultimately is the *source* of the enforced participation? Nothing, it appears. Examined closely these factors are merely *metaphors* of description. What, after all, does 'colonisation' mean? The fact that at present the elements of compulsion simply fall apart, simply form a list, indicates, I think, an important point—namely, that we regard watching, as in essence, free activity, free participation, not compelled. Any factor that seems to limit this freedom is not grasped as part of the essence of watching but only as an external limitation on an essentially free activity. This is why each limitation that is discovered is isolated from the others, why there is no unity among them. For instance, Marie Winn (1977, p. 217) concludes her book by saying:

For although we may be powerless in the face of the abstract machine that modern society has become, we can still assert our will in the face of that real and tangible machine in our homes, the television set. We can learn to control it so that it does not control us.

In watching TV, we see free participation of the audience as essential, limitations only as contingent.

This is not specific to theories of television watching alone but structures the way in which leisure time, broadly speaking, has thus far been conceptualised. Work is compelled while leisure time is free. For instance, Dumazedier (1960, p. 557), a major mainstream theorist of leisure believes that

Leisure consists of a number of occupations in which the individual may indulge of his own free will—either to rest, to amuse himself, to add to his knowledge or improve his skills disinterestedly or to increase his voluntary participation in the life of the community after discharging his professional, family and social duties.

Chris Rojek in *Capitalism and Leisure Theory* (1985) sharply disagrees with such a perspective. He sees leisure as not free time but 'an effect of systems of legitimation' and considers the example of housework to see if the compelled–free distinction is analytically valuable. For those involved in house, husband and child maintenance outside of the traditional wage relationship it is very difficult to distinguish free time and work time. The expectations that accompany the occupation of housewife structures the entire waking time of many women and the notion of 'time off' is an abstract and much sought-after fantasy. Rojek (1985, p. 18) writes:

The case of women reveals the limitations inherent in the concept of free time as the basis for leisure theory and research. The leisure or 'free' time of women is conditioned by their position in a male-dominated society. The housewife can have time off only when her household duties have been satisfactorily fulfilled. Even then she is subject to the ethos of sexism which supports some female activities and dismisses others.

Instead leisure time should be examined in a historical and concrete context to discover its characteristics. For Rojek modern leisure is structured by four major tendencies: privatisation, individuation, commercialisation, and pacification.

For watching activity the notion of free time remains the true blindspot. And it is produced by accepting the structuring of time by wage labour in the capitalist mode of production. Wage labour structures our time, all our time, into labour and leisure: this is peculiar to the capitalist mode of production. Leisure, therefore, is produced as, in essence, free activity time. We know, of course, that much of this free activity winds us up for and winds us down from the time of labour, from the time in which our activity produces value for capital. In such a way does the time of compelled activity subordinate the time left to us for free activity. But this subordination of free time has been recognised only in *formal* terms (see Chapter 3). Thus the discussion has been about 'colonisation'. It has generally been overlooked that capital in fact can not only formally subordinate this time but that it can directly *valorise* it, that it can *really* subsume the activity of watching and make it produce value. As long as we remain blind to this possibility, any discovered limitations on free watching will remain separated, a mere list of limits. Consequently the source of the compulsive character of watching will remain mysterious: 'It makes me watch it'. The social relations of compulsion will remain fetishised in the technology that mediates it. If we can break through this fetishism and demonstrate that watching is in essence compelled, it can also be demonstrated that surplus-watching exists. If watching is formally free but practically compelled (as wage labour is) the valorisation of this activity would become more clearly understandable.

## The culture of consumption and the crisis of meaning

The literature that I have examined so far in this chapter calls into question in a significant way the free nature of watching. However, the authors examined stop short of grasping the essence of this time as unfree. The elements based on technological (addiction), organisational (colonisation) and material (time and money) factors are all correct but partial explanations. They miss the source of the compulsion. While many theorists talk about the psychological needs that television provides, they misconstrue the compulsive character of watching. Television is merely one easily available means for this fulfilment. It is the source of the compulsion to watch that I wish to address in this section.

The nature of compulsion in other areas of non-work activity has been more readily recognised. The working class is compelled to channel the reproduction of labour-power through the commodity market—shelter, clothing, food, and so on, must be bought. There is no alternative to this activity of consumption. The creation of these consumer markets for subsistence goods lies at the heart of the development of capitalist industrialisation. The compulsion of work is based on this need to gather sufficient currency to reproduce labour-power, for the working class to reproduce itself as a class. However, traditional views of the reproduction of labour-power have focused on its *material* character and have largely ignored questions of *cultural and symbolic* reproduction within the context of compulsion. In Chapter 1 I stressed the need to understand both the material and symbolic character of human needing and while there is a great deal of discussion about the power of symbols and ideology, the question of the *basis* of this power is not often posed. (When it is asked, the answer is that it is derived from the content of the messages.) The answer that I would like to give here is that the power of symbols in modern society derives not only from the technological virtuosity of the creators of messages but from the human need to search for *meaning*, from the need for *cultural process*. We need both material and cultural reproduction, both bread and circuses. As Raymond Williams writes (cited in Garnham 1979, p. 128):

From castles and palaces and churches to prisons and workhouses and schools; from weapons of war to a controlled press: any ruling class, in variable ways though always materially, produces a social and political order. These are never superstructural activities. They are the necessary material production within which an apparently self-subsistent mode of production can alone be carried out.

Material production, then, involves an ideological element; similarly, ideological reproduction involves a material element. The cultural element of human needing, then, is just as important in the reproduction of labour-power as its physical element. Meaning is not secondary. It is constitutive of human experience.

If this much is granted, then the next question is: How is this meaning mediated in capitalist society and what is the role of consumption, advertising and the media in these movements? The social historian Jackson Lears (1983) has attempted to provide an answer to this question by examining the period in the late nineteenth century and early twentieth century when a culture of puritanism, work and self-denial was replaced by a culture of hedonism, leisure and self-fulfilment. The moral and religious fabric of American society was progressively dissolving under the strains bought on by modernity. 'Feelings of unreality stemmed from urbanization and technological development; from the rise of an increasingly interdependent market economy; and from the secularization of liberal Protestantism among its educated and affluent devotees' (Lears 1983, p. 6). The anonymity of the city brought with it feelings of depression and loss (even if only of repressive but traditional and familiar relations). Similarly the spread of a national market economy brought more and more people into relations of interdependence, such that 'liberal ideals of autonomous selfhood became ever more difficult to sustain'. Within the new context the self was not defined in terms of something inherent within the individual (something one was born with such as character) but was tied up with elements that could be manipulated by the individual for display to others.

As success became more dependent on evanescent 'impression management', selfhood lost coherence. The older ethic had required adherence to an internalized morality of self-control; repressive as this 'inner-direction' had been, it helped to sustain a solid core of selfhood. The new ethic of 'other-direction' undermined that solidity by presenting the self as an empty vessel to be filled and refilled according to the expectations of others' (Lears 1983, p. 8).

Coupled with this, religious beliefs waned in strength and influence also, as a 'softening Protestant theology undermined commitments and blurred ethical distinctions'.

As a result of these feelings of unreality within the new context provided by modern institutions, Lears argues that there arose longings for bodily and emotional strength and a revitalised sense of the self. In earlier times this quest for health had taken place within larger communal, ethical or religious frameworks of meaning that by the late nineteenth century were eroding. At the turn of the century the search for health had become almost entirely a secular process. Lears claims to detect a new 'therapeutic ethos' emerging as a result of these social movements, and further, that advertisers had picked up on this to exploit the emotional needs that Americans had now developed. Advertisers then both drew upon as well as created the process of the decline of traditional institutions of meaning and celebrated the new ethos of personal development.

A dialectic developed between American's new emotional needs and advertisers' strategies; each continually reshaped and intensified the other . . . Their motives and intentions were various but the overall effect of their efforts was to create a new and secular basis for capitalist cultural hegemony . . . By the 1920s the symbolic universe of national advertising markedly resembled the therapeutic world described by Philip Rieff—a world in which all overarching structures of meaning had collapsed . . . It is important to underscore the role of advertising in accelerating this collapse of meaning. The decline of symbolic structures of meaning outside the self has been a central process in the development of a consumer culture, joining advertising strategies and the therapeutic ethos (Lears 1983, p. 4 and 21).

In one of the first large-scale sociological studies of modern life, Robert and Helen Lynd traced through the changes that industrialisation and the expansion of the commodity market had wrought on community life in the opening decades of this century. In their book *Middletown* (1929) they reported the results of the research they had conducted in the town of Muncie, Indiana, and examined what life had been like in the 1890s and how that had altered by the mid-1920s. The Lynds paint a picture of a town which by 1924 saw the weakening and decline of the old community institutions, especially those of religion, family and work and their replacement by marketplace transactions. Money exchange replaced emotional commitment as the currency of social life. Richard Wightman Fox (1983, pp. 124–5) writes:

High-speed machine production had not only largely erased the distinction between skilled and semiskilled labor, it had also undermined the apprenticeship system that had guaranteed continuity within the family from father to son. The home was no longer a center of economic production or even family social life but a base from which each family member set out for leisure-time consumption with his own peer group . . . In 1924 Middletowners no longer assembled to debate ideas, values, or goals in their churches, clubs and union halls. The men and women of the 1890s—business-class men and women and working-class men—gathered regularly to discuss philosophical, ethical and political questions. Religion, previously a 'spontaneous and pervasive part of the life of the city', was now an institution struggling to regain some semblance of its earlier power through the latest techniques of advertising publicity.

As work and community life provided fewer satisfactions, people looked elsewhere for 'compensatory fulfilment' and found it in the most important institution of the developing consumer society—the consumer marketplace. Consumption replaced community, class and religion as the defining feature of social life. In these movements we are seeing a shift in the basic ways in which meaning was constituted. Advertising and the developing media of broadcasting absorbed much of the energy of these activities.

Raymond Williams, in *Television: Technology and Cultural Form* (1974), has written perceptively of the role that broadcasting played in the process of capitalist industrialisation and the reconstitution of family and class.

In a changing society, and especially after the Industrial Revolution, problems of social perspective and social orientation became more acute. New relations between men, and between men and things, were being intensely experienced, and in this area, especially, the traditional institutions of church and school, or of settled community and persisting family, had very little to say . . . In a number of ways, and drawing on a range of impulses from curiosity to anxiety, new information and new kinds of orientation were deeply required (Williams 1974, p. 22).

Within the developments of the first twenty years of the twentieth century, radio broadcasting played a unique and indispensable role. Williams identifies two parallel yet seem-

ingly contradictory tendencies of an emerging urban industrial culture: 'on the one hand mobility, on the other hand
the more apparently self-sufficient family home'. Broadcasting (both radio and television) was a product of this tendency
towards *mobile privatisation* and responded to the needs for
new kinds of communication.

The new 'consumer' technology which reached its first decisive
stage in the 1920s served this complex of needs within just these
limits and pressures . . . [Broadcasting was] the applied technology
of a set of emphases and responses within the determining limits
and pressures of industrial capitalist technology (Williams 1974,
p. 27).

There has been then an increasing recognition that the void
left by the erosion of the influence of traditional institutions
of the mediation of meaning has progressively been filled by
marketplace institutions, especially those of mass communication. The 'colonisation' of time outlined by Sahin and
Robinson is one indication of this dynamic. More specifically,
what these changes highlight is the manner in which increasing areas of social life are directly brought under the
control of commodity relations of production. Culture and
commodity are indistinguishable in advanced capitalism.
Nicholas Garnham (1979, p. 142) writes:

The development of the capitalist mode of production and its
associated division of mental and manual labour has led to the
development of the extraction of the necessary surplus for the
maintenance of cultural production and reproduction directly via
the commodity and exchange form.'

This has led to what Garnham calls the *industrialisation of
culture*, whereby surplus capital looking for profitable investment opportunities increasingly invests in the cultural
realm and thus provides the marketplace with cultural goods
to satisfy needs that had taken place before within localised
communities. As Asa Briggs (1960) says, 'massive market
interests have come to dominate an area of life which until
recently was dominated by individuals themselves.'
Garnham (1983, p. 14) writes:

It is a development that goes back at least 150 years in Britain, part of a wider process by which commodity exchange invades wider and wider areas of social life and the private sphere expands at the expense of the public sphere, driven by capital's restless and relentless search for new areas in which to realise surplus-value, thus introducing the 'dull compulsion of economic relations' to more and more spheres of social life.

The necessity of culture is integrated into the commodity marketplace. Yet this recognition does not go beyond the *formal* subsumption of cultural production and reproduction under commodity production. It is as buyers of goods that the working class enters into the process. In the production and movement of value it is in terms of realising surplus-value that the working class enters. The possibility that this formal subsumption to capital could be utilised in the *real* subsumption to capital has not yet been explored in the literature. It is precisely this shift from formal to real subsumption that I believe explains the dynamic element at the heart of modern media.

## Advertising, religion and magic

This book started with a philosophical consideration of the relationship between people and things and the various dimensions within which it is cloaked and can be studied. I end the book also with a consideration of the person–object relationship and an integration and summary of the major themes of the analysis. In the broadest terms we have to understand the various ways in which the relationship has been cloaked and the ways in which it has changed in response to wider social, economic and cultural changes. Much of the discussion in this chapter has contrasted old with modern modes of life. This dichotomy, however, is somewhat misleading for what we have in historical perspective is not two stages of society but three. Further the three can be distinguished from one and other along the dimensions of the person–object relationship.

The first stage, *traditional pre-industrial society* was based on a rural and agricultural lifestyle where local community, religion and the extended family were hugely important and where work and leisure were integrated within a coherent whole. The relationship between people and things was mediated by old ethnic cultures. Objects were given meaning by being integrated within older forms of cultural life based around family, religion and community. This can be represented in the following way:


PEOPLE -------- ETHNIC CULTURE -------- OBJECTS


The second stage is *industrial society*. The move to an industrial setting destroys the vitality and significance of older ethnic cultures based around rural life as people are transplanted into a new world and a new mode of production. Urban living, factory labour and the separation of work and leisure destroy the older traditions based around coherence and community. The unity and continuity of daily life in village settlements could not be sustained amid increasing urbanisation, especially when workplace, domicile and commerce were separated. Linked intimately with craft labour, the old ways of life could not stamp their accumulated meanings on the anonymous products that were beginning to pour off the assembly lines. And the highly restrictive codes of personal behaviour shaped by the closed worlds of religious values and distinct ethnic communities could not survive the more subtle blows of industrialism: the cultural relativism resulting from the quick amalgamation of so many different groups; the erosion of the economic function of the extended family; and the dawning of a new type of leisure time, highly individualised and privatised in nature and no longer bound to the traditional collective forms of popular entertainment or domestic routines. Industrial society is a transitional society, neither able to draw upon the past or to construct its own structures of meaning. A cultural void is created where the old and new ways of living collide: in Stuart Ewen's words, a 'social crisis of industrialisation'. This can be represented in the following way:

OLD WAYS OF THOUGHT
PEOPLE ----- NEW RELATIONS OF PRODUCTION -------- OBJECTS
CULTURAL VOID

The third stage is *consumer society*. The consumer society resolves the tensions and contradictions of industrial society: the market place and consumption take over the functions of traditional culture. Into the void left by the transition from traditional to industrial society comes the 'discourse through and about objects' and the reconstitution of the population not into social classes as the primary mode of identification but into consumption classes. (See *SCA* for a much fuller discussion of this historical development.) These transitions are literally revolutionary movements that are accomplished in the space of fifty years. As already discussed, *Middletown* by Robert and Helen Lynd is a description of the momentous changes taking place in cultural life as a result of these developments. This period can be represented in the following way:

MARKETPLACE
PEOPLE ---------- ADVERTISING ---------- OBJECTS
POPULAR CULTURE

Consumption, then, is the mode of living of modern culture. How does advertising fit into this scenario of compelled activity? I wish now to pick up a point from Chapter 2: wherein lies the *power* of advertising? I described earlier that in non-market pre-capitalist social formations a large part of the meaning of objects was derived from the knowledge of who produced them. Objects were embodied with the spirits of the producers. By contrast, a capitalist society creates a separation between object and producer and so little meaning can be derived from this sphere. In Chapter 2, I phrased this in terms of capitalism's 'emptying' of the true meaning of goods, and advertising's inserting its meaning into the hollow shell. Given the central role of objects in the constitution of human societies, human culture and human meaning, one can provide an answer as to where the power of advertising comes from: it derives not from the ingenuity of advertisers but from the need for meaning. If goods are ritual adjuncts and rituals 'make visible and stable the categories of culture' (Douglas and Isherwood 1978), then advertising, and the meaning it provides, is indispensable for the stability of capitalism. Its real ideological role is not to create demand, to affect market share or even to dispense ideology—it is to give us meaning. That is why it is so powerful. If it is manipulative, it is manipulative with respect to a real need: our need to know the world and to make sense of it, our need to know ourselves. As Richard Wightman Fox (1983, p. 103) comments:

Americans were not passive creatures subject to direct manipulation by wily agents of capital. They became consumers through their own active adjustment to both the material and spiritual conditions of life in advanced capitalist society. Through consumption . . . they continued the quest for 'real life' which earlier generations had sought in the transcendent religious realm.

The function just described, if it were attributed to an institution in non-capitalist society, would indeed be clearly seen for what it is—*religion*. But critical thinkers have not explored this possibility when examining advertising and its functions. In combating the old religion, Marxism was forced into a bland utilitarianism which tended to see religion as having been superseded, as a thing of the past. This occurred despite the fact that in the notion of fetishism one has the conceptual tool required for understanding advertising as a religion.

I argued earlier that capitalism empties products of their social meaning: in other words, exchange-value *exhausts* the social powers of use-value (meaning). In fact it does more than this. The social powers of use-value are transformed into the social powers of exchange-value. The social powers of human interaction in activity are transferred from use-value to exchange-value—from the commodity to capital. Thus when we consider a commodity, we start by thinking about its *uses*. But when we consider *capital* we start by describing its powers to *command activity*. Bill Livant (1983a, p. 2) writes:

As we know, the Marxian approach to religion is that it is a fetish, an inverted, upside-down, representation of real relations. It escapes from confronting the sphere of real powers on earth, to invest symbolically a heaven with powers it does not possess. This approach to religion is valid; we can now put it to use . . . The fundamental point is this: the new religion does not arise on the basis of the aspect which is growing in real powers. It arises on the basis of the aspect which is being exhausted, which is being emptied. It is in the *destroyed* domain of the *real* that the religious fetish of symbolic powers arises . . . This means that the religion of capitalism, the fetish, arises not in the sphere of Exchange Value but in the sphere of Use Value. It is in the sphere of uses that we shall expect to find all the major confusions, inversions, mysteries.

In fact, we can find a similar argument in the work of one of the most sophisticated defenders of advertising, Staffan Linder (1970). It is his claim that advertising provides a basis for some choice, however irrational, in a context where any real basis of choice is impossible. Jackson Lears, too, notes that information is replaced by feeling in advertising. If the basis of advertising is to make us feel good and it has surrendered any objective basis for this feeling, in what way is it different from religion? As Livant (1983a, p. 1) remarks:

But why not also tea leaves, ouji boards, black cats, dice, sounds that go bump in the night? Why not God? All these too can 'satisfy' us, can 'justify' our choices? What else is Linder's defence but a *secular* version of God, what else is it in practice but the ritual of a religion?

From such a perspective one can characterise more adequately the fetishism that is present in advertisements as measured in the empirical study reported in Chapter 5. The issue here is not merely symbolisation but product use and results. The commodity of advertising plays a mixture of psychological, social and physical roles in its relations with people. The object world interacts with the human world at the most basic and fundamental of levels, performing magical feats of enchantment and transformation. And yet no basis is offered to support the claims except for the anonymous sacraments of the producers themselves. It is not a question of mere irrationality in terms of persuasion but of the acceptance of *blind faith* that the product can fulfil this sacred role in secular life. Then where does the power of the commodity derive from? What makes us accept the groundless (not untrue) assertions of the advertisements? What is the glue that holds the system of modern fetishism together? It is certainly not 'technological rationality' for, as I showed in the last chapter, very few commercials give any detailed description of the product under consideration or any objective basis for its superiority. While technological rationality does not offer an answer to these questions, a belief in technology itself does. There is clearly no rationality in the strict sense in the system, no rationality of information. But this does not preclude the belief in technology itself. It is in the religion of technology 'where anything is possible', where anything can be 'fixed', where science can bestow miracles. Raymond Williams (1980), indeed, calls his article 'The Magic System' and writes (Williams 1980, p. 185): 'The short description of the pattern we have is *magic*: a highly organised and professional system of magical inducements and satisfactions, functionally very similar to magical systems in simpler societies but rather strangely coexistent with a highly developed scientific technology.' Varda Leymore (1975) describes advertising as a form of myth, while Martin Esslin (1976, p. 271), in comparing advertising with Greek drama, writes more directly of advertising as a fetishistic religion where commercial personalities can be seen as demigods and mythical heroes akin to characters such as Hercules, Ulysses, Dionysos and Aphrodite.

The TV commercial, exactly as the oldest known types of theater, is essentially a religious form of drama which shows us human beings as living in world controlled by a multitude of powerful forces that shape our lives ... The moral universe ... is essentially that of a polytheistic religion. It is world dominated by a sheer numberless pantheon of powerful forces, which literally reside in every article of use or consumption, in every institution of daily life. If the winds and waters, the trees and brooks of ancient Greece were inhabited by a vast host of nymphs, dryads, satyrs, and other local and specific deities, so is the universe of the TV commercial. The polytheism that confronts us here is thus a fairly primitive one, closely akin to animistic and fetishistic beliefs.

In the mythical universe of advertising it is the spirits of technology that invade the body of the commodity and supply the basis for a belief in its power. In older African cultures the same phenomenon can be observed. In this there is no fundamental difference between the old and the new fetishisms. Both rely for their power on the system of religious belief that surrounds the use of certain sanctified objects. In this context what is advertising if not the new religion of modern life, the religion indeed of use value? As Martin Esslin (1976, p. 271) writes:

We may not be conscious of it, but this *is* the religion by which most of us actually live, whatever our more consciously and explicitly held beliefs and religious persuasions may be. This is the actual religion that is being absorbed by our children from almost the day of their birth.

Advertising does not of course exist in isolation from the rest of society, it mirrors in some way the 'reality' that surrounds it. The Jesuit scholar, John Kavanaugh (1981), believes that advertising is part of the way of life based upon the commodity-form—a world where people are identified through the things they consume as well as being dominated by them. Kavanaugh (1981, pp. 15–16) compares this to a life based on more human values, the personal form, which is more closely related to justice and spirituality.

A 'gospel' is a book of revelation, an ultimate source of reference wherein we find ourselves revealed. A gospel is a response to the questions of who we are, what we may hope for, how we may aspire to act, what endures, what is important, what is of true value. A gospel then is an expression of who or what is our functional god . . . We will inevitably be confronted with at least two competing gospels or books of revelation in American society . . . They serve as ultimate and competing 'forms' of perception, through which we filter all of our experience. Each form, moreover, provides a controlling image for our consciousness in apprehending our selves and our world. These competing life-forms can be expressed as the 'gospels' of Personhood and Commodity: the Personal Form and the Commodity Form; the Person-god and the Thing-god. Each has its own 'church', you might say, its own cults and liturgical rites, its own special language, and its own concept of the heretical.

The dominant 'gospel' in capitalism is clearly that based on the possession of things, on the satisfaction of needs predominantly through the consumption of commodities. For Kavanaugh the religion of modern society based on the commodity-form is quite clearly a form of *idolatry*, an illustration of what Marx called the fetishism of commodities wherein the world of humans is dominated and controlled by the very things that they produce.

Kavanaugh, however, casts his conceptual net too broadly and thus misses the differences within the commodity-form of life as well as the different forms in which the commodity life has been cloaked through this century. In *SCA* we developed four distinct chronological stages in the evolution of the cultural meanings of products as reflected in advertising. Looked at from another perspective this perhaps can be viewed as the development of different religious frameworks for the commodity-form. The question is: if we saw these relations in older, more traditional societies, what anthropological terms would we use to describe them?

Stage 1 (1890s–1920s) is product utility (*idolatry*). In this first stage of the development of industrial culture, the products of the new technology are venerated, almost worshipped. Advertising acts as a form of celebration of the products of the new age. Advertisements focus on what goods do, their utility, and there is a great sense of discovery in the exploration of the new world of things. Text is the dominant mode of communication.

Stage 2 (1920s–1940s) is symbolisation (*iconology*). Icons are symbols, they mean something and are representative of something else. In this stage the focus in advertising moves from the worship of commodities to their *meaning* within a specific social context. There is a shift away from the product alone and towards the consumer, but this movement stops half-way. Although the qualities of goods were in this period much more abstract and less focused on pure utility, these qualities were still bound tightly to the things themselves. For example, motor cars were in and of themselves expressions of modernity, or products could capture and tame the very forces of nature (freshness, sunshine, and so on). People, too, were not really concrete but were embodiments of reigning social values such as status and elegance. Because of this, both persons and objects seem to be frozen in space and time—in a twilight world of abstract significance that is neither wholly thing-based or person-based.

Stage 3 (1940s–1960s) is personification (*narcissism*). (Narcissus was a character from Greek mythology who fell in love with his own reflection.) In this stage the shift towards the person is completed, and not just in abstract terms—people are presented as real rather than symbolic representations. This is aided by the increasing use of colour photography to make people more real and concrete. In the advertising of this period, the product puts its power at the disposal of the individual and consumers are encouraged to consider what the product could do for them, personally and selfishly. This power can be manifested in many ways, but largely through 'black magic' where persons undergo sudden transformations or where the commodity has power over other people as well. The world of objects here enters the everyday world of people and performs in magical ways. (This stage could also be called *fetishism*.)

Stage 4 (1960s–1980s) is lifestyle (*totemism*). Totemism in older societies refers to the correlation between the natural world and the social world where natural differences stand for social differences (see Chapter 1). In modern advertising goods take the place of natural species. This last phase draws together and synthesises the other three phases: products are freed from only being utilitarian things, or abstract representations of social values, or tied up with the world of personal and interpersonal relationships. Here, utility, symbolisation and personalisation are mixed and remixed under the sign of the *group*. Products are badges of group membership. (See *SCA*, Chapter 11, for a fuller discussion of these four stages of advertising development.)

The different stages in the development of this religion are based, then, upon the *uses* of goods. Indeed, if use-value is the ideological sphere of this religion, then there is little wonder that there is so much confusion about it. (Is it 'natural' or 'social'? Is there one use or many? And so on.) As Livant (1983a, p. 3) writes:

These questions, like those about the nature of the Trinity . . . can be expected to flourish in a domain which is mystified, in which all sorts of magical powers appear and disappear like fireflies. We will never sort out these questions until we remember that, today, when we are putting our minds to use-value . . . we are thinking in church.'

In fact, seen from this perspective, the historical tracing of the person–object relation in advertisements as just outlined above takes on new meaning. As Livant (1983a, p. 3) notes about the four-stage development:

Aren't they (in *SCA*) tracing out steps in the history of the rise of the new religion? Is it an accident that advertising messages have moved historically from a centre on physical function . . . to a centre on desire . . . to a centre on personal and small group lifestyle . . . to a centre on the form of being-in-the-world of a whole social formation? And that these messages addressed to individuals are about the expanded world of *uses* . . . Is it an accident that the messages have moved historically from a centre on the verbal to a centre on the visual? Yes, these are the graven images, the icons that mark a 'real, old-time' religion! And the rise of *repetition*?!

It may seem a little strange to suggest that the ideology that holds together the most technologically-advanced civilisation in history is a form of old-fashioned religion. But note that it is the social relations of the technology itself that provides the impetus to this movement. It is in the emptied and hollow husk of the commodity-form, drained of its social powers, that the spirit of technology is able to foster its own fiction concerning the relation of people and things, to make things 'come alive' with new social powers. Seen from the other direction, it is the social relations of capitalism that compel people to search for meaning in the domain of the commodity-world. Within this context of a world without meaning wherein people search for meaning arises the religion of use-value, the religion of advertising. The ultimate power of advertising does not rest on its creative ingenuity or its ability to manipulate (which is not to deny its effectiveness in those areas), but on its ability to mediate the dialectic of emptying and needing.

The understanding of advertising as a religion, though, should not be left at this most general of levels for, as previous chapters have shown, the meaning of advertising is mediated through the value form of time. The empirical study in Chapter 5 demonstrated the way that different audiences are constituted as audiences in relation to differing systems of messages. Put in more provocative terms: writers such as Kavanaugh have identified the general form of the religion that dominates modern society while in my analysis I have shown the different denominations and congregations that the population is divided into (and in *SCA* we showed the different stages of the development of these religious forms).

## Conclusion: use-value and exchange-value

In market societies, the exchange-value of commodities dominates their use-value. This point has not often been explored in a concrete way and I attempted here to understand the precise nature of this relation and the role of advertising within it. In fact in our society it is the double subsumption of use-value to exchange-value that helps us understand the *meaning* of commodities. The first subsumption takes place in the realm of production, where the social relations of capitalism hide the real relations of production and thus hide the true (complete) social meaning of commodities. It is only within this context that we can understand the symbolism of advertising. This explains why the world of use-value in advertising resembles ancient religions in its portrayal of the relation between persons and things. The second subsumption takes place in the realm of communication, where the form and content of advertising messages is constrained by the exchange-value of audience time in commercial broadcasting. This is the major hypothesis underlying the empirical study and is substantially upheld by the results. The depictions of fetishism were themselves affected by the exchange-value of audience time. The addition of the compulsive nature of watching, caused by the search for meaning directed towards the marketplace as the only means of meaning-fulfilment, further develops the notion that in capitalism, symbolic processes are dominated by economic ones and, more specifically, the attempt to generate increasing amounts of surplus value for private producers.

There is an unhealthy tension between the social production of meaning and the manner of its private appropriation.

In fact, advertising functions as a mirror, highlighting the major elements of capitalism as a system of production. In capitalism, the symbolic processes connected to goods are collapsed into one sphere (the market), and the institution of advertising reflects this duality. This reflection is not superficial but reaches the fundamental level on which capitalism is organised—the production of surplus-value. The movement of value *invades* the symbolic/material processes of human needing and destroys any idea of the separation of superstructure and base. Advertising not only reflects, but is itself a part of the extraction of surplus-value (in addition to realising it). Capital invades the process of meaning construction—it valorises consciousness itself.

# Bibliography

Albion, M., and P. Farris (1981). *The Advertising Controversy*, Auburn House, Boston.

Althusser, L. (1971). *Lenin and Philosophy*, NLB, London.

Andrén, G., L. Ericsson, R. Ohlsson, and T. Tannsjö (1978). *Rhetoric and Ideology in Advertising*, AB Grafiska, Stockholm.

Andrew, J. (1981). 'Need to Convey More Data? Squeeze 36 Second Message into 30 Seconds', *Wall Street Journal*, 14 May.

Ansbacher, H. (1958). 'Fetishism: an Adlerian Interpretation', *Psychiatric Quarterly*, vol. 32.

Arlen, M. (1981). *Thirty Seconds*, Penguin, New York.

Arriaga, P., (1983). 'Broadcasting: Monopoly Profits or Differential Rent', unpublished paper.

—— (1984). 'On Advertising: A Marxist Critique', *Media, Culture and Society*, 6.

Bak, R. (1953). 'Fetishism', *Journal of the American Psychoanalytic Association*, no. 1.

—— (1974). 'Distortions of the Concept of Fetishism', *Psychoanalytic Study of the Child*, vol. 29.

Baker, S. (1968). *The Permissible Lie: The Inside Truth About Advertising*, World Publishing Co., Cleveland, OH.

Balint, M. (1935). 'A Contribution on Fetishism', *International Journal of Psychoanalysis*, vol. 16.

Baran, P., and P. Sweezy (1964). 'Theses on Advertising', *Science and Society*, Winter, vol. 28.

—— (1966). *Monopoly Capitalism*, Penguin, London.

Barnouw, E. (1978). *The Sponsor: Notes on a Modern Potentate*, Oxford University Press, New York.

Barthes, R. (1973). *Mythologies*, Paladin, London.

Baudrillard, J. (1975). *The Mirror of Production*, tr. M. Poster, Telos Press, St Louis, MO.

—— (1981). *Critique of the Political Economy of the Sign*, tr. C. Levin, Telos Press, St Louis, MO.

Bauxbaum, E. (1960). 'Hair Pulling and Fetishism', *Psychoanalytic Study of the Child*, vol. 15.

Belakaoui, A., and J. Belakaoui. (1976) 'A Comparative Analysis of the Roles Portrayed by Women in Print Advertisements, 1958, 1970, 1972', *Journal of Marketing Research*, vol. 13, May.

Bell, D. (1960). 'The Impact of Advertising' in Sandage and Fryburger (1960).

Bell, M. (1966). *Marketing: Concepts and Strategy*, Houghton Mifflin Co., New York.

Berelson, B. (1952). *Content Analysis in Communication Research*, Free Press, New York.

Berger J. (1972). *Ways of Seeing*, Penguin, London.

Bergreen, L. (1980). *Look Now, Pay Later*, Mentor, New York.

Berman, R. (1981). *Advertising and Social Change*, Sage, Beverly Hills and London.

Bernstein, P. (1979). 'Psychographics Is Still an Issue on Madison Avenue' in Wright (1979).

Betty, J. (1971). 'A Clinical Contribution to the Analysis of a Perversion', *International Journal of Psychoanalysis*, vol. 52, no. 4.

Bogart, L. (1973). 'As Media Change, How Will Advertising?', *Journal of Advertising Research*, vol. 13, no. 5.

—— (1976). 'Mass Advertising: The Message Not the Measure', *Harvard Business Review*, September/October.

Boorstin, D. (1974). 'Advertising and American Civilisation' in Brozen (1974).

Borden, N. (1947). *The Economic Effects of Advertising*, Richard Irwin, Chicago.

Braverman, H. (1974). *Labour and Monopoly Capital*, Monthly Review Press, New York.

Brewster, B. (1976). 'Fetishism in *Capital* and *Reading Capital*', *Economy and Society*, vol. 5, no. 3, August.

Briggs, A. (1960). 'Fisher Memorial Lecture', University of Adelaide.

Brown, L. (1971). *Television: The Business Behind the Box*, Harcourt Brace Jovanovitch, New York.

Brozen, Y., ed. (1974). *Advertising and Society*, New York University Press, New York.

Bugler, J. (1969). 'The Sex Sell', *New Society*, 15 May.

Burke, J. (1979). 'Reification and Commodity Fetishism Revisited', *Canadian Journal of Political and Social Theory*, vol. 3, no 1.

Busch, T. and T. Landeck (1980). *The Making of a Television Commercial*, Macmillan, New York.

Buzzi, G. (1968). *Advertising: Its Cultural and Political Effects*, tr. D. Germize, University of Minnesota Press, Minneapolis.

Carey, J. (1960). 'Advertising: An Institutional Approach' in Sandage and Fryburger (1960).

Chibnall, S. (1977). *Law and Order News*, Tavistock, London.

Cohen, G. (1978). *Karl Marx's Theory of History: A Defence*, Princeton University Press, Princeton, NJ.

Cohen, S., and J. Young, eds (1973). *The Manufacturers of News: Deviance, Social Problems and the Mass Media*, Constable, London.

Courtney, A., and S. Lockeretz (1971). 'A Woman's Place: An Analysis of the Roles Portrayed by Women in Magazine Advertising', *Journal of Marketing Research*, vol. 8, February.

Courtney, A. and T. Whipple (1974). 'Women in TV Commercials', *Journal of Communication*, vol. 24, Spring.

Csikszentmihalyi, M. and E. Rochberg-Halton (1981). *The Meaning of Things: Domestic Symbols and the Self*, Cambridge University Press, New York.

Curran, J. (1981). 'The Impact of Advertising on the British Mass Media', *Media, Culture and Society*, vol. 3, no. 1.

Curti, M. (1967). 'The Changing Concept of "Human Nature" in the Literature of American Advertising', *Business History Review*, vol. 41, Winter.

D'Amico, R. (1978). 'Desire and the Commodity-Form' *Telos*, no. 35, Spring.

David, P. and M. Reder, eds (1974). *Nations and Households in Economic Growth*, Academic Press, New York.

Debord, G. (1970), *Society of the Spectacle*, Black and Red, Detroit.

Demsetz, H. (1974). 'Advertising in the Affluent Society' in Brozen (1974).

Dennert, R. (1906). *At the Back of the Black Man's Mind*, Macmillan and Co., London.

Divita, S., ed. (1974). *Advertising and the Public Interest*, American Marketing Association, Chicago.

Douglas, M., and B. Isherwood (1978). *The World of Goods*, Basic Books, New York.

Dumazedier, J. (1960). 'Current Problems in the Sociology of Leisure', *International Social Science Journal*, no. 4, p. 527.

Dyer, G. (1982). *Advertising as Communication*, Methuen, London.

Easterlin, R. (1974). 'Does Economic Growth Improve the Human Lot? Some Empirical Evidence', in David and Reder (1984).

Easton, L. and K. Guddat, eds (1967). *Writings of the Young Marx on Philosophy and Society*, Anchor, New York.

Echeveria, R. (1978). 'Critique of Marx's 1857 Introduction', *Economy and Society*, vol. 7, no. 4.

Eidelberg, L. (1968). *An Encyclopedia of Psycho-Analysis*, Free Press, New York.

Ellis, A. (1887). *The Tshi-Speaking Peoples*, Benin Press, Chicago (republished 1964).

Engel, J., H. Fiorillo, and M. Cayley, eds (1972). *Market Segmentation: Concepts and Application*, Holt Rinehart and Winston, New York.

Epstein, E. (1979). *News From Nowhere: Television and the News*, Random House, New York.

—— (1982). *The Rise and Fall of Diamonds*, Simon and Schuster, New York.

Esslin, M. (1976). 'Aristotle and the Advertisers: The Television Commercial Considered as a Form of Drama' in H. Newcomb, ed., *Television: The Critical View*, Oxford University Press, New York.

Ewen, S. (1976). *Captains of Consciousness*, McGraw-Hill, New York.

Ewen, S., and E. Ewen (1978). 'Americanization and Consumption', *Telos*, Autumn.

—— (1982). *Channels of Desire*, McGraw-Hill, New York.

Fiber, B. (1984). 'Tuning Out Ads, a Growing Trend', *Globe and Mail*, 31 October.

Fiske, J. and J. Hartley (1978). *Reading Television*, Methuen, London.

Fliess, R., ed. (1948). *The Psychoanalytic Reader*, Indiana University Press, Indianapolis.

Forde, D. (1958). *The Context of Belief*, Liverpool University Press, Liverpool.

Fox, R. W. (1983). 'Epitaph for Middletown' in Fox and Lears (1983).

—— and T. J. Lears (1983). *The Culture of Consumption*, Pantheon, New York.

Frank, R. (1972). 'Market Segmentation Research: Findings and Implications', in Engel *et al.* (1972).

Freud, S. (1935). *A General Introduction to Psychoanalysis*, Liveright Publishers, New York.

—— (1953). *Standard Edition of the Complete Works of Sigmund Freud* (ed. J. Strachey), Hogarth Press, London.

Friedman, J. (1974). 'The Place of Fetishism and the Problem of Materialist Interpretation', *Critique of Anthropology*, Spring.

Galbraith, J. K. (1958). *The Affluent Society*, Houghton Mifflin, Boston.

—— (1967). *The New Industrial State*, Houghton Mifflin, Boston.

Garnham, N. (1979). 'Contribution to a Political Economy of Mass-Communication', *Media, Culture and Society*, no. 1.

—— (1983). 'Public Service versus the Market', *Screen*, vol. 24, no. 1, January/February.

Gehr, R. (1983). 'The MTV Aesthetic', *Film Comment*, vol. 19, no. 4.

Geras, N. (1971). 'Essence and Appearance: Aspects of Fetishism in Marx's *Capital*', *New Left Review*, no. 65.

Gershman, H. (1970). 'The Role of Core Gender Identity in the Genesis of Perversions', *American Journal of Psychoanalysis*, vol. 30, no. 1.

Gillespie, W. (1940). 'A Contribution to the Study of Fetishism', in Ruttenbeek (1940).

—— (1964). 'The Psycho-Analytic Theory of Sexual Deviation with Special Reference to Fetishism' in Rosen (1964).

Gitlin, T. (1980). *The Whole World is Watching*, University of California Press, Berkeley.

—— (1983). *Inside Prime-Time*, Pantheon, New York.

Godelier, M. (1977). *Perspectives in Marxist Anthropology*, Cambridge University Press, Cambridge.

Goffman, E. (1979). *Gender Advertisements*, Harper and Row, New York.

Goldman, M. (1960). 'Product Differentiation and Advertising: Some Lessons from Soviet Experience', *Journal of Political Economy*, August.

Goldway, D. (1978). 'Appearance and Reality in Marx's *Capital*', *Science and Society*, vol. 31, no. 4.

Gossage, H. (1967). 'The Gilded Bough: Magic and Advertising' in Matson and Montague (1967).

Greenacre, P. (1953). 'Certain Relationships Between Fetishism and Faulty Development of the Body Image' *Psychoanalytic Study of the Child*, vol. 8.

—— (1955). 'Further Considerations Regarding Fetishism', *Psychoanalytic Study of the Child*, vol. 10.

Greyser, S. (1972). 'Advertising: Attacks and Counters', *Harvard Business Review*, vol. 50, March/April.

Griff, M. (1969). 'Advertising: The Central Institution of Mass Society', *Diogenes*, vol. 68, Winter.

Halberstam, D. (1979). *The Powers That Be*, Dell, New York.

Hall, S. (1973). 'The Determination of News Photographs' in Cohen and Young (1973).

—— (1980). 'Encoding/Decoding', in S. Hall *et al.* (1980).

Hall, S., and P. Whannel (1965). *The Popular Arts*, Pantheon, New York.

Hall, S., D. Hobson, A. Lowe, and P. Willis, eds (1980). *Culture, Media, Language*, Hutchinson, London.

Hanson, P. (1974). *Advertising and Socialism*, Macmillan, London.

Harvey, D. (1982). *The Limits to Capital*, Cambridge University Press, New York.

Heller, A. (1976). *The Theory of Need in Marx*, Allison and Busby, London.

Hirsch, F. (1976). *Social Limits to Growth*, Harvard University Press, Cambridge, MA.

Hirschman, A. (1982). *Shifting Involvements: Private Interest and Public Action*, Princeton University Press, Princeton, NJ.

Holsti, O. (1969). *Content Analysis for the Social Sciences and Humanities*, Addison-Wesley, Reading, MA.

Horowitz, I. (1977). 'Sports Telecasts: Rights and Regulations', *Journal of Communication*, vol. 27, no. 3.

Hoste, W. (1921). *Fetishism—in Central Africa and Elsewhere*, Westminster, London.

Howard, J. A. and J. Hubert (1974). 'Advertising and the Public Interest', *Journal of Advertising Research*, vol. 14, no. 6.

Hurwitz, D. (1984). 'Broadcast Ratings: The Missing Dimension', *Critical Studies in Mass Communication*, June.

Inglis, F. (1972). *The Imagery of Power: A Critique of Advertising*, Heinemann, London.

Jacoby, J. (1974). 'Consumer Reaction to Information Displays, Packaging and Advertising' in Divita (1974).

Jacoby, R. (1980). *The Dialectic of Defeat*, Cambridge University Press, Cambridge.

Janowitz, M. (1978). *The Last Half-Century*, University of Chicago Press, Chicago.

Janus, N. (1981). 'Advertising and the Mass Media: Transnational Link Between Production and Consumption', *Media, Culture and Society*, vol. 3, no. 1.

Jhally, S. (1982). 'Probing the Blindspot: The Audience Commodity', *Canadian Journal of Political and Social Theory*, vol. 6, nos. 1–2.

—— (1984). 'The Spectacle of Accumulation: Material and Cultural Factors in the Evolution of the Sports/Media Complex', *The Insurgent Sociologist*, vol. 12, no. 3, Summer.

——, S. Kline and W. Leiss (1985). 'Magic in the Marketplace: An Empirical Test For Commodity Fetishism', *Candian Journal of Political and Social Theory*, vol. 9, no. 3.

Johnson, C. (1980). 'The Problem of Reformism and Marx's Theory of Fetishism', *New Left Review*, January/February.

Johnson, W. (1971). *Super Spectator and the Electric Lilliputians*, Little Brown and Co, Toronto.

Kaatz, R. (1982). *Cable: An Advertiser's Guide to the New Electronic Media*, Crain Books, Chicago.

Kaplan, D. (1972). 'The Psychopathology of TV Watching', *Performance*, July/August.

Kavanaugh, J. (1981). *Following Christ in a Consumer Society*, Orbis, New York.

Keys, B. (1972). *Subliminal Seduction*, Signet, New York.

—— (1976). *Media Sexploitation*, Signet, New York.

Kline, S. (1983). 'Images of Well-Being in Canadian Magazine Advertising', paper prepared for CCA meetings in Vancouver.

—— and W. Leiss (1978). 'Advertising, Needs and Commodity Fetishism', *Canadian Journal of Political and Social Theory*, vol. 2, no. 1

Kontos, A. (1977). 'Review of *The Limits to Satisfaction*', *Canadian Journal of Political and Social Theory*, vol. 1, no. 1.

Kress, G. (1976). 'Structuralism and Popular Culture', in C. Bigsby, ed., *Approaches to Popular Culture*, Popular Press, Bowling Green University.

Kuhn, A. (1985). *The Power of the Image*, Routledge and Kegan Paul, London.

Lancaster, K. (1971). *Consumer Demand: A New Approach*, Columbia University Press, New York.

Lane, R. (1978). 'Markets and the Satisfaction of Human Wants', *Journal of Economic Issues*, vol. 12, no. 4, December.

Lasch, C. (1979). *The Culture of Narcissism*, Warner Books, New York.

Lebowitz, M. (1984). 'Comment on "The Valorization of Consciousness"', unpublished paper, Simon Fraser University.

Lears, T. J. (1983). 'From Salvation to Self-Realization', in Fox and Lears (1983).

Lefebvre, H. (1971). *Everyday Life in the Modern World*, Harper and Row, New York.

Leiss, W. (1976). *The Limits to Satisfaction*, Marion Boyars, London.

—— (1978). 'Needs, Exchanges and the Fetishism of Objects', *Canadian Journal of Political and Social Theory*, vol. 2, no. 3.

—— (1983a). 'The Icons of the Marketplace', *Theory, Culture and Society*, vol. 1, no. 3.

—— (1983b). 'Things Come Alive: Economy and Technology as Modes of Social Representation in Modern Society', paper prepared for *Table Ronde Internationale sur les Representations*, Montreal, October.

——, S. Kline and S. Jhally (1986). *Social Communication in Advertising: Persons, Products and Images of Well-Being*, Methuen, Toronto.

Levitt, T. (1960). 'Are Advertising and Marketing Corrupting Society? It's Not Your Worry' in Sandage and Fryburger (1960).

214   *Bibliography*

—— (1970). 'The Morality (?) of Advertising', *Harvard Business Review*, vol. 48, no. 4, July/August.

Levy, S. (1983). 'Ad-Nauseum: How MTV Sells Out Rock & Roll', *Rolling Stone*, 8 December.

Leymore, V. (1975). *Hidden Myth: Structure and Symbolism in Advertising*, Heinemann, London.

Lichtman, R. (1975). 'Marx's Theory of Ideology', *Socialist Revolution*, 23 April.

Lindblom, C. (1977). *Politics and Markets: The World's Political-Economic Systems*, Basic Books, New York.

Linder, S. (1975). *The Harried Leisure Class*, Columbia University Press, New York.

Livant, B. (1979). 'The Audience Commodity: On the "Blindspot" Debate', *Canadian Journal of Political and Social Theory*, vol. 3, no. 1.

—— (1981a). 'The Value-Form of Time', unpublished xerox, Brooklyn College.

—— (1981b). 'On a Historical Turning-Point in Making Audiences as Commodities', unpublished xerox, Brooklyn College.

—— (1982). 'Working at Watching: A Reply to Sut Jhally', *Canadian Journal of Political and Social Theory*, vol. 6, nos 1–2.

—— (1983a). 'On the Religion of Use-Value', unpublished xerox, University of Regina.

—— (1983b). 'On the Defence of Advertising', unpublished xerox, University of Regina.

—— (1985). 'Urban Time and the Valorization of Consciousness', unpublished xerox, University of Regina.

Lorand, S. (1930). 'Fetishism in Statu Nascendi', *International Journal of Psychoanalysis*, vol. 11.

Lukács, G. (1967). *History and Class Consciousness*, Merlin Press, London.

Lynd, H. and R. Lynd (1929). *Middletown*, Macmillan, New York.

MacGaffey, W. (1977). 'Fetishism Revisited: Kongo *Nkisi* in Sociological Perspective', *Africa*, vol. 47, no. 2.

MacLachlan, J. and H. Siegel (1980). 'Reducing the Costs of TV Commercials by Use of Time Compression', *Journal of Marketing Research*, vol. XVIII, February.

Mandel, E. (1978). *Late Capitalism*, NLB, London.

Mander, J. (1978). *Four Arguments for the Elimination of Television*, William Morrow and Co., New York.

Mankiewicz, F., and J. Swerdlow (1978). *Remote Control*, Ballantine, New York.

Marcuse, H. (1972a). *One Dimensional Man*, Abacus, London.

—— (1972b). 'The Foundation of Historical Materialism' in *Studies in Critical Philosophy*, NLB, London.

Marshall, A. (1920). *Industry and Trade*, Macmillan, London.

Marshall, D. (1984). 'Videomusic and Interface: The Conforming Nature of Technological Innovation and Cultural Expression', unpublished paper, Simon Fraser University.

Marx, K. (1934). *Letters to Dr. Kugelman*, International Publishers, New York.

—— (1952). *Wage, Labour and Capital*, Progress, Moscow.

—— (1956). *The German Ideology*, International Publishers, New York.

—— (1964). *The 1844 Paris Manuscripts*, International Publishers, New York.

—— (1970). *Contribution to a Critique of Political Economy*, International Publishers, New York.

—— (1973). *Grundrisse*, tr. M. Nicolas, Penguin, London.

—— (1976). *Capital* (Vol. 1), tr. B. Brewster, Penguin, London.

Matson, F. and A. Montague, eds (1967). *The Human Dialogue*, Free Press, New York.

Mauss, M. (1967). *The Gift*, tr. Ian Cunnison, Norton, New York.

Mayer, M. (1961). 'The American Myth and the Myth of Advertising', in Sandage (1961).

McArthur, L. and B. Resco (1975). 'The Portrayal of Men and Women in American Television Commercials', *The Journal of Social Psychology*, vol. 97, no. 2, December.

McCracken, G. and R. Pollay (1981). 'Anthropology and the Study of Advertising', unpublished xerox, University of British Columbia.

McLuhan, M. (1951). *The Mechanical Bride*, Vanguard, New York.

Meehan, E. (1983). 'Neither Heroes Nor Villains: Towards a Political Economy of the Ratings Industry', unpublished PhD dissertation, University of Illinois at Urbana-Champaign.

—— (1984). 'Ratings and the Institutional Approach: A Third Answer to the Commodity Question', *Critical Studies in Mass Communication*, June.

Melody, W. (1973). *Children's Television: The Economics of Exploitation*, Yale University Press, London.

Mepham, J. (1972). 'The Theory of Ideology in *Capital*', *Radical Philosophy*, no. 2.

Mepham, J. and D. H. Ruben, eds (1979). *Issues in Marxist Philosophy*, Vol. 1, Harvester Press, London.

Milligan, R. (1912). *The Fetish Folk of West Africa*, AMS Press, New York.

Mills, C. W. (1956). *The Power Elite*, Oxford University Press, New York.

Millum, T. (1975). *Images of Women*, Chatto and Windus, London.

Mitchell, A. (1983). *The Nine American Lifestyles*. Macmillan, New York.

Moore, S. (1979). 'Seven Notes on Commodity Fetishism', *Canadian Journal of Political and Social Theory*, vol. 3, no. 1.

Morely, D. (1980). 'Texts, Readers, Subjects', in Hall *et al.* (1980).

Moskin, J., ed. (1973). *The Case for Advertising*, American Association of Advertising Agencies, New York.

Murdock, G. (1978). 'Blindspots About Western Marxism: A Reply to Dallas Smythe', *Canadian Journal of Political and Social Theory*, vol. 2, no. 2.

Nassau, R. (1904). *Fetishism in West Africa*, Negro University Press, New York (republished 1969).

Nelson, J. (1983). 'As the Brain Tunes Out the TV Admen Tune In', *Globe and Mail*.

Nelson, P. (1974). 'Advertising as Information', *Journal of Political Economy*, no. 82.

Nielsen, A. C. (1983). *Report on Television for 1983*, Nielsen, Chicago.

O'Kelly, C. and L. Bloomquist (1976). 'Women and Blacks on Television', *Journal of Communication*, vol. 26, no. 4.

Oliver, R. (1981). 'Advertising and Society' in Zarry and Wilson (1981).

Ollman, B. (1976). *Alienation*, Cambridge University Press, Cambridge.

Packard, V. (1960). *The Hidden Persuaders*, Penguin, London.

Parkin, A. (1963). 'On Fetishism', *International Journal of Psychoanalysis*, vol. 44.

Parrinder, G. (1961). *West African Religion*, Epworth Press, London.

Payne, S. (1948). 'The Fetishist and his Ego', in Fliess (1948).

Peto, A. (1973). 'The Olfactory Forerunner of the Superego: Its Role in Normalcy, Neurosis and Fetishism', *International Journal of Psycho-Analysis*, vol. 54, no. 3.

Plummer, J. (1979). 'Life-Style Patterns', in Wright (1979).

Pollay, R. (1984). '20th Century Magazine Advertising: Determinants of Informativeness', *Written Communication*, vol. 1, no. 1, January.

Pope, D. (1982). *The Making of Modern Advertising*, Basic Books, New York.

Potter, D. (1954). *People of Plenty*, University of Chicago Press, Chicago.

Price, J. (1978). *The Best Things on TV: Commercials*, Penguin, New York.

Querles, R., L. Jeffres and A. Schnuerer (1980). 'Advertising and the Management of Demand: A Cross-National Test of the Galbraithian Argument', paper presented at the International Communication Association, Acapulco, Mexico.

Rachman, D and E. Romano (1980). *Modern Marketing*, Dryden Press, Hinsdale, IL.

Rattray, R. (1923). *Ashanti*, The Clarendon Press, Oxford.

—— (1927). *Religion and Art in Ashanti*, The Clarendon Press, Oxford.

Ray, M. (1982). *Advertising and Communication Management*, Prentice-Hall, Englewood Cliffs, NJ.

Ray, M. and P. Webb (1978). *Advertising Effectiveness in a Crowded Television Environment*, Marketing Science Institute, Report no. 78–113.

Reel, F. (1979). *The Networks: How They Stole the Show*, Charles Scribner's Sons, New York.

Rey, P. and G. Dupre (1973). 'Reflections on the Pertinence of a Theory for the History of Exchange', *Economy and Society*, vol. 12, no. 1.

Rose, N. (1977). 'Fetishism and Ideology: A Review of Theoretical Problems'. *Ideology and Consciousness*, no. 2, Autumn.

Robinson, J. (1977). *How Americans Use Time*, Praeger, New York.

Rojek, C. (1985). *Capitalism and Leisure Theory*, Methuen, London.

Rosen, I., ed. (1964). *The Pathology and Treatment of Sexual Deviation*, Oxford University Press, New York.

Rosengren, K., ed. (1980). *Advances in Content Analysis*, Sage, London.

Rotzoll, K., J. Haefner, and C. Sandage (1976). *Advertising in Contemporary Society: Perspectives Towards Understanding*, Copywright Grid Inc., Columbus, OH.

Roucek, J. (1971). 'Advertising as a Means of Social Control', *International Behavioural Scientist*, vol. 3, no. 4, December.

Ruben, D. H. (1979). 'Marxism and Dialectics' in Mepham and Ruben (1979).

Rubens, W. (1984). 'High-Tech Audience Measurement for New-Tech Audiences', *Critical Studies in Mass Communication*, June.

Ruttenbeek, G., ed. (1940). *The Psychotherapy of Perversion*, Citadel Press, New York.

Sahin, H. and J. Robinson (1981). 'Beyond the Realm of Necessity: Television and the Colonisation of Leisure', *Media, Culture and Society*, vol. 3, no. 1.

Sahlins, M. (1976). *Culture and Practical Reason*, University of Chicago Press, Chicago.

Samarajiwa, R. (1981). 'The Audience Commodity Centred Theory of Communication: A Critique', unpublished xerox, Simon Fraser University.

—— (1983). 'The Canadian Newspaper Industry and the Kent Commission: Rationalization and Response', *Studies in Political Economy*, no. 12, Autumn.

Sandage, C. and V. Fryburger, eds (1960). *The Role of Advertising*, Richard Irwin, Homewood, IL.

Sandage , C. (1961). *The Promise of Advertising*, Richard Irwin, Homewood, IL.

—— (1973). 'Some Institutional Aspects of Advertising', *Journal of Advertising*, vol. 1, no. 1.

Sartre, J. -P. (1976). *The Critique of Dialectical Reason*, tr. A. Sheridan-Smith, NLB, London.

SCA—see Leiss *et al.* (1986).

Scheibe, C. (1979). 'Sex Roles in TV Commercials', *Journal of Advertising Research*, vol. 19, February.

Schudson, M. (1984). *Advertising, The Uneasy Persuasion*, Basic Books, New York.

Schultze, Q. (1981). 'Professionalism in Advertising: The Origin of Ethical Codes', *Journal of Communication*, Spring.

Schwartz, T. (1974). *The Responsive Chord*, Anchor, New York.

Scitovsky, T. (1976). *The Joyless Economy*, Oxford University Press, New York.

Sepstrup, P. (1980). 'Methodological Developments in Content Analysis', in Rosengren (1980).

—— (1981). 'Information Content in Advertising', *Journal of Consumer Policy*, vol. 5, no. 4.

Sexton, D, and P. Haberman (1974). 'Women in Magazine Advertisements', *Journal of Advertising Research*, vol. 14, no. 4.

Shanks, B. (1977). *The Cool Fire: How to Make it in Television*, Vintage, New York.

Simon, J. (1970). *Issues in the Economics of Advertising*, University of Illinois Press, Urbana.

Simon, R. (1980). 'Advertising as Literature: The Utopian Fiction of the American Marketplace', *Texas Studies in Literature and Language*, vol. 22, no. 2, Summer.

Skelly, G. and W. Lundstrom (1981). 'Male Sex Roles in Magazine Advertisements 1954–1970', *Journal of Communication*, Autumn.

Smith, H. (1975). *Strategies of Social Research*, Prentice-Hall, Englewood Cliffs, NJ.

Smith, W. (1972). 'Product Differentiation and Market Segmentation as Alternative Marketing Strategies' in Engel *et al.* (1972).

Smythe, D. (1977). 'Communications: Blindspot of Western Marxism', *Canadian Journal of Political and Social Theory*, vol. 1, no. 3.

—— (1978). 'Rejoinder to Graham Murdock', *Canadian Journal of Political and Social Theory*, vol. 2, no. 2.

—— (1980). *Dependency Road*, Ablex, Norwood, NJ.

Socarides, C. (1960). 'The Development of a Fetishistic Perversion', *Journal of the American Psychoanalytic Association*, vol. 8.

Spencer, H. (1879). *The Principles of Sociology*, vol. 1, Appleton and Co., New York.

Spitzer, L. (1962). *Essays in English and American Literature*, Princeton University Press, Princeton, NJ.

Springborg, P. (1981). *The Problem of Human Needs and the Critique of Civilisation*, Allen and Unwin, London.

Stigler, G. (1961). 'The Economics of Information', *Journal of Political Economy*, vol. 69, June.

Sumner, C. (1979). *Reading Ideologies*, Academic Press, London.

Swingewood, A. (1977). *The Myth of Mass Culture*, Macmillan Press, London.

Szalai, A., ed. (1972). *The Use of Time*, Mouton, The Hague.

Taussig, M. (1980). *The Devil and Commodity Fetishism in South America*, University of North Carolina Press, Chapel Hill.

Truchill, B. (1984). 'Comments on Sut Jhally's "The Spectacle of Accumulation"', *The Insurgent Sociologist*, vol. 12, no. 3, Summer.

Turner, E. (1952). *The Shocking History of Advertising*, Penguin, New York.

Tylor, E. (1871). *Primitive Culture*, Harper, New York, (republished 1958).

Veblen, T. (1953). *The Theory of the Leisure Class*, Mentor, New York.

Warne, C. (1962). 'Advertising—A Critic's View', *Journal of Marketing*, vol. 26, October.

Warren, D. (1978). 'Commercial Liberation', *Journal of Communication*, vol. 28, no. 1.

Williams, R. (1974). *Television: Technology and Cultural Form*, Fontana, London.

—— (1980). 'Advertising: The Magic System' in *Problems in Materialism and Culture*, NLB, London.

Williamson, J. (1978). *Decoding Advertisements*, Marion Boyars, London.

Winn, M. (1977). *The Plug-In Drug*, Viking, New York.

Winship, J. (1981). 'Handling Sex', *Media, Culture and Society*, vol. 1, no. 3.

Wright, J., ed. (1979). *The Commercial Connection: Advertising and the American Mass-Media*, Dell, New York.

Zarry, P. and R. Wilson (1981). *Advertising in Canada: Its Theory and Practice*, McGraw-Hill Ryerson, Toronto.

Zeicher, A. (1983). 'Rock'n'Video', *Film Comment*, Vol. 19, no. 4.

# Index